Complete Book of Effective Personal Letters

by Robert and Elaine Tietz

PRENTICE HALL
Paramus, New Jersey 07652

Library of Congress Cataloging-in-Publication Data

Tietz, Robert.
    Complete book of effective personal letters.
       p. cm.
    Includes index.
    ISBN 0-13-156414-5—ISBN 0-13-156019-0 (pbk)
    1. Letter-writing. 2. Letters. I. Tietz, Elaine.
  II. Title.
PE1497.T53   1984   83-15949
808.6   CIP

Printed in the United States of America

10

The characters, businesses, places, and situations in this book are fictional. Any resemblance to actual firms, locales, events, or persons, living or dead, is entirely coincidental.

ISBN 0-13-156414-5   ISBN 0-13-156019-0(PBK)

ATTENTION: CORPORATIONS AND SCHOOLS

Prentice Hall books are available at quantity discounts with bulk purchase for educational, business, or sales promotional use. For information, please write to: Prentice Hall Career & Personal Development Special Sales, 240 Frisch Court, Paramus, New Jersey 07652. Please supply: title of book, ISBN number, quantity, how the book will be used, date needed.

 PRENTICE HALL
Career & Personal Development
Paramus, NJ 07652
A Simon & Schuster Company

On the World Wide Web at http://www.phdirect.com

Prentice-Hall International (UK) Limited, *London*
Prentice-Hall of Australia Pty. Limited, *Sydney*
Prentice-Hall Canada Inc., *Toronto*
Prentice-Hall Hispanoamericana, S.A., *Mexico*
Prentice-Hall of India Private Limited, *New Delhi*
Prentice-Hall of Japan, Inc., *Tokyo*
Simon & Schuster Asia Pte. Ltd., *Singapore*
Editora Prentice-Hall do Brasil, Ltda., *Rio de Janeiro*

How This Book Can Help You Write Better Personal Letters

Many otherwise sophisticated people have trouble writing a letter, not for lack of any worthwhile ideas, but because they feel they just can't quite come up with the right words.

It needn't be that way. In the chapters that follow, we'll show you how to initiate or respond in a wide variety of circumstances ranging from routine matters to difficult and sensitive situations. You'll never again draw a blank when confronted with pen and paper.

If you've ever been intimidated by a letter from a lawyer, an IRS auditor or a collection agent, you know the effect created by the ring of authority. We'll show you how to turn the tables and put adversaries on the defensive. Unreasonable landlords or neighbors, unfair insurance claims agents, unprincipled politicians will soon feel the sting of some of their own medicine.

Just as often, the occasion may call for a message of appreciation, reconciliation or sympathy. A thoughtful note to a caring nurse after a hospital stay, to a Little League coach who helped your son bloom, or to an inspirational clergyman can convey a depth of feeling far beyond the "canned" message of a store-bought greeting card.

TIME-SAVING METHOD SIMPLIFIES LETTER WRITING

For every occasion, we've prepared model letters you can use practically as is, changing perhaps just a few words. Often you'll find that the samples contain the essence of what you want to say. With minor adaptations you'll be able to compose an appropriate letter geared to your exact circumstance in a matter of minutes. Hundreds of samples cover every imaginable situation. All are categorized by subject, and are right at your fingertips.

Letter writing, like just about anything else, gets easier as you do more of it. Soon it will become a pleasure rather than a chore. You'll find that self-expression follows self-confidence. Once you've acquired both, you're on your way to becoming an accomplished wordsmith.

Your letters will become the medium for renewing and nurturing old friendships, and for tactfully handling every social occasion. They'll open the way to solutions of problems that seemed insurmountable at first. And you'll soon experience the heady feeling that comes with the realization of the influence your letter can bring to matters of importance.

NOW THAT YOU'RE READY TO WRITE THE PERFECT LETTER . . .

Is there anything that can still be called "perfect" in this age of compromise? You bet there is . . . and it doesn't have a thing to do with punctuation or grammar or style. The perfect letter is one that accomplishes its purpose—obtains an elusive refund, secures an important interview, gets a nit-picking teacher off your child's back, brightens a good friend's day.

Unlike most books, this one needn't be read from the beginning. Each model letter stands on its own. When the occasion calls for a particular type of letter, turn to the pages covering that situation. Copy the letter, modify it, go off on a tangent of your own. But remember, the final product will be *yours*, not ours.

Now go ahead and write that perfect letter.

Robert and Elaine Tietz

Contents

Part I

LETTERS FOR EVERYDAY OCCASIONS

Part II

LETTERS COVERING SPECIAL SITUATIONS

Part III

LETTER WRITING IS EASY ONCE YOU KNOW HOW

Part I

Letters for Everyday Occasions

1

Keeping in Touch

When a good friend or loved one moves away (or you do the moving), good-bys are often accompanied by promises to keep in touch. After the move is made, and time begins to pass, it's up to one of you to show that you care and that you value the relationship. All it takes is a letter.

Usually the hardest part is just getting started. This chapter is designed to give you model letters as well as sample beginnings to use as stepping-stones.

MISS YOU/OLD FRIEND

Dear Karen,

All of us are miserable since you've moved. The kids keep complaining, "There's no one to play with," Fred misses carpooling with Cliff each day, and I fight back tears each time I see your empty house next door.

After your letter, Fred and I came up with an idea—how 'bout both our families spending a week's vacation together this summer? There must be some lake or lodge halfway between South Dakota and Georgia where we could meet. July would be the best month for us, but we're pretty flexible all summer. Talk it over with Cliff and see what he thinks.

The winter weather is getting to be a drag. The kids never tire of the snow, and Fred and I have gotten a lot of use out of our cross-country skis, but I'm longing for spring at this point.

Write soon!

Fondly,

MISS YOU/OLD FRIEND

Dear Sandy,

It's taken a fantastic amount of self-control to fight the temptation to pick up the phone and, just like old times, call you. You are my dear friend, but those long-distance rates are murder.

I have an idea . . . see what you think. The telephone rates are lowest on Saturday mornings. Let's talk the first Saturday of each month at 10:00 a.m. One month I'll call you; next month you call me, etc. I'll start by calling you next Saturday. I can hardly wait!

Sincerely,

MISS YOU/OLD FRIEND

Dear Valerie,

You've been on my mind a lot the past few days, so I felt it was time to sit down and write. Are you settled in yet? How are the kids adjusting to school? Have you met any of your new neighbors?

It seems as if you've been gone forever. One sad fact about human nature is that we don't seem to appreciate what we have till it's gone. That's how I'm feeling today.

So much has happened since you left; I haven't had time to get too down in the dumps. Billy has been to the emergency room twice—once for stitches after falling off his bike and again for a cast on his broken wrist after "flying" off a swing at the school playground. Susie auditioned for the fall Children's Theater production and got a good part, so I'm busy chauffeuring her to and from rehearsals.

Brian's still travelling about one week a month. I hate having him gone, but I'll admit that hot dogs for dinner are a lot easier that roast beef.

Be sure to write soon. I'm eager to hear from you.

Affectionately,

MISS YOU/FATHER TO SON AT COLLEGE

Dear Neil,

It was good to hear from you last night. Sounds as if college life is agreeing with you.

Your mother and I sat up for hours after your call talking about old times. Believe it or not, it's quite an adjustment for parents when their oldest son is away from home for the first time.

We're so pleased that you're happy at U of X, and we're proud of your performance there. Keep up the good work and keep calling—we love to hear from you.

Mom is getting another "care" package ready to send which should hold you over till you come home at the end of the month. Debbie is thrilled that you'll be home for her birthday.

Miss you,

MISS YOU/FATHER TO DAUGHTER AT COLLEGE

Dear Marcy,

I imagine your first reaction when you opened this bulging manila envelope was disappointment since it contains no snacks.

Instead, I hope you'll put the enclosed stationery to good use along with the accompanying supply of envelopes, stamps and list of addresses.

You wouldn't believe how many people are asking about you. And an occasional phone call home, welcome as it is, hardly begins to describe campus life. Please take a few minutes to drop Grandma a line. Uncle Gus would probably re-read your letter ten times. And a note from her big sister personally addressed to Trudy would certainly wind up on her bulletin board.

Meanwhile, all's well at this end. Ginger hangs around your empty chair at the dinner table as if a juicy tidbit might magically appear.

We're all looking forward to seeing you at Homecoming. The football game and other events sound like fun. Till then, drop any of us a line when you have a spare moment.

Love,

MISS YOU/GRANDMOTHER TO GRANDCHILD

Dear Brandon,

Well, I'm back home now in my own little apartment, and I'm having fun getting in touch with all my old friends and catching up on what I missed while I was gone.

I had a wonderful time visiting with you and your mom last month, but now I miss you very much. I also miss going to your basketball games and being a part of the excitement. You keep doing your best, and you'll be a star someday. Of course, you'll always be a star in my eyes.

Your loving grandma,

WHY I HAVEN'T WRITTEN

Dear Sharon,

No, I haven't run away from home, or broken both arms, or had a bout of amnesia. I must admit I have just been downright lazy lately. I cringed when I noticed the date on your last letter. I'm sorry I've been such a slow-poke in responding.

My new position with the company involves a bit of travelling which was hard to get used to at first, but I love it now. When I'm home, I seem to be busy catching up or just collapsing in a heap for a cat-nap here and there.

Janet has finally found her "one and only." You'll probably be getting a wedding invitation one of these days. For her sake, I hope it works out. She's been dying to get married since she was four. He's a sharp guy—a lawyer with Jones & Biddle. Keep your fingers crossed!

Write soon?

WHY I HAVEN'T WRITTEN

Dear Andrea,

Here I am finally answering your letter of weeks ago. You are probably wondering what happened to me. To be honest, I haven't written because I have been so depressed. Brent and I broke up right after New Year's and I've been in the dumps. It's a long story and not worth going into right now, but I'm feeling much better and I was eager to let you know I haven't forgotten you.

I got sick of feeling sorry for myself and took a wonderful vacation with a friend from the office. We went to Lake Tahoe for a week, and we had a ball. It was just what I needed.

Forgive me for making this so short. I've been working overtime lately and trying to have a social life too.

I'll write more soon.

Fondly,

WHY I HAVEN'T WRITTEN

Dear Lynn,

I'm sorry I've taken so long to answer your last letter. We have had a round of the flu bug in our house. It was a wicked bug that kept each of us down for a few days. Of course the kids bounced back in no time, but I was beginning to think I'd never get over being tired.

So now that I'm back in full swing and thinking of you, I'm eager to write and tell you all our other news. And I also want you to be assured that I haven't forgotten you.

(Continue with news and answer Lynn's letter, commenting on her news, asking questions, etc.)

WHY HAVEN'T YOU WRITTEN?

Dear Theresa,

I know there's not a postal strike. I know that paper is still available in all 50 states. All the stores seem to have ample supplies of pens and pencils. The post office is still selling stamps. So why haven't I heard from you in three months?

There can only be two reasons—either you have been kidnapped and are being held hostage in a small cage, or you have given up letter writing for Lent. If you've been kidnapped I will be glad to chip in toward the ransom. On the other hand, let me remind you that Lent ended a month ago.

If this idiotic letter doesn't prod a response, I'll really get depressed. I'm waiting to hear from you!

Impatiently,

WHY HAVEN'T YOU WRITTEN?

Dear Pat,

I've decided that either you don't love me anymore or your post office went out of business.

Starting today I refuse to read the funnies till I hear from you. (I was going to hold my breath, but changed my mind.)

Sincerely,

WHY HAVEN'T YOU WRITTEN?

Dear Ann,

My mailman is beginning to get ideas. I greet him eagerly at the door each day hoping for a letter from you. I haven't heard from you yet, but he's getting friendlier each day. If you want to save my reputation, you'd better write soon!

> Your impatient friend,

FRIEND COMING TO TOWN

Dear Keith and Donna,

I will be in Houston attending a convention during the first week of May, and I'm hoping to get to see you while I'm in town. The meetings end at 1:00 p.m. on Friday so I could come by that afternoon and spend the evening. Would you be able to get me to the airport for the 10:00 p.m. flight?

It would be fun to see you two again. Let me know if this works out okay with you.

> Cordially yours,

WANT FRIEND TO VISIT

Dear Doug,

We were delighted to hear you will be coming to Houston and will be able to visit us. We'll be happy to take you to the airport Friday night as you asked, but if you could, we'd like you to stay for the weekend.

The Astros are going to be in town, and Keith can get great seats through his office. Have you ever been to the Astrodome? It's quite an experience. Please plan to spend the weekend with us. We'll have a great time.

> Sincerely,

MOVING BACK TO TOWN

Dear Jack,

It's hard to believe four years have passed since I left Beantown and headed for California with a new job and a new wife. The job worked out well beyond expectations, but the marriage did not.

As part of our divorce settlement, Carol kept the condo, and I began to put together the pieces. Last week I was told I'm being transferred back to Boston—with a promotion to boot.

I'll be looking forward to seeing you and the rest of the guys again. There's one favor I'd like you to do for me before I return. Do you remember Corrie Jensen, the stewardess, I went with in the late seventies? Last I heard she was still single. I'd like to look her up when I get back into the swing of things, but don't know her whereabouts. She always had a thing about an unlisted phone number, and you know how stewardesses move about. You might start by asking Pete Brown's wife.

Meanwhile, I'll get my act together and see you next month.

Your ol' buddy,

PARENT'S WORD OF ENCOURAGEMENT

Dear Kevin,

I share your disappointment with some of the grades you received this past semester. And I agree that they don't accurately reflect your ability to handle a full college workload.

Missing a week of classes with that virus halfway through the semester certainly didn't help. And the noise in the dorm doesn't permit much concentration. Better days are ahead though—as a sophomore you'll probably be assigned two to a room rather than four. Meanwhile, make more use of the library . . . it's quieter and provides a more conducive atmosphere for serious studying.

On the plus side, I'm encouraged to hear you've made some good friends and that the classes are interesting. Believe me, Kevin, no freshman sails through that first year without an occasional setback. You'll soon be surprised to see how quickly things begin to fall into place.

Till then, keep pluggin' away. Your mom and I are proud of you and confident that everything will turn out just fine.

Love,

PARENT TO HOMESICK DAUGHTER

Dear Sarah,

I'm sorry you're so homesick and that it's affecting your studies. Please believe me when I say that I know this is a temporary problem. It's also very normal, so don't get down on yourself.

Your roommate sounds like a great gal. Don't be afraid to be honest with her. Talking things over with her would be a good outlet for you. Keep calling home as often as you wish, and I'll keep calling you. Before you know it you'll be flying home for the winter holidays. I can hardly wait!

You are very much loved, appreciated and missed.

Lovingly,

VALENTINE/MOTHER

Dear Mom,

Instead of a card this year I thought I'd write you a Valentine letter so I could tell you myself, as best I can, that I love you and appreciate you.

Now that I'm grown and can look back at the years when you had to raise Craig and me on your own after Dad died, I'm realizing how hard it must have been for you. I didn't realize it then because you were always so strong and able to calm any fears or frustrations I had with a hug and just the right words. You must have had fears and frustrations of your own, but Craig and I never knew of them, because you beamed confidence through your faith in God.

Thank you for being firm with me while I went through my rebellious stage. It must have hurt you very much to see me make a fool of myself, but thanks to your consistent, firm hand it was only a stage, not a way of life.

O Mom, I love you so much. I'm sorry for the times I let you down, and I'm thankful that you always love me.

Your loving daughter,

VALENTINE/HUSBAND

Dear Hon,

On this Valentine's Day, instead of a card, I'm writing a letter to tell you how much I love you and appreciate you.

I thought I was reasonably happy before you became a part of my life, but now I see those years as a very self-centered, empty span. Your love has helped me discover things within myself that I didn't know were there. I never realized giving of myself to another could be so exciting and fulfilling.

We've had our ups and downs these past two years, but through it all, you have always put our relationship first—before anything else. I love you for your patience and most of all for your willingness to hear my side.

Never change your far-out sense of humor or your intense compassion.

All my love,

LETTER LEVERAGE

Suppose you've just received a breezy, newsy letter from an old friend. You sit down at the kitchen table to read it, pour yourself another cup of coffee and then read it again, not bothering to suppress an occasional chuckle. One of life's better experiences, but what do you do for an encore?

Write back with some news of your own, that's what! No need to do it right away, but be sure to save your friend's letter in your stationery box or in some other handy place.

Then when the spirit moves you, take it out and have it in front of you when you begin. Answer any questions that may have been asked, comment on the events your friend has related, and add some news of your own.

The following pages contain a variety of sample openings to letters to get you started. Choose one that sounds most like you and go from there.

If you feel you don't have enough to say to justify a letter, write a short note instead. It's better to send a note in response to a letter than to write nothing. But whatever you do, don't procrastinate forever.

ANSWERING A LETTER/OPENING PARAGRAPH

Dear Ruth,

Your letter was like a glass of ice-cold lemonade on a hot, sunny day—refreshing, stimulating, and good right down to the toes. I'm sure glad you enjoy writing letters, because I certainly appreciate receiving them.

ANSWERING A LETTER/OPENING PARAGRAPH

Dear Carla,

One advantage to moving far from home is receiving your interesting letters. Now that I'm settled in and feeling as if I belong, I love to hear the latest from back home. I'm so glad you're a good letter writer!

ANSWERING A LETTER/OPENING PARAGRAPH

Dear Helen,

It was a real treat to receive your nice, long letter. Your timing was perfect. I was getting frustrated with the project I was working on (refinishing a second-hand desk) and was in need of a boost. I went out on the patio and sat down and enjoyed each page.

ANSWERING A LETTER/OPENING PARAGRAPHS

Dear Connie,

So you thought you'd make up for the four-month delay in answering my letter by writing an eight-page "book" eh? Well, it worked!

Yes, I was beginning to think you had forgotten me, but now that I know all that's been going on in your life I understand. I thoroughly enjoyed reading each page.

ANSWERING A LETTER/OPENING PARAGRAPH

Dear Dorothy,

Your letters are very much appreciated. You'd be surprised how few of my old friends have kept in touch since we moved to Dallas. The first few months when I was really homesick your letters kept me going. Thank you for being a faithful correspondent and a good friend.

ANSWERING A LETTER/OPENING PARAGRAPH

Dear Marty,

It's always good to hear from you, but your last letter was something else! The news about your new job (especially the salary) blew my mind. It did my heart good to hear about a good guy coming out on top for a change. Most of those who graduated with us are having a devil of a time finding a decent job.

ANSWERING A LETTER/OPENING PARAGRAPH

Dear Becky,

When I received your letter I was so happy! You sure know how to brighten your grandma's day. I think about you very often, wondering what you're up to, so I enjoy hearing your news.

ANSWERING A LETTER/OPENING PARAGRAPHS

Dear Tony,

I really enjoyed your letter and the newspaper story about the Yanks. Thanks for keeping me up-to-date on everything that's going on back in the Big Apple. That Little League team you're on sure sounds promising.

When your grandma and I come to visit next month, we plan to come and watch your games. After all, it isn't every day we get to see a future Yankee pitcher do his thing ten years before he puts on his pinstripes.

We'll be bringing up a box of mangoes in the car. I'll also have along my fishing gear, so we can cut out some afternoon and try our luck at Lake Swallowhook.

LETTER LEVERAGE

For those of you who send Christmas cards, take advantage of this opportunity to catch up on your correspondence. Christmas cards are fun to send as well as receive, and they express your sentiment for the season. But they will mean much more to the recipient if you include a personal note.

Since Christmas comes at the end of the year it's the perfect time to give your friends a short summary of the year just past. And, since Christmas is a season of peace and love, it's also a good time to write in a line or two letting someone know why you appreciate them. The spirit of peace may also inspire you to contact a person with whom you've had a falling out in the past. Life is too short to waste on grudges and hard feelings. Your card may be returned unopened if the other party isn't ready to mend fences, but don't let that stop you.

CHRISTMAS NOTE/UPDATE

Dear Kent and Diana,

Hope this Christmas season finds you in good health as well as in good spirits.

This past year has been an interesting one for us. It started out with the birth of our second child, Jodie, our beautiful, blue-eyed daughter. Things took a turn for the worse in spring when we learned that Ross was going to be laid off at the end of April. We struggled through May and before we really got too discouraged, he found a new job that has turned out to be fantastic. It's closer to home, and there's good opportunity for advancement.

In the fall we were able to get away for a long weekend while my parents took care of the kids. If it were up to me I'd say, "Second honeymoons for everyone!" We had a great time.

Have a Happy New Year.

> Merrily,

CHRISTMAS NOTE/APPRECIATION

Dear Aunt Sheila,

Christmastime brings many happy memories, and you are always a vital part of them. As far back as I can remember you have always been there when I needed you. At family gatherings you always took time to spend with me. And the weekends I spent with you over the years were always times when I felt especially important because I had you all to myself.

Thank you for helping an awkward, shy little girl feel like a princess, and for guarding my secrets as if they were as earth-shaking as I thought they were. I'm going to become an aunt this year when Sherry has her baby, and I hope to be the kind of aunt you are.

I'll be driving up to the home to visit you on Christmas Eve, and I'll bring some of those delicious gingerbread cookies you taught me to make years ago.

> Much love,

CHRISTMAS NOTE/PEACE

Dear Mary Ann,

As Christmas gets closer, and I hear the carols and read these lovely cards I'm sending and receiving, I realize more than ever that I do not have peace in my heart.

It's been eight months now since we had our blow-up. We haven't spoken to each other since, and that has been fine with me up till now.

I'm either getting sentimental in my old age or finally getting some sense in my head, but I can't bear the thought of Christmas with this knot in my heart. I want to say I'm sorry for my part in this mess, and I hope you will forgive me.

If this card is returned unopened I'll know you aren't ready to reconcile yet, and I'll try again next year. If it doesn't come back and I don't hear from you, I'll assume you read this and are considering getting in touch with me.

May the Christmas season touch your heart as it has mine.

> Sincerely,

2

Thank You Letters

Thank you letters are easy to write. Unfortunately, they are also easy to put off. After promising yourself for two weeks to thank Aunt Clara in Cleveland for that new quilt, you get pen and stationery ready, put on the TV to occupy the kids and hope somehow to dash off a couple of paragraphs and get the darned thing in the mail before the casserole comes out. But the casserole comes out before the words come out.

Speechless . . . pen-struck . . . call it what you like . . . the same warm, wonderful you who can talk on the phone for half an hour at the drop of a hat can't summon up whatever it takes to commit a few thoughts to paper. So you throw in the towel, get on with the business of life, and wonder why you detect a faintly reticent attitude in the usually bubbly Aunt Clara when you see her six months later.

Next time try a rough draft of the letter instead. Use a pencil and a scratch pad. Your best stationery can look formidable if you aren't sure what to say.

Start with one of the sample letters and mix in a few ingredients of your own. Cross out what doesn't suit you and have another crack at it. When you're satisfied, pick up a pen and copy the letter on stationery. No one need know these weren't flowing, spontaneous words. Given a little practice, they soon will be.

THANK YOU FOR HOSPITALITY

Dear Carmen and David,

I thoroughly enjoyed your hospitality during my three-day stay in Miami. Your new house is spectacular, and, Carmen, your cooking is out of this world. All in all, a far cry from the out-of-town accommodations this old traveling salesman is accustomed to.

The trip was a success in every way. We landed the contract, and it should provide a substantial chunk of business.

It was great getting together with you two once again. Don't forget the standing invitation to pop in on me the next time you're in New York.

Thanks again . . . and say hello to the twins.

All my best,

THANK YOU FOR HOSPITALITY

Dear Jack and Gerry,

The only bad part about staying at your house for a week was that we had to leave! Thanks again for a wonderful time—lotsa laughs, lotsa sights to see, lotsa good food—but best of all, the pleasure of all of us being together again.

The kids are still talking about the rides on JC's go-cart and the canoe races. Now that we've seen that our two families can have such a good time together, why don't all of you plan on coming up here for a visit next summer? We'd love to see you again.

Thanks loads for a super week.

Love,

THANK YOU FOR CHRISTMAS GIFT

Dear Mom and Dad,

Your Christmas gift check was much appreciated, though somehow I feel that as a parent myself I'm too old to be still getting presents.

Cathy and I splurged and spent it all on ornaments and lights for our Christmas tree. It's quite a sight. Steve Jr. has eyes as big as saucers as he takes it all in. In a week or so, when the snapshots are developed, we'll send some your way.

We're finally getting settled after the move, but it will take awhile before we can really call Atlanta home. The job is turning out to be better than we expected, and although our new home and neighbors are great, I still miss the old white Christmases of Vermont.

Spring comes early down here, I'm told. So if you'd like to thaw out sooner than usual, give some thought to heading south and spending some time with us. There's plenty of room for everyone, and we'd love to see you.

Cathy and Steve Jr. join me in wishing you a wonderful New Year.

Love,

THANK YOU FOR CHRISTMAS GIFT

Dear Uncle Paul,

I've thought so often about writing to thank you for the Christmas gift that I'd begun to think I had! I'm sorry to have taken so long.

We are thoroughly enjoying the preserves you sent from Oregon. In fact, there's only one jar left, so you know they're going over big.

All is well here. We've been making the most of the snowy weather by going skiing each weekend. We're still planning to stop and see you in June. I'll write later with details.

Love,

THANK YOU FOR WEDDING GIFT

Dear Dan and Laura,

Jim and I want to thank you for the beautiful salad bowl set. We're looking forward to getting lots of use out of your thoughtful and practical wedding gift.

We're having fun getting organized in our little apartment. Soon we'll be ready for company, and we'll be giving you a call. After all the times you've had us over for dinner, we'll get to play host for a change.

Thanks again for the lovely gift.

Fondly,

THANK YOU FOR WEDDING GIFT

Dear Bill and Terry,

Thank you so much for your generous wedding present. We used the money to purchase a lovely lamp for our living room.

We're slowly getting settled in our apartment. After the whirlwind of the wedding and our honeymoon on the slopes, it's been a delight to just relax each night after work and take our time about getting organized.

Thanks to good friends like you, our little nest will be well equipped right from the start.

Affectionately,

THANK YOU FOR BRIDAL SHOWER GIFT

Dear Christy,

Every time I bake a cake I'll think of you. The set of stainless steel cake pans you gave me is fantastic. I can't wait to try them out with my favorite recipes.

Thank you, Christy.

As ever,

THANK YOU FOR BRIDAL SHOWER GIFT

Dear Muriel,

You are incredible. The set of bath towels you personally monogrammed for us is beautiful. Thank you very much for this precious gift. Hand-made presents are always special because they are created with time, talent, and more than anything else—love.

Ted was thrilled to finally see something with "HIS" name on it. He said to be sure to say thanks from him, too.

With love,

THANK YOU FOR BABY SHOWER GIFT

Dear Barb,

I can't wait to see our baby-to-be bundled up in the darling "snow-sack" you gave me at the baby shower. He/she will be cozy and warm no matter what the weather, thanks to you.

I really appreciate it, Barb. I know we'll get lots of use out of it, especially since it has growing room.

Fondly,

THANK YOU FOR BABY SHOWER GIFT

Dear Sallie,

The beautiful baby afghan you gave me at the shower is a gift I'll always treasure. It must have taken you hours to create.

I'll be taking the afghan to the hospital with me to wrap our precious bundle in when we come home. Thank you very much.

Sincerely yours,

LETTER LEVERAGE

When you've sent a gift and have never received an acknowledgement you have every right to know the reason. Wedding presents, in particular, have a way of disappearing if delivered to the doorstep of an unoccupied home or apartment. And even first class mail occasionally gets sidetracked.

More often than not, the recipient has simply forgotten to acknowledge the gift. A certain degree of subtlety is required here. You don't want to embarrass the person with even a mild reprimand for failing to respond.

On the other hand, you've probably already paid for the item and are entitled to know whether it was even received. Following are several letters which are sure to evoke either a belated thanks or let you know it's time to put a tracer on the gift.

GIFT NOT ACKNOWLEDGED

Dear Rita and Glenn,

Happy six-month anniversary! You two look happier each time we see you.

We have been concerned that you have not mentioned our wedding gift. If it's an oversight we understand, but if you have never received it we'll have to investigate. We selected a set of glassware at the Fragile China Company and requested that it be delivered to your apartment.

Please let us know if it has been lost so we can check into it.

Fondly,

GIFT NOT ACKNOWLEDGED

Dear Pete,

Did you ever receive the check I sent for your birthday? My monthly bank statement came today, and as I was balancing my account I noticed that the $20 check I mailed to you two months ago has never cleared, nor do I recall your ever mentioning it.

I think I know my only nephew well enough to realize he didn't just stuff it in a drawer and forget about it.

If the check never arrived, let me know and I'll send another one your way as soon as I hear from you.

Your favorite uncle,

LETTER LEVERAGE

If there ever existed an occasion warranting a letter of thanks, it's when someone goes out of his way to do you a favor. It could be a friend, a neighbor, a relative, or someone you hardly know.

Written thanks for such a favor is rarely expected, but does demonstrate that it is thoroughly appreciated.

In the letter to the store manager complimenting one of his employees the writer is, in turn, returning the favor by putting in a good word for the bag boy with his boss. The ripple effect of a good deed spreads far.

THANK YOU FOR FAVOR

Mr. Harold Wells
Store Manager
Mighty Fine Foods
street address
city, state ZIP

Dear Mr. Wells:

Our family has shopped at your supermarket for several years. The quality of the food has been consistently good, the prices reasonable, and the staff friendly and helpful.

One of your employees is particularly outstanding, and I thought I'd drop you a line and say a word on his behalf.

Freddy, who bags groceries and brings them out to the car, frequently goes out of his way to help. Yesterday he had finished loading my car and was heading back to the store. I tried to pull out but found myself stuck in the snow. When he heard my wheels spinning Freddy came back and gave me a push. That certainly beat calling a tow truck!

It's nice to find someone these days who's willing to go that extra mile to please a customer. That young man will go far in life.

Yours truly,

THANK YOU FOR FAVOR

Ms. Emily Green
Fairview Public Library
street address
city, state ZIP

Dear Ms. Green:

You may remember me. One night last week I asked your help in trying to locate a stack of reference material, for an adult education course I'm taking in geology.

Before our paths crossed, I had searched high and low without success. Then at the Fairview library I struck gold. The books you suggested were exactly what I needed and countless hours were saved.

I appreciate your spending so much time with me on this project.

Yours truly,

THANK YOU FOR FAVOR

Dear Mom and Dad,

Thanks so much for taking care of the children last week so that Hal and I could have that wonderful time together in Phoenix. What a pleasure it was to know that the kids were happy and in good hands. They are still talking about the fun they had. The highlight of the week seems to have been getting to stay up late the night you were all pulling taffy.

We are very fortunate to have you. Your availability and, most of all, your T.L.C. are very much appreciated.

All our love,

THANK YOU FOR FAVOR

Dear Judy,

You'll never realize how much your visit meant to me on the day Roy left and how grateful I am for all the time you spent with me during the hard weeks that followed.

Now that I'm back on my feet and realize that divorce isn't the end of the world, I want to let you know how much I appreciated your support.

Tell Carl how much I appreciate his not getting impatient with me for taking up his wife's time over and over again.

"Time heals all things," is a well-worn phrase, but I see its truth already. Having good friends available certainly speeds up the process.

Thank you for being you.

Most sincerely,

THANK YOU FOR FAVOR

Dear Carolyn,

Thank you so much for taking good care of Ginger while we were on vacation. She was such a happy dog when we got home, we knew she'd had lots of loving attention. When we used to pick her up from the kennel she would whimper and carry on for hours.

You not only saved us some money, you also spared us the worry of how she was doing while we were gone. Your help is very much appreciated not only by Ginger, but also each one of us as well.

Fondly,

THANK YOU FOR FAVOR

Dear Ginny,

The many meals you fed Al and the girls and the times you baby sat while I was in the hospital were *soooo* appreciated! Thank you for being such a big help.

Because of you, Al was able to save his vacation time for later and I was able to relax, knowing the girls were under your wing.

Thanks again.

All our love,

THANK YOU FOR FAVOR

Dear Sam,

I had to drop you a line to let you know that the two box-seat tickets you gave me were very much appreciated.

I took my dad along and it tickled me to see his face as we sat right behind the dugout, and he got to see "his" Red Sox up close after watching them from the bleachers for 40 years. He almost burst with excitement when Jim Rice waved at him after Dad yelled, "Hit one for me, Jim!"

Thanks from me and my dad.

Sincerely,

THANK YOU FOR FAVOR

Dear Cindy,

Your kindness at the time of my mother's death meant more than I can express in words. The old saying, "a friend in need is a friend, indeed," is a perfect description of you.

Thanks for being available and understanding.

Affectionately,

THANK YOU FOR FAVOR

Dear Mark,

You will never know how much we appreciated your kind and practical help. With all the trips back and forth to the hospital in the past weeks, it has been good to know that we didn't have to worry about our lawn.

The enclosed check is not a payment—it's a token of our thanks and appreciation.

Lovingly,

THANK YOU FOR CONDOLENCE NOTE

Dear Alice,

Your expression of love and concern was very much appreciated during our time of grief. Nothing will be able to erase our fond memories, we will nurture them forever. The presence of good friends like you was especially comforting.

Thank you.

Yours sincerely,

THANK YOU FOR CONDOLENCE NOTE

Dear George,

Thank you for the letter you sent when you heard the news of Sue's death. The scriptural passage of John 14:1–3 seemed especially appropriate at this time. It's reassuring to know that we'll all be together again some day.

The thoughtfulness of old friends is very comforting in this time of grief, and I do appreciate it.

Very sincerely,

THANKS FOR FAREWELL PARTY

To the Accounting Department:

I want to thank each and every one of you for the wonderful retirement party and the dandy hammock. There couldn't have been a more memorable way to cap off a long career with the company.

Thirty years with any one firm is a long time and I'll take many happy memories along with me. The scrapbook you prepared, Larry, will be a reminder forever of the good times we shared.

As Evelyn and I get ready for our move to Florida, I want you all to know I consider it a privilege to have had such good friends. Let's keep in touch.

Thanks again for everything.

Fondly,

THANKS FOR FAREWELL PARTY

Dear Peggy,

I don't know about you, but I had a ball at my farewell party. I understand you planned it and created the hilarious card recounting my years at Jimco. Thank you for coordinating a fun event, saving me from sad good-byes and teary speeches.

It's hard to explain what it's like to be free and easy after years of the nine-to-five routine. I guess if I had to describe it in one word I'd say . . . fantastic! I do miss all of you, but I'm having a good time and have plenty to keep me busy.

Many thanks, old friend.

Affectionately,

TEACHER'S THANKS FOR CLASSROOM DEMONSTRATION

Dear Mr. Bishop,

Thank you for the marvelous talk and demonstration you gave my fourth-grade class yesterday. You held the children's attention right from the start, and your hands-on demonstration with your pets made lasting impressions.

The hour you spent in our classroom was worth more than a month with a textbook. The chapter on reptiles in our science book is always a fascinating one, but most of the children have never seen one up close, nor had a chance to touch or hold a snake or lizard.

Your thorough knowledge of the subject and your live specimens were invaluable also in helping the children understand how to recognize poisonous reptiles.

Thank you for sparking the children's minds with the pleasure of learning and experiencing new things. I hope you'll be able to arrange a return visit again next year.

Yours sincerely,

3

How to Pry Loose a Refund or Adjustment

There is frequently an honest difference of opinion about whether a refund or adjustment is in order. And the vote usually goes along party lines. Trouble is, the one who already has your money tends not to want to give it back.

When you encounter a faulty product or unsatisfactory service and ordinary efforts to reconcile the problem have fallen on deaf ears, a letter is the best way to communicate. The odds, of course, favor the person who has saved all receipts and can briefly summarize a convincing case for a fair settlement.

In certain gray areas where the policy on refunds isn't clearly defined, it's essential to be tactful and appeal to the recipient's sense of fair play.

In cases involving questionable sales tactics, the law is on your side *if you write promptly.* In order to secure a refund or nullify a contract, you *must* give written notification within a specified time period.

WHEN DELIVERY IS UNACCEPTABLE

Dear Mr. Moore:

Your products are of high quality and fairly priced. But there's a weak link in the system that you should know about.

The desk I purchased from the Bingo Supply Store was delivered to my apartment yesterday. The two men who brought it were quite annoyed when I insisted that they bring the desk into the bedroom rather than just leave it in the hallway. While grudgingly carrying it into the bedroom they gouged out a 3″ chunk of paneling in the doorway. My protest was ignored, and I was told it's "no big deal, just sand it down and it'll look good as new."

The janitor in our building can't or won't fix it, and has assured me that about $40 will be deducted from my security deposit to have a carpenter fix the paneling.

It will take a check for $40 payable either to me or to Ace Realty Company and transmitted through me to undo the damage caused by your careless delivery men and restore my faith in Bingo.

Yours truly,

NEVER GOT YOUR REBATE CHECK?

Gentlemen:

Three months ago I purchased one of your smoke detectors because I believed your promise of a $10 rebate. This offer was clearly stated in advertising at the time and on the package.

In case my box top, receipt and rebate form got lost in the mail, I am enclosing a copy of my sales receipt. Please forward my rebate immediately.

Thank you.

Yours truly,

Enclosure

ASKING NEWSPAPER'S CONSUMER COLUMN FOR HELP

Dear Consumer Action Column,

Three months ago I ordered a set of personalized stationery through Green's Mail Order Catalog and enclosed a personal check for $10.89. I have since received my cancelled check, but no stationery.

Six weeks after I placed my order I sent an inquiry. Green's replied that they were behind schedule. After 12 weeks I wrote again and asked for a refund. So far, no word from them.

I would appreciate your intervention and advice as to what I should do next.

Sincerely,

REQUESTING DEPOSIT REFUND FROM STORE MANAGER

Dear Mr. Fox:

For many years I have maintained an active account at Feathers & Pipp, and have long regarded it as a high-quality clothing store. This favorable impression lasted until yesterday when I went in to pick up the three-piece worsted suit I had ordered four weeks ago during your annual fall sale.

Some minor alterations were to be made, as is usually the case when I purchase off-the-rack clothes. But when I tried on the suit, I was not prepared for what I saw in the mirror. The coat felt and looked several sizes too small, and the vest fit so tightly I couldn't button it.

Admittedly, Bill Bickel, the salesman who sold me the suit, and the tailor who marked the alterations were very busy on the day of the fall sale, but it was their carelessness that produced this ill-fitting garment.

I expressed my astonishment to Mr. Bickel and told him I considered the suit unacceptable. When I asked him to return my $25 deposit, he said that would be impossible since he couldn't sell the suit to anyone else. And that may well be, unless some pencil-thin individual with a taste for worsted comes through the door. I asked to see the store manager but was told you weren't in.

I left without the suit and without my $25. I am enclosing a copy of my receipt and would appreciate a prompt refund of my deposit.

Yours truly,

Enclosure

REQUESTING DEPOSIT REFUND FROM CAMP DIRECTOR

Dear Mr. Hoving:

In early April I sent a check for a $50 deposit for my son, Brad, to attend summer camp. Brad has been looking forward to going to camp for years.

Two days ago he had an accident with his bicycle. He broke his right wrist and sprained his left ankle and, needless to say, is in no shape to attend camp next week.

I am enclosing a note from Dr. Tappan outlining the extent of Brad's injuries. I realize you've had a space reserved for him, but in view of his accident and my prompt notification I would appreciate your refunding my $50 deposit.

Cordially yours,

Enclosure

CANCELLING A DOOR-TO-DOOR SALES CONTRACT

Gentlemen:

The purpose of this certified letter is to cancel the order I placed yesterday with one of your door-to-door salesmen for a set of encyclopedias. He was pushy; I was gullible, and the morning after, I had cause to regret my action.

Fortunately a neighbor pointed out that there was a recourse. The Attorney General's office informed me that the law allows a 3-day "cooling off" period in this state during which buyers may rescind orders placed through door-to-door salespersons. I am enclosing with this letter (for which I have a return receipt) a copy of the contract for the purchase. I also have directed my bank to stop payment on the check I wrote for the down payment.

I'm assured this will conclude the matter. I regret the inconvenience caused you. It has been a sobering lesson for me and one which I'll never repeat.

Yours truly,

Enclosure

COMPLAINT TO REGIONAL DIRECTOR
ABOUT HOME DEMONSTRATION

Dear Miss Wright:

On July 14 a "Forever Painting" demonstration and party was held in my home. My friends ordered over $400 worth of paintings, and each person prepaid the entire amount of her order that night.

Three months have passed and still no merchandise! As you can imagine, my friends are getting quite impatient and more than a bit apprehensive.

My attempts to get a satisfactory explanation from the demonstrator, Juliet Pender, have gotten me nowhere. I had this party in my home because I had heard such good things about your organization. I trust you will either come through with the merchandise, or forward refunds to these people who paid their money in good faith.

I am enclosing photocopies of each order, with amounts itemized. I look forward to hearing from you.

Yours truly,

Enclosure

WHEN LANDSCAPER BOTCHES THE JOB

Dear Mr. Jones:

Four times a year a Jones & Smith truck and crew come by to do a chemical application which until two weeks ago made my lawn the envy of the block.

THEN THE GRASS BEGAN TURNING BROWN

Two days after the last application it was apparent that something was very wrong. It was four more days before a Jones & Smith foreman finally came out to take a look. He could hardly speak English, but managed to convey the message, "not to worry."

Several days later, at my insistence, the local branch manager, Mr. Graves, inspected the lawn and admitted that a mistake had been made in the treatment formula. He apologized for what had happened and offered to re-seed the lawn in the fall, saying that was as far as he was authorized to go.

Not good enough, Mr. Jones. The devastated lawn should be taken up and replaced with sod at once. This will, of course, be more costly than re-seeding, but as chairman of a publicly-held company which spends millions each year to advertise the magic of the Jones & Smith process, I'm sure you'd agree that nothing less would be equitable.

I am enclosing color photos of the ruined lawn and a copy of the contract with your company. I'm inclined to believe your Mr. Graves when he said this sort of thing has never happened before. That's all the more reason to correct the mistake as soon as possible.

Yours truly,

Enclosures

LETTER LEVERAGE

When seeking a refund or adjustment from a large corporation the initial contact should be made through conventional channels. Straightening out most billing errors is usually best handled by a call or a letter to people who deal with such things eight hours a day. It's usually the fastest way to get things done. But not always.

If there's some procedural complication or a computer-generated error, it's much harder to get the matter resolved at the initial contact level. Rather than continue to spin your wheels, write directly to the president of the company.

There's very little chance Mr. BIG himself will see your letter, but a ubiquitous corporate species known as an administrative assistant surely will. The Chief in the corner office usually has a number of them around at his beck-and-call to insulate him from problems such as yours. But regardless of who marks it "please handle," if it's transmitted to the appropriate department head on a sheet bearing the imprint, "From the Office of the President," things get done.

The matter invariably gets priority attention, and if there's a snag, the administrative assistant will follow up on it.

The guidelines here are simple. State your grievance concisely, and in a non-combative tone. Indicate that you've tried to resolve the matter at a lower level, but for whatever reason, couldn't. Be clear about what you expect done, and be reasonable. If you still can find it in your heart to put in a good word for the product or retailer generally, do so. End on a positive note by hoping that his intervention will right the wrong and restore your faith in the company.

TO PRESIDENT OF UTILITY

Dear Mr. Cedar:

I'm sure that most customer complaints about high electric bills are usually resolved at a lower level than that of the Office of the President. I've tried to do just that, but after repeated attempts to get a reasonable explanation from your customer service department proved futile, I'd appreciate a few minutes from your busy day.

I have lived with my wife and one child in the same six-room house since 1980. We have not changed our habits, nor added any major appliances.

What follows is a comparison of my electric bills for the month just passed and the same period a year ago:

	This Year	Last Year
Days of Service	32 (June 6–July 8)	32 (June 5–July 7)
Kilowatt Hours	970	822
Amount Due	$156.28	$70.43

Your customer service people, including a supervisor, explained that rates are up 14% from last year and, due to the hotter weather and increased air conditioning use, consumption is up about 20%. These are facts I accept and understand, but at this point communication breaks down.

No one can tell me why my bill has more than doubled. I have suggested they re-check their computations but no one is willing to do so.

My neighbors in similar-sized homes are receiving electric bills roughly 30–40% higher than last year. Several have suggested I complain directly to the State Public Service Commission, but I thought I'd try once more by asking you to help before taking such action.

I'd appreciate your looking into this matter.

Yours truly,

TO PRESIDENT OF MANUFACTURING COMPANY

Dear Mr. Steele:

One year ago today my husband and I purchased a beautiful new Town & Country refrigerator. We researched refrigerators through consumer publications and the Better Business Bureau and chose Town & Country for its high quality and dependability.

It seems our research was a futile exercise. We have had nothing but problems with our refrigerator and now that our warranty has run out we won't be able to afford the repair bills.

Two weeks after we purchased the refrigerator, I came into the kitchen in the morning and found a huge puddle on the floor. That time the problem was with the in-door water dispenser. From that day till now we have had ten service calls (copies of repair receipts enclosed).

All the problems seem connected to the freezer section. This has caused not only inconvenience and frustration, but costly loss of food as well. I am also enclosing a record of my phone calls and letters which will give you an idea of the hours I've spent trying to get this situation resolved.

This letter to you is my last resort before asking the Better Business Bureau for binding arbitration. My husband and I have borrowed a tiny portable refrigerator which does not meet our needs to say the least. Yes, our beautiful Town & Country refrigerator is on the blink again—now there is a roaring sound whenever the motor is on.

Because of our research, we still believe that Town & Country has a good product and that we happened to get a lemon. We would appreciate your intervention and hope you conclude that we are to be given a replacement as soon as possible.

Yours truly,

Enclosures

UNTANGLING THE MEDICARE MAZE

Rata-Data, Inc.
street address
city, state ZIP

Attention: Mr. H.R. Schneider
                 Chairman of the Board

Dear Mr. Schneider:

I am writing to you in desperation after learning that Rata-Data, Inc. is under contract to administer and process Medicare claims in this metropolitan area.

On September 6 I had cataract surgery with an intra-ocular lens implant. I paid the doctor his fee of $1700 in full (copy attached) and submitted the bill to Rata-Data for reimbursement. Evidently they misread the amount as $17.00 (seventeen dollars) and sent me a check not for the $1360 to which I am entitled after my insurance company's payment, but for $13.60 (thirteen dollars and sixty cents). A copy of the form which accompanied the $13.60 check is attached. I'm also including a copy of my supplemental private insurance company's explanation of benefit payments since they paid the $340 difference on the claim. My Medicare number is 00000 00.

Numerous inquiries and protests have brought nothing but frustration as the computer indicates the reimbursement has been paid in full.

I am 70 years old, widowed and a retired school teacher living on a small pension and receiving no social security. The money due me is very much missed, and I would appreciate anything you could do to expedite payment on this claim.

Yours truly,

Enclosures

TO HEAD OF RESTAURANT CHAIN

Dear Mr. Dewey:

The food in your restaurants is delicious, but your wonderful barbecue sauce is disastrous on my clothes.

On October 24 my friend and I were in your restaurant at 620 Main Street in Fairview, managed by Bud Andrews. When the waiter brought our food, he tripped and my barbecued rib dinner went down the front of my clothes, landing in my lap. Mr. Andrews was very apologetic and gave each of us a free dinner that night.

That was the costliest "free" dinner I've ever had. I was wearing a brand-new wool skirt and sweater and after numerous attempts by my dry cleaner to remove the food stains, we have concluded that it is hopeless. The skirt and sweater are a total loss.

I am enclosing copies of my sales receipt and cleaning bills which total $101.87. Mr. Andrews tells me he doesn't have the authority to give me a check for that amount, and he won't tell me whom I should contact. So, Mr. Dewey, I've come straight to the top. I would appreciate it if you would see that full restitution is made.

Thank you.

Yours truly,

Enclosures

TO PRESIDENT OF CARPET CLEANING FIRM

Dear Mr. Middlebury:

We recently hired your firm to clean the wall-to-wall carpeting in our living room and dining room. The results were appalling.

Before the workmen left, I expressed my dissatisfaction. Not only had they failed to remove stains, but they had somehow managed to smear them across a much larger area. I was assured that in 24 hours after everything had dried, a quick sweep of the vacuum cleaner would remove the last traces of dirt and stains. It did nothing of the kind.

The next day I called Norman Nelson, manager of your local facility, and told him what had happened. Mr. Nelson said he'd send someone over to take a look, but no one ever came. He has since refused to return my calls.

I am left with two rooms of carpeting which look worse than before the so-called "cleaning." At the very least I would expect a complete refund of the $75 it cost me.

If you take pride, Mr. Middlebury, in the firm that bears your name, you'd arrange to have someone inspect the carpeting and then clean it again The workmen would be instructed not to leave until the job had been satisfactorily completed. Then my faith in Middlebury Carpet Cleaners would be restored.

Yours truly,

LETTER LEVERAGE

Millions of Americans are aware of the advantages of shopping with a plastic card instead of with cash. Countless others who have been the victims of a billing error would tell quite a different story.

Often their stories would begin with dozens of attempted phone calls made to register the complaint, each resulting in a busy signal. If the caller is persistent enough, eventually some harried individual will come on, and, more often than not, spend a great deal of time trying to explain and justify the incorrect bill.

There's a better way. If you have access to a photocopying machine, make copies of both your monthly statement and the receipt you received at the time of the purchase. Send the copies along with a brief cover letter. Always retain the originals for your records.

If it isn't possible to make copies, a letter is still the best way to straighten things out. State all pertinent information as it appears on your receipt and specify the differences between the receipt and your statement.

BILLING ERROR ON BANK CHARGE

Dear Mr. Russell:

Through numerous phone calls I have tried for several months to resolve a billing error on my bank charge account 123-456-789, but each subsequent monthly statement repeats the mistake and the interest keeps accumulating.

Your account representatives, while courteous and patient, remain convinced that the computer is infallible. I know otherwise and, at the suggestion of my banker at Liberty National Bank, am appealing to you directly in the hope that you'll be able to straighten out this matter.

Enclosed are copies of my past four monthly statements, plus copies of the two charges in question—$40.15 for Sid's Shoes on April 4 and $46.50 for Acme Motor Lodge on April 8. In addition, I am sending copies of each side of my cancelled check #406 dated May 2 in the amount of $86.65. As you can see, it has been cashed, but I have not been credited with payment.

Repeated attempts to correct this error have been time consuming and annoying. Now I fear my credit rating may soon be impaired if this confusion continues.

Will you please help?

Sincerely,

Enclosures

BILLING ERROR ON BANK CHARGE

Gentlemen:

Please note the discrepancy between one item on my latest monthly statement and the corresponding receipt issued by the store at the time of the transaction (copies enclosed).

As the copy indicates, on May 25 I made a purchase from Green & Green for $302.17. Inexplicably, the monthly invoice shows $312.84 for that transaction.

I believe the new balance should be $423.15, not $433.82 as shown. If you agree, please issue a corrected bill.

I would appreciate your prompt attention to this matter since I am going on vacation next week and do not wish to incur a finance charge.

Thank you,

Enclosures

DON'T SEND CHECK ON DISPUTED INVOICE

Gentlemen:

I am enclosing a copy of my current bill and have circled in red a portion of it which I know to be incorrect.

On October 4 I did indeed make a purchase from Barrett Brothers. However, as the enclosed photocopy of my receipt covering that transaction indicates, the amount was for $11.00, not $110.00. By prior arrangement I have for some time authorized Overland Charge to collect payment automatically each month from my checking account #000–000 at your affiliate, Second National Bank at Fairview.

Please stop payment before a check is issued for the amount due on my current bill until the above billing error is corrected.

Yours truly,

Enclosures

CHARGE ACCOUNT ERROR

Account #000 000

Dear Credit Manager:

The enclosed photocopies of a receipt and a corresponding credit to my account will make clear to you that on September 17 I purchased a sweater for $40.19 and on September 20 I returned it for a full refund.

For the past two months that amount has been carried on my account and the finance charges are growing. I would appreciate a prompt reconciliation of my account.

Sincerely,

Enclosures

CHARGE ACCOUNT ERROR

Account #000 000

Dear Mr. Bigby:

I have been a regular customer at the Big Drugstore for 15 years. Your location, friendly service and prompt delivery in emergencies have always been appreciated.

Until this year I have also appreciated having a charge account with you. In the last six months there have been two annoying errors on my account. In January an interest charge was added to my bill for nonpayment of the December invoice.

I photocopied my December cancelled check plus my December invoice and sent them with a note of explanation when I paid my January bill minus the interest charge. My account then was credited correctly, but the interest charge remained. I paid it rather than get into a stew, since it was the first problem I'd ever had.

Well, here we are in June and the same problem has occurred again. This time I will *not* pay the interest charge I do not owe. Consider my account closed unless you can straighten out this matter at once. It's not worth the aggravation and added expense.

Sincerely,

PACKAGE NEVER DELIVERED; DELETE CHARGE

Dear Credit Manager:

I received a bill (copy enclosed) for a package that never came. It all began with your summer sale. I called and ordered a toaster, charged it to my account and arranged to have it delivered to my apartment.

Since I have a full-time job and am not home on weekdays, I asked what day it would be delivered so I could have someone accept the package for me.

I was informed that it would arrive on Tuesday or Thursday of the following week. I put a note on my mailbox on those two days indicating that my neighbor, Mrs. Adams, would take the package.

Mrs. Adams was at home on both days, and says that her doorbell never rang. At this point I assume your delivery man left the package in the foyer that I share with 20 other families. There's no telling who is enjoying the new toaster, but I'm certainly not going to pay for something I never received.

Please credit my account for the full amount of the toaster, $31.68. Thank you.

Yours truly,

Enclosure

4

Getting It Off Your Chest

Life's little and not-so-little annoyances needn't be borne with resigned acquiescence. Not when, for the price of a stamp and a few minutes of your time, you can get in a few licks of your own.

Certainly no book could begin to cover every imaginable situation, but the following model letters typify the sort of responses appropriate to some common circumstances.

When a product or service no longer satisfies, most people simply switch to another, and wonder why they find themselves switching again before long. Better to drop a line to the manufacturer or retailer and let your disappointment hang out.

Tradesmen working in and around your house come in varying ranges of ability and affability. If one becomes overbearing, let the boss know so that he can send someone else next time.

For city dwellers relying on public transportation, getting there is rarely half the fun. The next time you encounter a crazed cab driver, keep in mind that he is licensed by the city. Your letter describing and documenting his behavior can lead to a hearing that could put him out of business for a while at least. Should you encounter his exact opposite—cheerfully and competently getting you from here to there—tip generously if he's driving a cab; write a note of praise to his employer if he's a bus driver or train conductor.

If you're disappointed with a meal in a restaurant, drop a line to the owner and tell him why. It's not uncommon to receive an invitation to return for another visit—on the house this time—in an attempt to mend fences.

Finally, the Action Line or Consumer Column of many newspapers affords you the opportunity both to zap your tormentor in print and draw on the paper's investigative staff to straighten out a problem.

The heavy volume of mail to this ombudsman reduces any one letter's chance of appearing. Odds improve, however, if you state all facts and dates clearly and concisely and include copies of receipts. Be sure to also include your business and home phone numbers.

WHEN YOU CAN'T OPEN A CHILD-PROOF CONTAINER

Pharma-Facture, Inc.
street address
city, state ZIP

Attention: Marketing Vice President

Dear Pharma-Facture:

For many years I have been buying and using your product even though I've heard that all aspirins are pretty much alike. However, when my current supply runs out, I intend to switch to another brand permanently.

The reason is that it is all but impossible for me to open your new child-proof container. The devil himself must have invented this bottle cap. I understand that safety requires some modifications of the conventional cap, but your package designers must have callously written off that segment of the market that suffers from arthritis.

Your challenging container falls short of being one of life's major irritations, but it is more than I care to confront again.

Sincerely,

CONSTRUCTIVE SUGGESTION ON PRODUCT DESIGN

XYZ Manufacturing Co.
street address
city, state ZIP

Gentlemen:

Four years ago we purchased your top of the line washer and clothes dryer. While both appliances have performed reliably, I have a complaint about the design of the dryer (Model D-80).

The hinged door in front that provides access to the pilot light is located where it invites the curiosity of toddlers and crawling infants. Last week my 2-year-old daughter opened the door and was about to reach in when I saw what was happening and just managed to stop her in time.

A liberal supply of criss-crossed masking tape applied to the door and surrounding surface should prevent a recurrence, but is unsightly at best.

I would hope your designers get to work at once on relocating this door on future models. If you share my concern, you might even consider issuing a warning to present owners of the D-80. Nothing so drastic as a product recall is indicated, but a letter alerting them to the potential danger and suggested remedial measures could prevent some child from suffering tragic consequences.

Sincerely,

CRITICISM OF PACKAGE DESIGN

Crunchee Snax Co.
street address
city, state ZIP

Attention: Sales Manager

Dear Sir:

Why did you feel you had to redesign the package for Crunchee Crackers? I have been pleased with your product for years, but now I'm just plain frustrated.

The new package is attractive, but I find it impossible to reclose. As a result the contents soon become stale. I'll have to settle for second best in crackers that come in a package I can reseal.

Formerly yours,

WAITED ALL DAY FOR DELIVERY THAT NEVER CAME

Mr. Frank Fine
Fine Furniture
street address
city, state ZIP

Dear Mr. Fine:

Yesterday I received a phone call assuring me that the new bedroom set I purchased from your store would be delivered today. It was inconvenient for me to stay home all day, but well worth it to receive the long-awaited furniture.

By 4:00 p.m. I began to have my doubts that the delivery would be made. I called Mr. Solomon who sold me the furniture, and he said he'd check into it. He called back at 4:40 to inform me that my furniture was still sitting in the warehouse because somebody goofed. He added that I will have to wait until next week when deliveries are made again in my area.

It made me wonder whether any establishment so indifferent to its customers' time wouldn't also display the same callous disregard if I were to complain that the furniture was defective in any way on arrival.

So, cancel my order. My husband and I have decided to purchase a comparable set from a store that lets you take the furniture home yourself. I will expect a full refund of my deposit at once.

Yours truly,

BAD-MOUTHING THE BOSS

Dear Mr. Vaughan,

The painting of my condo turned out beautifully and I am pleased with the results. Your price was fair and the workmanship satisfactory, but there was one "fly in the ointment."

Dick claims to be your top man. He also told me over and over again how incompetent you are and how, if it weren't for him, nothing would be done right. I did my best to avoid him and his constant chatter, but I always managed to get an earful of his griping.

You may have heard this complaint before, but I urge you to do something about it. At this point, if one of my friends asked me to recommend a decorator I would warn him about the unpleasant side effects of dealing with Vaughan's Decorating.

Sincerely yours,

INCOMPETENT REPAIR MAN

Dear Mr. Platt,

For the past 15 years we have received prompt, efficient service from Platt Plumbing Service & Supply.

Last Wednesday your man, Judd, was out to fix our sump pump. He was rude and extremely slow. As you can see on the copy of the enclosed bill, he was here for 1 1/2 hours and replaced one part. In that time he made two trips "back to the shop" (so he said) to pick up something he needed.

I would appreciate it if you would look over this bill, Mr. Platt, and see if it looks fair to you. I'll be anxious to hear from you.

Yours truly,

Enclosure

BLOWING THE WHISTLE ON A BAD CAB DRIVER

Ms. Dorothy Daniels, Director
Bureau of Consumer Service
street address
city, state ZIP

Dear Ms. Daniels:

Since the Bureau regulates taxi service in this city, I am writing to register a complaint against the Ace Cab Company and, in particular, against Lucifer Gross, driver permit number 620.

At about 2:30 this afternoon I hailed an Ace Cab and was picked up on the 600 block of Broadway by Mr. Gross. I told him I was going to 1400 Park Lane—about eight blocks north and two blocks east. It soon became apparent that the driver either didn't know the way or was determined to take me to my destination by a circuitous route.

I pointed out that he was going west instead of east and he brusquely retorted that he knew where he was going. As a lifelong resident of this city I knew otherwise, and insisted he turn around and take me to 1400 Park Lane by a direct route. Mr. Gross became increasingly abusive, and when he finally headed in the right direction I indicated that I would pay only the $2.60 fare I'm usually charged for this trip.

At this point Mr. Gross unleashed a torrent of obscenities and physically threatened me if I didn't pay the charge indicated on the meter (now approaching $5.00). I was already late for an appointment and, quite frankly, frightened of this hysterical driver so I agreed.

As I left the cab I noted the license plate number: 41539.

This individual is a disgrace to the city as well as to his employer. What's more, anyone driving while turned around cursing a passenger in the back seat is a hazard to other vehicles and pedestrians.

I expect a hearing to be scheduled and the driver called. If my appearance is necessary or if an affidavit describing these events is required, I'll be glad to cooperate.

Yours truly,

COURTEOUS BUS DRIVER APPRECIATED

Municipal Transit Authority
street address
city, state ZIP

Gentlemen:

You no doubt receive many letters and calls of complaint each day. Well, I'd like to turn the tables and say a kind word on behalf of one of your bus drivers.

His name is Ed, he wears badge 4406, and he can frequently be seen driving east on Sheridan Road—Route 160—during the morning rush hour.

Ed greets passengers cheerfully, calls out the stops and is especially considerate of older riders. In short, Ed is a rare commodity these days and he's much appreciated.

Cordially yours,

THOUGHTLESS TRAIN CONDUCTOR

Mr. Orval Worthington, President
Old Smoky Railroad
street address
city, state ZIP

Dear Mr. Worthington:

One rather annoying aspect of the otherwise satisfactory commuter train service from Lancaster to downtown Manchester is the playing of the radio over the loud speaker system.

This was particularly objectionable this morning on train 610 where riders were subjected to the incessant blaring of KIOU for nearly the entire trip. Evidently whoever calls the stops is unaware that the background noise of his radio accompanies his announcements. Worse yet, he apparently forgets to press his off switch, and a thousand passengers are forced to hear this clatter.

Noise pollution on city buses is usually confined to an individual carrying a loud radio. Old Smoky Railroad does it on a grand scale. I think it should stop.

Yours truly,

COMPLAINT TO RESTAURANT OWNER

Dear Mr. Cartier:

My wife and I had heard from friends that dining at The Seville was an enjoyable experience. The review by the Clarion's restaurant editor a week ago made much of the superb cuisine and attentive service in elegant surroundings.

We reserved a table for last Saturday night and invited another couple to join us. Things got off to a shaky start when no table was ready when we arrived. After a 40-minute wait we were finally seated.

The waiter seemed hurried and annoyed. Two of us ordered the vichyssoise and were disappointed. The salmon with crabmeat stuffing fell short of expectations.

Since our guests included my law firm's most important client, I avoided any complaint about the food or confrontation with the irritable waiter, but I'm disappointed nonetheless.

From the reputation you've built, I can only conclude that our experience was an exception. It was, however, enough to keep us from ever returning.

Yours truly,

A GUIDE CAN MAKE OR BREAK A TOUR

Mrs. Chester Summers
Coordinator of Tours
Art Museum
street address
city, state ZIP

Dear Mrs. Summers:

Our two 5th-grade classes from Jefferson School were looking forward to their guided tour of the Art Museum. Even those who had been there before were eager to have a knowledgeable person give them insights on the art we would be seeing.

I have been teaching 5th grade for seven years, and our school's annual Art Museum tour has always been a worthwhile field trip—until this year. I understand your guides are volunteers, people who have taken a course at the Museum to prepare them for this job. And the guides we've had so far were good with children, another vital qualification. I don't understand how Mrs. Prunewell became a guide at all.

She was condescending to the children (who were very well-behaved) and didn't have all her facts straight.

From the vast selection of pieces you have at the Museum, she chose 15—nine of which were religious objects from European cathedrals. Half the children in our group are of the Jewish faith, and this was new to them. When one boy asked, "Who is that?" she gave him a withering look and answered, "St. Francis of course . . . *every*one knows who St. Francis is!"

I suggest you speak to Mrs. Prunewell and perhaps limit her services to parochial school groups. Before our tour next year I will especially mention her by name as the guide we do *not* want for our children.

Yours truly,

WHO SPEAKS FOR THE REST OF US?

Mr. Lionel Hancock, Manager
Classified Advertising Department
The Bugle
street address
city, state ZIP

Dear Mr. Hancock:

As a long-time subscriber to the Bugle, it should come as no surprise that I found my present home through one of your classified ads six years ago, and last Wednesday found my new home through an ad in the July 9 Bugle.

I immediately placed an 8-line ad in the Sunday, July 16 paper. It appeared exactly as requested with one exception. Your Ad-Taker told me that I was unable to specify "No Realtors," because such a restriction was discriminatory.

In attempting to save several thousands of dollars which otherwise would be paid in commissions, I prepared myself for a certain amount of aggravation, including the predictable onslaught of solicitations from real estate agents seeking a listing.

I was particularly puzzled and annoyed by the three intrusive calls from realtors *occurring between 11:00 a.m. and 1:30 p.m. Saturday*, hours before the papers hit the newsstands.

Would it not appear that someone is leaking names to realtors? If I'm wrong, please correct me so I may once again regard The Bugle as favorably as I had until the past weekend.

One final observation . . . if the "No Realtors" designation discriminates against a small but influential and cohesive group, what safeguards are taken to protect the unorganized thousands of individual advertisers against such a breach in ethics?

Yours truly,

CORPORATE ARM-TWISTING NOT APPRECIATED

Mr. Mitchell Morris, President
Brickton Industries, Inc.
street address
city, state ZIP

Dear Mr. Morris:

Now that I am retired I feel free to speak out on what I have for some time felt to be the darker side of an otherwise fine company. I am, of course, referring to the subtle yet coercive methods used each fall to extract from employees the maximum amount of pledges for contributions to the annual charity appeal.

If the end justifies the means, I'm sure you consider this method of fund raising an unqualified success. Because without the screws being turned, there is no doubt that payroll deductions for what is labeled a "voluntary" contribution would be substantially lower.

Imagine, if you will, the effect upon an employee when his supervisor informs him—in terms of specific dollars-and-cents—what he is expected to give out of each paycheck. He is handed a pledge card to be filled out, signed, and put in a sealed envelope addressed to his department head.

The huge progress charts displayed prominently in the lobby during the entire campaign intimidate further. As the red lines resembling the mercury in a thermometer move toward 100% participation for each department, you couldn't be unaware of the pressure being applied by bosses on the remaining holdouts. It's clear that no department head wants to risk your displeasure by presiding over a section that fails to make its goal.

At the conclusion of the campaign you are invariably pictured in the newspaper proudly sporting a donor button on your lapel, smiling and shaking hands with other officials, and boasting about your generous employees. How enthusiastic your people are about the whole thing could perhaps be measured by the percentage who wear *their* donor buttons. I've always thrown mine away and just about everyone else does likewise.

I'll try to end on a constructive note. The annual charity appeal is indeed a worthy project and deserving of community support—on a truly voluntary basis. If the company would increase the size of its corporate contribution to offset the somewhat lower level of giving from employees who no longer feel threatened, the end result would be the same and morale would improve noticeably.

Yours truly,

ABUSED CUSTOMER STRIKES BACK

Mr. Fidoo Chiari, President
First National Bank
street address
city, state ZIP

Dear Mr. Chiari:

There are established in my name at First National a savings account, a checking account, two certificates of deposit, an IRA account and a safe deposit box.

While I customarily transact business during lobby hours, I had occasion this morning to use the walk-up facility before regular banking hours. It was my misfortune to encounter the only person on duty at the time—a heavy-set girl of about 20 with straight blond hair.

When I asked her to cash four $20 traveler's checks, she asked me to sign them. This, of course, I was prepared to do in her presence, but she said she had no pen and motioned me to the counter 20 feet away which is used for filling out forms. After endorsing the checks I had no choice but to go back to the end of the line.

Eventually I worked my way up to the teller again. She said I now had to go back for the pen to fill in the name of the bank as the payee. I asked her if she had ever seen an instrument of this sort before and she retorted that she's been with the bank nearly two months and had seen everything. At my insistence she picked up the phone and minutes later evidently received word from someone on the other end that a stamp could imprint the bank's name on the line indicating payee.

But I wasn't finished yet. She said I now had to sign the back of the checks once more, repeated that she didn't have a pen and again pointed to the faraway counter. By now the checks had been stamped and it was too late to retrieve them and go elsewhere. Back again to the counter, then to the end of the line and finally to the window to again face my tormentor. She peeled off four $20 bills, slid them under the glass and grunted, "Have a nice day."

Fat chance I'll "have a nice day," when I start by wasting 40 minutes of it at your walk-up window on what should have been a routine transaction, and then spend another half-hour writing this letter of complaint.

I do so, not in an attempt to cut short the career of your young banker, but with the hope that you could take several remedial measures:

1) Explain to new employees what a traveler's check is and what to do with it.

2) Provide each teller with an inexpensive ball point pen.

3) Instill in trainees a certain respect for the time of your customers.

Sincerely yours,

WHEN YOU'RE PURPOSELY SHORTCHANGED

Mr. A. J. Girard, Manager
Handy Hardware Store
street address
city, state ZIP

Dear Mr. Girard:

For the second time in a month, one of your checkout clerks attempted to shortchange me. Earlier today I purchased several items totalling $8.40 and handed a $20 bill to a thin, dark-haired girl wearing a name tag which read Anna. She rang up the sale and handed me $1.60 in change.

I immediately pointed out that I had given her a $20 bill, not a ten. As she handed over the rest of my change she muttered, "Mistakes will happen; cool it." No apology, of course.

The entire episode was almost a repeat of a similar incident which occurred about a month earlier. At that time Anna had "mistaken" my $10 bill for a five and, when it was called to her attention, she simply shrugged and handed me the $5 bill.

As I was driving home from the store, I wondered how many times Anna gets away with it. If the scheme succeeds with only one or two customers an hour, she has by the end of the day made quite a haul. Until it happens to the same customer more than once, it may indeed be considered to have been an honest mistake. Always in her favor, of course.

What you choose to do with this piece of information, Mr. Girard, is entirely up to you. I, for one, will avoid shopping in your Handy Hardware store as long as this individual remains behind the cash register.

Yours truly,

cc: President, Handy Hardware Stores, Inc.

A STICKY REBATE PROBLEM

Bottomz-Up Importers, Inc.
street address
city, state ZIP

Gentlemen:

For years I have enjoyed your fine product. Now this absurd $2.00 rebate offer has me livid. What sadist specified the glue with which you affix the front label? Several hours of soaking, peeling off with a razor blade and leaving on a napkin to dry overnight have produced the messy thing you'll find enclosed.

Most people would give up in disgust after trying. And they'll curse you for it. I am just persistent enough to carry it on to completion—though it's been some time since I worked this long for $2.

Your records doubtless show what a small percentage of people actually claim their mail-in rebate. What they don't show is the frequency with which Bottomz-Up leaves a bad taste in their mouths.

Yours truly,

Enclosure

SEEKING HELP FROM CONSUMER ACTION COLUMN

Action Line
The Crestwood Gazette
street address
city, state ZIP

Dear Action Line:

For the past year the City of Crestwood has been issuing parking tickets to a car which evidently has the same license plates as mine, except that I drive a Plymouth and my alter ego a Ford. I live and work in suburban Ferndale and have little occasion to go into the city.

I explained all this in a letter to the Crestwood Police and returned the tickets to them. No response ever came until last week when I received word that unless fines for the parking violations are paid at once, they will issue a warrant for my arrest.

Numerous phone calls have failed to break the impasse. Can you help?

Sincerely,

LETTER LEVERAGE

It's an exhilarating feeling to see your letter reprinted in a newspaper or magazine. Not just because your name appears below but, more importantly, because your views are being exposed to a vast audience.

Your letter has a better chance of being printed if it comes right to the point. Be certain of your facts and dates, especially if your letter takes exception to an article or editorial which appeared earlier in that publication. In *every* case, sign your correct name and furnish your exact address. Some editors will call and verify the identity of the writer before printing a letter.

Don't be surprised or disappointed if parts of your letter are omitted or changed somewhat. The editor must be the final judge of length and style. Rest assured, though, that it will convey the meaning you intended.

Be sure to keep copies of your letter for future reference. Also, keep copies or notes of whatever item prompted you to write.

LETTER TO EDITOR OF NEWSPAPER

Letter to the Editor
Daily Herald
street address
city, state ZIP

Dear Editor:

If the police are to begin ticketing jaywalkers, it's time they also paid more attention to some rarely enforced traffic laws.

For example, why are tickets seldom issued downtown to drivers who disregard the pedestrian's right of way at crossings when both have the green light? Another frequent violation observed countless times each day is that of drivers who enter an intersection knowing they'll never make it across before the signal changes. Finally, why do police issue tickets for following too closely only *after* there's been a rear-end collision?

Motorists, as well as pedestrians, should realize that traffic safety is a two-way street.

Yours truly,

LETTER TO EDITOR OF MAGAZINE

Letter to the Editor
Auto Enthusiasts Magazine
street address
city, state ZIP

Dear Editor:

Your recent Auto of the Year article sent me on the double to an Empire dealer. A huge poster in his window trumpeted AE's award and invited passersby to take a test drive.

Regrettably, though most of his demos came with several thousand dollars worth of optional equipment, none had the HeviDuty suspension you regarded as essential. Nor did the vehicles at any of the next three Empire dealers I visited, or the next half dozen in the surrounding area I called. The excuses were as plentiful as the HD equipped cars scarce: "It's not that great after all . . . You could have remote control mirrors for the same cost . . . It gives too rough a ride," etc. Most salesmen confessed they hadn't actually read the article.

I soon lost interest. My old car could suffice for a while longer. I wondered what good are the billions spent designing a new model if its success depends on the weakest link in the entire automotive distribution system—a salesman who doesn't know his product.

Yours truly,

cc: Mr. Harold D. Phillips
   Chairman, Empire Motors

LETTER LEVERAGE

The circumstances which justify sending an unsigned letter are few and far between. Most anonymous letters aren't taken seriously; the assumption being that if something is worth writing, it's worth signing.

A few exceptions follow. In each sample letter is a brief explanation for the anonymity. The postmaster might have disregarded his letter except that a carbon copy was sent to the U.S. Congressman for that district. Not knowing whether a follow-up inquiry might be made from the Congressman's office, he has no choice other than to investigate. Presto—the letter has served its purpose.

The letter to the automobile dealer is best left unsigned too, but for a different reason. Its overall complimentary tone and breezy, roundabout approach to the complaint isn't likely to get anyone fired. Nor was that the writer's intent. But it will probably be posted where mechanics can see it and that will accomplish its purpose.

More than vague generalities are needed if the IRS is to follow through on a report of tax evasion. Be as specific as you can with details after identifying the suspected cheater by name and address. Obviously, no reward for such information is possible if furnished anonymously.

ANONYMOUS LETTER TO POSTMASTER

Mr. Willard Smith
Postmaster
U.S. Post Office
street address
city, state ZIP

Dear Mr. Smith:

The new postal facilities planned for our village will certainly be a credit to the community. However, I believe that most residents are concerned more with the caliber of service than with architectural achievements.

I am referring specifically to the new letter carrier whose appointed rounds include Mountain Lane. For the past week he has made no effort to locate individual mailboxes. Instead while ambling along, he flings the mail in the general direction of the house (particularly vexing this past Thursday with 40 mph winds).

I have heard repeatedly that qualified postal employees are hard to find and retain in this town. And because this careless individual will, in spite of my complaint, probably remain on the U.S. Government payroll, I write an unsigned letter for the first time in my life . . . largely for fear of *never* getting mail again if he learns my identity.

My neighbors and I are not satisfied with this letter carrier, Mr. Smith, are you?

cc: Honorable Roger Matthews

ANONYMOUS LETTER TO CAR DEALER

Mr. O. Watson
Tara Motors, Inc.
street address
city, state ZIP

Dear Mr. Watson:

When I recently brought my car into your service department, I was greeted promptly and treated courteously. The work was satisfactorily performed and the job finished when promised. What's more, I'll return again to Tara Motors for future repairs in spite of one rather trifling complaint.

Because it caused me only minor annoyance and this letter requires no response, I'll leave it unsigned lest you folks consider it too nit-picking.

However, here goes. When I got home after picking up my car I noticed all three of my rear seat belts were completely out of sight and out of reach. Since they are used regularly by members of my family, I knew at once that this had happened at Tara Motors. Particularly curious, I daresay, because the car needed only engine work.

After lifting out the seat to get at the belts, I encountered several years' accumulation of dust, popcorn, and other assorted litter that gathers under car seats. Everything except the coins that usually reward one with such a search.

While I'd be the first to acknowledge that everyone in these inflationary times needs an ace in the hole, I think it might be a good idea to remind your people that after s̶t̶e̶a̶l̶i̶n̶g̶ acquiring coins in this fashion, common courtesy would dictate that they at least put the seat belts back where they found them.

ANONYMOUS LETTER TO IRS

Internal Revenue Service
Treasury Department
Washington, D.C. 20224

Dear IRS:

I am writing to report a clear-cut case of tax evasion. I wish to do so anonymously, and the knowledge that you will put a stop to this cheating will be reward enough for me.

Buford Bullwinkle of 642 Parkway Drive, Clover, Colorado, as your records will indicate, is employed as stockroom supervisor for the Aardvard Insurance Company of Denver. What you don't know is that for several years Bullwinkle has been conducting frequent garage sales—with a heavy emphasis on office supplies—from his home address.

Where he obtains these items is a matter of conjecture, but he boasts repeatedly that 100% of the proceeds goes directly into his pocket.

I am enclosing for substantiation five typical tear sheets of classified ads from various back issues of the Clover Clarion and have circled the notice of Bullwinkle's sales.

The rest is up to you!

Enclosures

5

Dealing With Neighbors

It would certainly simplify things if most differences with neighbors could be resolved in a peaceful, unemotional discussion over the back-yard fence. But it doesn't always work that way. Often small points of contention escalate in a most unneighborly fashion.

A letter, making your point without interruption or argument, has a better chance of getting results and a much lower likelihood of boiling over into a long-standing dispute.

It may be a simple request that you feel could best be made in writing. At the other end of the spectrum, a letter might be the only possible avenue of communication in a seemingly insoluble impasse.

In any case, stop short of drawing a line in the dirt. Allow your neighbor a face-saving way out of the dilemma. After all, you'll probably continue to be neighbors for some time whatever the outcome.

Finally, resist the temptation to save a stamp. Furtively dropping the letter in his mailbox is not only against postal regulations, but also can be an embarrassing disaster if you're spotted and asked for an explanation.

DOGS AND YOUR LAWN

Mr. Trundle:

Another disgusting pile was left on my front lawn by your dog this morning. And when I insisted that your son who was walking the dog at the time clean it up, he just shrugged his shoulders.

I went to the police station and asked Sgt. Campbell if there is any way to compel a thoughtless neighbor to discontinue this foul practice. It seems there is.

The next time your dog defecates on my property, the droppings will remain there as evidence till the police arrive. Then I will sign a complaint charging you with violation of the littering ordinance. An arrest warrant will be issued. You will be charged and doubtless post bond. A court date will be scheduled and I will take time from work to testify. And you will have to take time from work to respond. Perhaps with a good lawyer you might even be found innocent.

On the other hand, maybe you'll be smart enough to avoid all this. The choice is yours.

(sign)

WHEN SOMEONE TAKES YOUR PARKING SPACE
(to be placed under windshield wiper of car)

Dear Neighbor:

It took me half an hour to shovel the snow from this parking spot in front of the building where I live. I realize no one owns any part of a public street, but what you've done is a form of trespassing as I define it. Please don't park here again.

Thank you.

WHEN SOMEONE TAKES YOUR RESERVED PARKING SPACE

Mr. Howard:

While I've never been invited to one of your parties, I've come to feel like an unwilling co-host. Again last night, a car belonging to one of your guests—a red Mustang, license 1234—was in my clearly marked parking space when I returned home.

If I were as thoughtless as this individual, I suppose I could have taken someone else's spot. Instead I parked on the street nearly two blocks away. But never again!

I have just made arrangements with Ace Towing to remove any car that I find parked in my spot again. Next time it will cost your friend $40 to retrieve his car. That's cold cash . . . no checks or credit cards accepted.

A word from you in advance could spare your friends considerable expense and aggravation.

(sign)

ROWDY CHILDREN/APARTMENT

Dear Mrs. Edwards,

I came up to your apartment yesterday and was surprised to see that your girls were home alone. Pam told me you had started working full time last week. That explains why it's been so noisy upstairs the last few days. I explained to the girls that our newborn usually sleeps from 3:00 to 4:30, but that the noise from upstairs has been so bad he just fusses instead and is completely off his schedule.

I asked Pam to turn down the stereo and stop the gymnastics. Both she and Penny said they'd quiet down. Here it is the next day and just as noisy as before.

Please speak to the girls about this. I would appreciate it.

Sincerely,

ROWDY CHILDREN/HOUSE

Dear Mrs. Aspen,

Now that you're working full time and your boys are on their own after school, life has become an adventure around here. Apparently you have told Rick and Todd they cannot bring anyone into the house. Instead, a group of boys gathers in your backyard each day and their horsing around invariably spills over into our yard as well.

So far they have trampled a bed of tulips, knocked down our bird feeder and broken a branch off our birch tree. I've spoken to them more than once, and though your sons are always polite and apologetic, in no time at all it happens again.

I would appreciate it if you would suggest they go to the school playground or to nearby Belmar Park. Thank you.

Yours truly,

HIGH-RISE SNOOPING

Occupant
Apt. 22-A
Twin Towers
street address
city, state ZIP

Dear Occupant:

I'm not certain whether this letter is to be directed to you or to your next door neighbor. If you are not the owner of a high-powered telescope that is frequently trained on my window, please pass this along to the person next door.

If you are the one whose curiosity about his high-rise neighbors exceeds normalcy, I suggest that you point that thing in some other direction before it gets you in trouble. Peeping Toms, even at this lofty level, are not suffered gladly by the police.

(no signature)

WARNING ON A ZONING VIOLATION

Dear Mr. Goodman:

You may remember me, the neighbor who lives in the apartment building across the alley from you and who drives a blue Pontiac. From time to time we used to exchange a brief greeting if we happened to be pulling our cars in or out of our respective garages at the same time.

In recent months I haven't been able to use my garage when I'd like to, because the alley is frequently cluttered with the cars of your sons' friends and "customers." It's no secret in the neighborhood that your boys are using your entire 3-car garage to perform minor automotive repair work. From what I've heard, they're quite good at it which doubtless accounts for the line of cars waiting for service. Trouble is, they interfere with the movement of other cars that have legitimate reasons to be in the alley.

Zoning ordinances in this city were enacted to prevent such occurrences. May I suggest that you are not doing the boys a favor by allowing them to run a car repair shop from your garage. It's time they learn that one of the costs of doing business is the rent for space in an area zoned for commercial, not residential, use.

I certainly don't mean to stifle initiative, but you and your sons must understand that the convenience and low cost of running such a business out of your home is at the expense of others. It must stop.

I decided to write this letter to you rather than report the violation to the City Zoning Board. Hopefully your prompt action in correcting the matter will make the filing of a formal complaint unnecessary.

Yours,

ASKING A FAVOR

Dear Mr. Charles,

You may remember the day several weeks ago when I asked you to take down the wind chimes on your porch. Your bedrooms are at the front of your house and ours are at the back, so I realize that you probably aren't aware of how disturbing these chimes can be during the night.

Since my wife is in poor health and needs her sleep, I'd especially appreciate your doing something about this noise. Thanks in advance for your cooperation.

Yours truly,

ASKING A FAVOR

Dear Mr. and Mrs. Randall,

Our guests at backyard cookouts who once admired your remarkable vegetable garden are now asking what smells so bad. I didn't make the connection at first, but have recently concluded that your large and growing compost pile is responsible for both the successful garden and the disagreeable odor.

The far end of your lot line would seem to be the logical location for both your garden and the decaying matter; I probably would have done the same if I had a green thumb. But since our yard backs up against yours, the prevailing southwest winds bring more than the rustling of leaves.

I have several suggestions, any one of which could help relieve the problem at little or no inconvenience to you. Relocating the compost pile from its present spot to the far southeast corner of your property would continue to keep it near enough to the garden for easy access while, at the same time, the breeze would carry its reminder across the street toward the vacant lot. Another alternative would be to reduce the size of the pile to what apparently sufficed in the past. Finally, placing a tarpaulin or cover of some kind over the decaying material might help.

If the first suggestion sounds best, I'll have my oldest son lend a hand with wheelbarrow and shovel, if you'd like. Just give me a call.

Thanks in advance for your cooperation.

Sincerely,

LETTER LEVERAGE

Even the most recalcitrant neighbor will take notice when half the block is up in arms and confronting him with the threat of unified action. The following example shows how a group of people can apply pressure successfully when conventional appeals fail.

The threat of an avalanche of calls to one's place of business can be unsettling. The further hint of involving the boss, if need be, will in all likelihood make any such action unnecessary.

NEIGHBORS BANDING TOGETHER IN PROTEST

Mr. and Mrs. Barnes:

The time has long passed for still another appeal to reason in the matter of your dogs' barking at all hours of the day and night. You evidently don't care that this racket disturbs the entire neighborhood. And the police seem to view the matter as unimportant.

But the level of discontent among your neighbors has escalated to the point where you had better take notice. You may be oblivious to the noise when you're at home and unaware of it while you're at work, but we're sure you'll begin to understand the extent of our annoyance once we begin phoning you about it.

The undersigned intend to call you—whatever the hour—starting on May 5. The calls will come in the middle of the night if that's when the dogs are out in the yard barking. They may come during the day if the noise persists.

It is our understanding that you, Mr. Barnes, can be reached at the Cleaver Credit Co. at 426-5000, extension 302. If you're unavailable, your department head, Mr. Ross, on extension 300 could probably locate you in an emergency. Inquiries have established that you, Mrs. Barnes, are employed by the Roasty Toasty Co. and can be contacted at 647-2140, extension 14. We understand your supervisor, Mrs. Clemson on extension 20, would know of your whereabouts should we be unable to reach you.

Beginning on Monday, the six of us whose signatures appear below will take turns calling you when necessary.

Unless, of course, you're finally getting the message.

(signatures)

LETTER LEVERAGE

Subtle diplomacy is essential in approaching a neighbor with a suggestion that will cost him money.

Two points to be conveyed in such a letter are that your proposal will solve a problem and that it is a good investment for him.

FENCING OFF A PROBLEM

Dear Mr. Young:

When you and your family moved next door last year, Mrs. Tyler and I made every effort to be friendly. But evidently we're not your kind of people, and we accept that. What we find harder to accept are your dogs wandering into our backyard and your sons and their friends chasing each other across our property.

It's been said that good fences make good neighbors, and I'd like to make a proposal. We'd be willing to go 50-50 with you on a fence on the lot line separating our backyard from yours.

Many types of fences are available in a wide range of prices. Any one of them would increase the value of your property and mine, as well as make life a lot more pleasant for all concerned.

I would be happy to discuss this matter further with you at your convenience.

Cordially,

WHEN LEAVES BLOW YOUR WAY

Dear Mr. O'Neal,

Each fall I find myself somewhat bothered by a matter we discussed briefly last year. Perhaps it's slipped your mind, so I thought I'd put it in writing this time.

It concerns the leaves your sons rake up and put in piles at the curb. As you know the village's leaf sweep apparatus breaks down frequently, and it's often a matter of weeks between pickups. If, during that time the piles in front of your house seem to be shrinking, it's not an illusion. Many of those leaves blow right next door and wind up on my lawn. This, of course, means extra raking for me.

The favor is not returned when the wind shifts and blows from the east because, like most people on the block, I bag my leaves and put them at the curb for regular pickup by the garbage collectors.

May I suggest that you do likewise? The cost of lawn bags is minimal, and you'll notice the aesthetic improvement in no time. And I'd be most appreciative.

Best regards,

LETTER LEVERAGE

If the problems and solutions depicted in the preceding letters in this chapter don't yet have you packing for some remote uninhabited island, consider this. Most neighbors are pretty nice people. The better you get to know them, the sooner you'll realize that you have more in common than the same zip code.

These are the folks who are nearby when you need them . . . friends to whom you entrust the key to your home or apartment . . . who take in packages for you. And these neighbors respond as anyone else does to a friendly letter. The following examples show how a few minutes spent composing a note of appreciation for a favor done can go a long way.

THANKS FOR HELP WHILE HOSPITALIZED

Dear Rob and Randy,

After all these weeks in the hospital, I just received two pieces of good news. The doctor said that I can come home in a few days. And my wife told me how you two have been clearing the snow from our driveway and sidewalk just about as fast as it falls.

Believe me, that's one less thing to worry about. Having such good neighbors as you cheers me up no end.

My wife tells me you have refused to take any money for your efforts. But I think I've found a way around that. Please accept the enclosed check, not as payment for the snow shoveling, but as a sincere token of our appreciation for your thoughtfulness.

Thanks again . . . see you soon.

Sincerely yours,

THANKS FOR BRINGING DINNER

Dear Jackie,

You were so sweet to bring dinner over the night that I came home from the hospital with our new bundle of joy. The dinner was delicious, and I enjoyed the luxury of relaxing and enjoying the evening. Don did the cleanup, so I truly had the night off. Thanks a heap.

The best part about moving to Central City five years ago was moving next door to you!

Fondly,

THANKS FOR CHRISTMAS EXHIBIT

Dear Mr. and Mrs. Moran,

While we've never met, a note of appreciation seems appropriate. Your extraordinary outdoor Christmas displays have brightened many a holiday for our family and our guests. No Christmas gathering at our home ever ends without someone suggesting that we all drive by or walk past the house down the street with Santa Claus and the reindeer and the sleigh full of toys.

I'm sure no small amount of work goes into the preparation of this extravaganza (not to mention the hundreds of lights and music). But if you could see the wide-eyed expression on the faces of the youngsters, you'd know it's all worthwhile.

Thanks for keeping alive a grand tradition. Hope you and your family have a Merry Christmas and the happiest of New Years.

Yours truly,

COMMENDING PARENTS FOR THEIR HONEST CHILD

Dear Mr. and Mrs. Davis,

I'm enclosing a bill for the replacement of my dining room window. As I mentioned on the phone yesterday, your son Jeff came to my door and admitted he was the one who threw the ball that caused the damage. The other boys scattered when it happened, but Jeff offered to pay for the broken window out of the earnings from his paper route.

You are both to be commended for instilling such a sense of responsibility in your son. Point out to him that the bill is marked "PAID" because I was so impressed with his honesty. I do hope, though, that he'll be more careful in the future.

Sincerely,

6

Sorry, I Goofed

It's as true today as ever that "for lack of a nail . . . the war was lost." So, too, have many meaningful relationships been severed because neither party was willing to say, "I'm sorry." Saying those two little words can be quite difficult. Yet, the ability to say them is an indication of an inner strength—the strength to put one's pride aside for another's sake.

If you find yourself in this position, a letter of apology is an effective tool for getting to the heart of the matter. Taking the time to put your thoughts on paper will enable you to choose your words carefully and express yourself sincerely without being interrupted.

MISSED OUR DATE

Dear Nancy,

I could tell by the tone of your voice tonight that you are upset with me for forgetting our luncheon date, and I can't blame you.

There's no excuse for my stupidity; I forgot to look at my calendar. I would hate to have this slip-up cause a rift in our friendship. Please forgive me, Nancy.

To make up for the mess I've made, I'd like to invite you here for lunch next Wednesday, the 12th. Let's get together.

Cordially,

MISSED OUR DATE

Dear Elizabeth and Ron,

As you can see by the enclosed page from our calendar, I wrote your dinner party on the wrong date! After talking with you today and trying to explain, we long to be able to make this up to you somehow.

Please accept the enclosed tickets to the Jets game on December 2nd as a peace offering for the embarrassment our two empty chairs caused you Saturday night.

Fondly,

CARELESS REMARK

Dear Emily,

As I thought over our conversation yesterday at the PTA open house I began to feel terrible because I think I may have hurt your feelings. I cringe every time I recall the remark I made after you had shared your concern about joining Bruce in New Jersey rather than waiting for your house to sell.

I was encouraging you to go ahead since you dread being alone, especially at night. You mentioned that the realtor was urging you to stay because, when a house is being showed to a prospective buyer, it looks better furnished. When I said, "I don't see how it would look any worse unfurnished," you looked at me kind of funny. I didn't realize how awful it sounded.

Please forgive me for a stupid choice of words. What I was trying to communicate was, as long as Bruce's company is going to cover any moving expenses you have, why should you listen to a realtor? There's no need to stay behind and be unhappy when you could be in your new home with Bruce. I can see why you didn't get that message from my thoughtless comment.

I'll be calling you next week to make sure we have this ironed out.

Sincerely,

THE BEST OF INTENTIONS . . .

Dear Gabe and Lois,

Your wedding was beautiful, and the reception was elegant. Now that you're back from your honeymoon, you still haven't received a wedding gift from Don and me. We feel badly about it and want you to know what happened.

Six weeks before your wedding date I called Linden's Finer China to order a place setting of your dinnerware. I was assured the china would be gift wrapped and delivered immediately. Two weeks before the wedding I called again because I had not received an invoice. I was informed that your pattern was out of stock, but would be coming in any day.

Today I went to Linden's in person, saw that the china is in, watched them wrap it up and wrote a card to include with it.

"Better late than never," isn't much consolation because we tried so hard to be on time. Many happy years to you.

Fondly,

A MISUNDERSTANDING

Dear Joan,

Let's not let a little misunderstanding come between us. I was sure you had said you would pick up a gift for Holly, and you thought that I was taking care of it. When we both arrived at the bridal shower separately, each without the present, it was embarrassing for both of us.

I'm sorry I didn't check with you before the shower. Holly was very understanding, but I'm eager to get her a gift soon. I suggest we each get our own gift this time so there won't be any more confusion.

Sincerely,

FAMILY FEUD

Dear Aunt Karen,

The first family reunion in 15 years was an event I looked forward to for months. Till then, it seemed the only time our relatives gathered was at funerals. Finally, we were gathering for a festive occasion.

I'm still in despair over the day ending on such a sour note. I personally want to extend an apology to you for my part in the harangue over old and distorted differences.

You were gracious to invite us all to your house, and I know you worked very hard to make the day a success. I'm truly sorry it was ruined by personality conflicts. For my part, I will do my best to make up with those I locked horns with.

Thank you for your efforts and your affection for all of us. I hope to see you again soon.

Love,

CLUMSY ME

Dear Marlene,

I'm still sick over the way I shattered your beautiful antique cut-glass pitcher. You were very gracious at the party, and I thank you for that.

I realize that particular pitcher is irreplaceable, but I hope you will use the enclosed check to purchase a similar one.

Sincerely,

WE'LL UNDO WHAT OUR PET DID

Dear Mr. and Mrs. Osterman,

Although I apologized in person for the damage our dog did to your yard yesterday, I want you to know how badly we feel about it and to assure you that it will not happen again.

The chain that had secured Bonehead for the last two years snapped, and I wasn't aware that he was loose until he had dug that huge hole in the middle of your yard. If you incur any expenses repairing the damage, let us know, and we will cover them. We have purchased a new chain, twice as thick, so Bonehead surely will be confined to our yard.

Thank you for being good neighbors and for being patient with us and our dog.

Sincerely,

BROKEN TOY

Dear Mrs. Aberdeen,

Jennifer came home from your house yesterday and burst into tears as she told me how she had accidentally broken Amy's "Music Box Tick Tock Clock." You were very kind to not even mention it to me, but Jennifer feels terrible and we would like to make it up to Amy.

We went to Marshall Field's today and purchased a new one which will be delivered to Amy by the end of the week. Thank you for your hospitality and your understanding.

Cordially,

HERE'S THE MONEY I OWE YOU

Dear Sally,

Wow, is my face red! It just dawned on me that I had never returned the $40 I borrowed from you last month to buy that old porch swing at the garage sale we went to on Central Avenue.

I'm enclosing a check and apologize for the oversight. I wish you had reminded me.

The swing creaks and squeaks, but is very comfortable . . . a great place to sit and watch the world go by.

Be sure to let me know when you hear of another garage sale. I'll bring enough of my own money next time.

Fondly,

HERE'S THE MONEY I OWE YOU

Dear Red,

As I was emptying the pockets of my tan summer slacks before taking them to the cleaners, I came across a crumpled note. It was a reminder I had written myself to pay the $20 you loaned me.

It dawned on me that I hadn't worn those pants since we all were at the County Fair last Labor Day. In a flash I remembered tapping you for a loan before we went out to dinner.

Here, months later, is a check. Why on earth didn't you remind me? Oh, well, I'll bet you're more careful whom you lend to these days.

Apologetically,

WHEN CHECK BOUNCES

Dear Roll-Rite Company:

I've just received notice from my bank telling me that I didn't have enough in my account to cover the check for $160.75 which I gave you on May 16 in payment for two new tires.

I immediately deposited ample funds, and am assured that the check will be honored if you will re-submit it.

Please accept my apologies for this oversight.

Yours truly,

7

Communicating With School Officials

Most questions concerning your child's progress in school are discussed and answered at regularly scheduled parent-teacher conferences. And the open house each fall usually provides parents with a comprehensive overview.

However, there are times when problems arise. Perhaps the teacher fails to return your calls . . . or when it seems your child has been singled out for particularly harsh discipline . . . or when you disagree in principle with administration policy.

That's the time for a tactful letter to the next higher level of authority. Keep in mind, however, that such escalation shouldn't be overdone. The system couldn't function if every minor incident were appealed to the principal or superintendent.

You'll find that most school administrators are genuinely responsive to constructive suggestions. They, too, have an interest in seeing that things go smoothly, so don't keep a good idea to yourself.

PARENT-TEACHER CONFERENCE SUGGESTION TO PRINCIPAL

Dear Miss Collins:

I received the forms for scheduling parent-teacher conferences for this semester and noticed that again this year teachers are available only during school hours, and from 3:00 to 5:00 P.M. Those hours are obviously convenient for the faculty, but impose a real hardship on families where both husband and wife hold full-time jobs. Since this has become commonplace in recent years, I'd like to suggest that evening conferences be arranged to accommodate such families.

My husband and I are very interested in our children's progress and look forward to having an opportunity to meet with their teachers.

Yours truly,

PROPOSAL TO PRINCIPAL FOR AFTER SCHOOL CLUB

Dear Mr. Hill:

Now that I am working full-time, I am concerned about the unsupervised period my children have from the time they are dismissed from school until I get home each evening. I have discussed this with other parents in the same situation, and we have a few ideas that we would like to have you bring to the School Board.

Could the school district provide (for a fee) an After School Club for children who are too old for day care and too young to be home alone? We have a number of suggestions on what could be done for the two to three hours, things like crafts . . . a quiet room where kids could do homework . . . gym time . . . after school snacks . . . a creative corner where children could write, paint or practice their musical instruments. Maybe even a once-a-week emphasis on scholastic assistance in various subjects for any youngster who would like it.

We realize this would involve organization, availability of adult supervisors and instructors, etc. The revenue this much-needed program would generate from participating parents would more than cover the salaries of the people staffing this program. We would be happy to meet with you and talk over details.

Thank you for considering our proposal.

Yours truly,

ASKING THE PRINCIPAL TO HELP STOP ROWDYISM

Dear Mr. Bowen:

Many years have passed since my own children attended Maplewood School. Until recently I enjoyed exchanging a wave or greeting with the youngsters passing by on their way to and from school.

That's all changed. Since classes began in September, a group of young toughs who appear to be seventh or eighth graders have made life quite unpleasant for me and many of my neighbors on Elm Street. I particularly object to their taking a shortcut across my front yard. My shrubbery has been ruined and a path worn across what was once a respectable lawn.

When I reprimanded the boys, they responded with a torrent of obscenities. Yesterday I was pelted with snowballs by these thugs while walking my dog. The police arrived long after the boys had left and showed little interest.

I have an idea that might put an end to this harassment once and for all. If you could find the time, I'd be honored if you'd join me for tea any afternoon at 2:45. Within 30 minutes you'd see for yourself what I mean. I can just see the look on their faces when the principal of Maplewood School steps out on the porch and calls them over by name.

Yours truly,

LETTER LEVERAGE

When you feel your child has received unfair or harsh treatment at school, it's difficult to remain calm and rational because you're emotionally involved. A frantic phone call to the principal just isn't as effective as a carefully composed letter from a concerned parent with a justifiable complaint. The letter could even be addressed to the teacher, but be sure a copy of it finds its way into the principal's hands.

Make no demands and don't push too hard; the principal usually is, after all, the one who will determine how the issue will be resolved. Make it clear by the tone of your letter that he can handle the matter to your satisfaction, but don't hesitate to hint diplomatically that if he doesn't, he hasn't heard the end of it.

GOING BEYOND THE TEACHER WITH A COMPLAINT

Dear Mr. Green:

As principal of Wellspring School I'm sure you've had your share of input from parents over the years. As a member of the PTA board and through involvement in numerous volunteer projects at the school, I've enjoyed being a part of the Wellspring "family" and have had numerous opportunities to voice my opinions. However, this is the first time I come to you with a personal concern, and I know I can rely on you to be fair.

As you know, our daughter, Meg, is in the sixth grade. Until recently she has loved school. As you know, she has always been rather shy, and I was pleased at my parent-teacher conference when Miss Grundy said she was determined to bring Meg "out of her shell." Little did I know that her method would be to humiliate Meg in front of her peers in order to drive her to stand up and defend herself. Her efforts to toughen Meg have had the opposite effect.

My husband and I are quite concerned and want this bullying stopped. When I spoke to Miss Grundy she seemed quite annoyed and told me not to tell her how to run her classroom. I would appreciate it if you would speak to her.

If a noticeable improvement isn't apparent immediately, please advise us on the procedures to be followed with the superintendent's office to have Meg transferred to Mrs. Taylor's sixth grade class.

Yours truly,

COMPLAINT TO GYM TEACHER

Dear Mr. Strong:

My son, Ralph, sadly recounted the tirade you directed at him today, and I must take exception to your methods.

Ralph says he was berated in front of the entire gym class and called a sissy for his inability to do enough pushups or climb the rope ladder as quickly as you'd like.

You, Mr. Strong, of all people should know that not all children have equal physical strength and coordination. For what it's worth, Ralph has always given the best that was in him in gym as in everything else. He knows and I know that his efforts fall short of the achievements of some other seventh graders, and we both wish it were otherwise.

But instead of encouragement, he is showered with abuse, not by his peers, but by his instructor. I find it inexcusable.

Fortunately such insensitivity is the exception rather than the rule at Alton Junior High.

Yours truly,

cc: Mr. Jones, Principal

ALERTING PRINCIPAL TO PROBLEMS WITH BUSES

Dear Ms. Kenton:

These past two weeks have been nerve-wracking for us as our daughter, Michelle, leaves home each morning not knowing how long she will have to stand on a cold, blustery corner waiting for her bus. Seven out of the last ten days she has been late for school because of the bus. Classes still start on time, and she invariably misses some important instruction.

The school secretary tells us on the phone that you are aware of the problem and that the children will not be penalized. That's easy for her to say because she apparently doesn't realize that being late and nearly frozen is quite a penalty in itself.

If this continues, I will be contacting the district superintendent to see what can be done to solve the problem.

Sincerely,

FIELD TRIP SUGGESTION FOR PRINCIPAL

Dear Mr. McHenry:

Yesterday I accompanied my daughter's class (Mrs. Whitby's third graders) to the museum. It was my first experience as a volunteer mother on a field trip and was quite an eye-opener. Mrs. Whitby and I were the only adults trying to keep track of 25 children.

As we gathered to go to the bus at the end of our tour, we discovered that one of the children was missing. It was another 45 minutes before we were able to locate him.

It seems to me that this could have been avoided easily by having more adult supervision. From now on, I will make sure there is more supervision before I allow my daughter to go on another field trip.

You should be thankful there wasn't a tragic ending to this episode. I certainly am thankful that I had the opportunity to see first-hand what goes on. I have learned my lesson well—get all the facts before entrusting my child to others, even at school.

Yours truly,

URGING PRINCIPAL TO IMPROVE LUNCHROOM SUPERVISION

Dear Mr. Willow:

My son, Gary, has been anxiously awaiting the day he would be old enough to be in first grade and get to eat his lunch at school. Imagine my surprise when, after the fourth day, he cried in the morning and said he didn't want to go to school. I tried to get him to tell me what was wrong, but he wouldn't. I took him to school and told his teacher, Miss Holly, of the problem. She was surprised, and said she would see if she could get Gary to confide in her.

Two days later he finally broke down and told me he hated eating lunch at school because he was afraid of Mrs. Hemlock. I called a few other mothers and found that they had heard similar complaints from their children. I dropped in at lunch time and observed Mrs. Hemlock shouting at the top of her voice at the first, second and third graders, while the older children seemed to be managing pretty well under Mrs. Dash's supervision.

I would like to suggest that, if Mrs. Hemlock must be a lunchroom supervisor, she be placed in charge of the older children who could better cope with her outbursts. If you don't agree with this suggestion, several of the mothers who have the same complaint will join me in paying you a visit.

Sincerely,

TELLING PRINCIPAL ABOUT ABUSIVE PATROL BOY

Dear Mr. Duffy:

My second-grade son, Scott, told me something I think you will find of interest.

While we live only two blocks from the school, Scott goes considerably out of his way to avoid an intimidating sixth-grade patrol boy named Larry who "owns" the corner of Pine Street and Cadwell Road. He feels taking the longer four-block walk via Pine and Central is preferable to enduring the daily taunts and bullying.

Instead of viewing this alternate route as a long-term solution, I hope you will speak to Larry and straighten him out. Patrol boys certainly have an important job, and should be obeyed in the interests of safety. But the authority is evidently being abused in this case.

Perhaps a more careful screening of sixth graders in the future could weed out any candidates with a sadistic bent.

Yours truly,

LETTER LEVERAGE

On the rare occasion when a single letter can bring about significant change, it's not so much what you have to say as to whom the message is beamed. And sometimes it pays to go straight to the top in an attempt to change school administration policy. The writer addressed the following model letter to the one key individual she felt would be most sympathetic to her plea.

A heavy-handed approach with carbons to all school board members and the superintendent on such a sensitive issue would have, at best, polarized the pro and con advocates.

Instead, the writer is generally complimentary, and mentions in passing that the subject has already been discussed with the superintendent.

Finally, an appeal to the reader's sense of fair play follows, coupled with an observation that times are changing and School District 44 shouldn't lag behind.

Let us assume that the letter to Mrs. Stein succeeded in its purpose. And that five years later the pendulum has swung in the opposite direction. Read on page 80 how another parent might once again seek to achieve a proper balance.

The letter to the superintendent with responsibility for the school with the discipline problem has a better chance of getting his attention when you indicate you're sending copies to the mayor and school board.

Feel free to let the people in charge know when you feel that "business as usual" is unacceptable, especially when it's contract renewal time.

AN APPEAL TO THE SCHOOL BOARD PRESIDENT

Dear Mrs. Stein:

Our entire family looks forward to the winter musical program presented by the students of Madison Elementary School. I have one suggestion which, I think, would make it even better.

Last year's theme, "Silent Night," certainly seemed slanted toward the observance of Christmas. Since Hanukkah occurs at about the same time, I feel future winter musical programs should strike a fair balance and contain several numbers which would be of significance to Jewish children as well.

I spoke with Superintendent Powers about this, but was left with the impression he didn't agree. That's why I'm turning to you as President of the School Board.

I would hope that further consideration of this matter is warranted in view of the fact than an increasing percentage of children in District 44 are of the Jewish faith. So, too, are 3 out of 5 school board members. I hope you will agree with me that the old way is no longer the only way.

Yours truly,

ASKING THE SUPERINTENDENT TO REVIEW POLICY

Dear Dr. Powers:

The subtle evolution of the winter musical program as presented by the Madison Elementary School students over the years has not gone unnoticed. Without disparaging the enthusiastic efforts of the youngsters, I was disappointed with "Happy Holidays."

Evidently the mere mention of Christmas so infuriates some members of our community that all reference to the true meaning of the holiday has been effectively suppressed. Would not fairness then require that all numbers blithely refer (as most did) to such generalities as glistening snow, sleigh rides, bells and toys? Incredibly, the lighting of Hanukkah candles and other symbolic songs and rituals of the Jewish faith were interspersed throughout.

I believe it would be more appropriate to plan a program that would be meaningful to both Christians and Jews, or to exclude absolutely all references to religious ceremonies.

Yours truly,

HOW TO RESTORE DISCIPLINE IN A PROBLEM SCHOOL

Dr. H. W. Palmer
General Superintendent of Schools
street address
city, state ZIP

Dear Dr. Palmer:

Unless radical changes are made soon, things will be completely out of control at Madison High School. Each evening my sophomore son tells of the deplorable conditions in this school . . . gang recruiting in the hallways . . . frequent assaults on students and teachers alike . . . weapons carried by at least one-third of the students . . . drug transactions in the washrooms . . . and an atmosphere of chaos that makes learning all but impossible.

My personal appeals to the principal, Mr. Jefferson, have fallen on deaf ears. He is apparently unable or unwilling to attempt reforms. What's needed—and without further delay—is his replacement by a no-nonsense principal backed by a concerned and responsive administration.

Following are some suggestions which, if implemented by a firm and respected principal, could put Madison High back in the business of educating:

—Declare Madison a "closed campus" . . . only the front door to be open . . . no students permitted to leave the building for lunch or until his/her classes for the day are finished . . . no one who leaves the building to be readmitted that day.

—Prominently displayed laminated I.D. tags bearing the student's photo and signature.

—Hiring as many off-duty policemen as necessary to enforce the new regulations and put a stop to terrorism in the building.

—An end to the casual attitude about class attendance . . . 3, 4 or 5 (?) cuts meaning automatic suspension.

Admittedly, Dr. Palmer, such a commitment will mean a significant departure from the past and no small amount of work. But aren't the education and safety of the next generation at least worth giving it a try?

Cordially,

cc: Mayor J. J. Abbott
Members of Board of Education

DON'T SETTLE FOR SECOND-RATE SUPPLIERS OF SCHOOL SERVICES

Mrs. James H. Connelly
President
Board of Education
street address
city, state ZIP

Dear Mrs. Connelly:

School busing is causing quite a problem in Plainfield.

I'm referring, of course, to the deplorable service of the Class-A Transit Company. Buses invariably run late. They're cold in the winter, and are dirty and poorly maintained year 'round.

I urge you and the Board not to renew Class-A's contract when it expires next June. There are several competing school bus companies serving nearby communities satisfactorily. I'm sure these firms would be happy to enter a bid on serving Plainfield's school system.

Sincerely yours,

LETTER LEVERAGE

Chances are, you'll never have to or want to level both barrels at a faculty member with the intensity the writer summoned for her letter to the oppressive librarian. But when your patience is exhausted, and you know your cause is just, let loose with a real zinger.

Its effectiveness is enhanced with the carbon copy to the principal. If the letter and its copy are to be hand delivered by your child, instruct the youngster to bring the copy to the principal's office first lest the librarian take steps to dissuade delivery or offer to do so herself and conveniently "lose" it.

Poetic justice requires that the iniative be regained and the reader instructed to fill out the improvised form at the bottom of the letter.

If all goes as expected, Mrs. Bombard will be properly subdued and never again try to intimidate you or your youngster.

LOWERING THE BOOM ON A LAX LIBRARIAN

Dear Mrs. Bombard:

I was certainly disappointed to hear that you thought my son, Jonathan, had misplaced a library book again. As you may recall, a similar accusation was made last January which resulted in my sending you a check for $25.50, the purported value of the seven "missing" books. A week later you returned the check after finding the books in the library.

While Jonathan assures me that he returned "Greatest World Series Thrillers" to the bin in April, I have, as you brusquely put it, no choice but to pay for the book. Please indicate its value on the form below, detach and return to Jonathan.

Your threat to withhold Jonathan's report card until this missing book is paid for seemed particularly inappropriate in that I wasn't even made aware that the book hasn't been accounted for until your phone call this afternoon.

In order to avoid such confrontations in the future, I intend to personally return each and every one of Jonathan's library books myself. Not to the bin, but to you or one of your associates. I will then wait until I have seen the books properly checked in.

Yours truly,

cc: Mr. Peter Plunkett, Principal

The cost of replacing "Greatest World Series Thrillers" is _____ .
I will, of course, return the check if the book reappears in the library.

_____

LETTER LEVERAGE

Brevity will suffice for such routine matters as excuses for absences due to illness and requests for a gym excuse where there's no need for a doctor's authorization. It's also a good idea to let the teacher know in advance when you plan on taking your children out of school for a few days. The offer to make up any lost class time indicates you take seriously the matter of missed lessons, and usually sits well with the teacher.

When a teacher has gone beyond what's expected or produced very satisfactory results with your child, your complimentary letter can brighten the day.

NOTE OF ABSENCE

Dear Miss Coleman,

Tony was absent yesterday because he had 24-hour flu. He's feeling fine this morning and was eager to get back to school.

I'll be home all day. If there's any problem, feel free to call me and I'll pick him up.

Sincerely,

NOTE OF ABSENCE

Dear Mrs. Meyers,

Adam was absent yesterday because my mother suddenly became ill, and we had to drive into the city for the day. Because it happened so unexpectedly I didn't have a chance to make arrangements for him to come home to a neighbor's house.

Please send home any work that you would like Adam to make up. Thank you.

Yours truly,

GYM EXCUSE/INJURY

Dear Miss Cutler,

Please excuse Lisa from gym today and tomorrow. She twisted her ankle Friday after school while she was taking her ballet lesson.

Lisa will be happy to make up what she will miss. Thank you for your understanding.

Sincerely,

GYM EXCUSE/ILLNESS

Dear Mr. Campbell,

I would appreciate it very much if you would excuse Jimmy from gym class today. He had an asthma attack last night and shouldn't be involved in physical activity for 24 hours.

Thank you, and please let Jimmy know what he can do to make up the missed class.

Yours truly,

TAKING YOUR CHILD OUT OF SCHOOL FOR VACATION

Dear Miss Diamond,

Cheryl will be absent for three days before Thanksgiving because our family plans to fly to Florida that week to visit my parents. Ordinarily we wouldn't schedule a vacation during the school year, but that week was the only time my husband could get time off from his job.

If you would be so kind as to write up assignments for Cheryl, we will make sure she spends some time on her school work each day. Thank you for your help.

Cordially yours,

PRAISING HELPFUL TEACHER

Dear Mrs. Dover,

There has been a noticeable improvement in Terry's pronunciation of "S" and "TH" sounds since she entered your remedial speech class in the fall.

I especially appreciate your tactful way of working with the youngsters. Treating a slight impediment as a common but correctable variation of speech patterns helps overcome the self-consciousness which the child would have felt in a less enlightened atmosphere.

While the tax rate which supports School District 105 has come under frequent criticism, a closer look will show that taxpayers are getting their money's worth with programs like this.

Thanks for your help.

Yours truly,

LETTER LEVERAGE

If your mailbox seems fuller when you have a teenager in the junior or senior year of high school, it's because many of the 1,500 colleges and universities in this country have access to a list with your child's name on it and want to acquaint prospective applicants with what they have to offer. However flattering such solicitations may seem, they are but the tip of the iceberg.

To cover all bases your youngster should take the initiative and contact others, too. Reference books in high schools and public libraries list pertinent information about each college or university including the name of the person to contact in the admissions department.

Two or three paragraphs are sufficient to provide a brief introduction, request desired information and/or catalogs and name a field of particular interest if applicable.

Fairness requires that if your child has received a notice of acceptance and changes his mind, a prompt response declining the offer of admission be sent. And the sooner the better, so that the spot can be reassigned to another applicant.

REQUESTING INFORMATION FROM COLLEGES

Dear Admissions Director:

I am considering applying for admission to Stars and Stripes University. I am a junior at Handsome High in Los Angeles and will be entering college a year from September.

Please forward an application, a catalog and any other information you have for applicants, including application procedures for financial aid.

I'm interested in a career in architecture. Any additional information on that area of study would be helpful.

Thank you,

DECLINING COLLEGE ACCEPTANCE

Dear Dean Schultz:

The notice of acceptance to the University of Lore was very much appreciated. I enjoyed my visit to the campus last summer and my interview with Mrs. McCarthy was very helpful.

I have decided instead to enter the University of Knowledge in September. It was a difficult decision to make, because I like both schools.

Thank you again for your consideration.

Yours truly,

8

Coping With Sad Occasions

Into every life come times of separation, illness and death. As we witness friends going through these situations, we can either offer comfort or we can avoid them, wait till time passes, and then try to resume the friendship. If you choose to do the latter, don't be surprised if you get a cold shoulder.

When a person is going through a difficult time, the awareness that someone else cares and is available eases the pain. Don't hesitate to write to a friend at a time like this, even if you can't think of what to say. A long letter isn't necessary . . . just a note will do.

When you are with someone who is suffering, your silence is often more appreciated than empty words. The same goes for your note of sympathy or condolence—just say what comes from your heart, don't feel you have to add a lot of flowery phrases.

You may find a greeting card that says it well, but often only the name is read when a person is receiving a number of cards at a time. A handwritten note, however, will be noticed, read, and appreciated as an indication that your words are sincerely your own.

Read through the following samples, mix, match and add till you have a message that expresses your heartfelt sentiments. You can bring a ray of hope into someone's day.

TO FRIEND ON DEATH OF HUSBAND

Dear Doris,

It's hard for us to understand how Marshall's suffering has now turned into a time of celebration and joy for him now that he's in the land of "no more tears." It would be selfish for us to want to bring him back, but down deep how we wish we could.

It's good to know that your married children are close by and will be looking after you in the difficult days ahead. We're only a phone call away if there's anything we can do.

Lovingly,

TO FRIEND ON DEATH OF HUSBAND

Dear Gloria,

Heartfelt sympathy and much love to you, dear friend, as you go through this time of grief.

Stan was one of those extraordinary people who will never be forgotten. His life was like a sunbeam that lit up the world around him. Now we can bask in the rainbow of the memories that we'll nurture in the years ahead.

No, it won't be the same without him by any means, but we will go on as best we can and look forward to the day we will meet again in eternity.

Love,

TO FRIEND ON DEATH OF WIFE

Dear Jerry,

The news of Evelyn's death came as a shock. There isn't much one can say to ease your sense of loss, but I want you to know my thoughts are with you in this time of sorrow.

When Alice died four years ago, I felt the bottom had dropped out of my world, too. But there's nowhere to go but up from the depths of despair, and, little by little, you'll find that time begins to heal your grief.

Please accept my deepest sympathy.

Your friend,

TO FRIEND ON DEATH OF MOTHER

Dear Lucy,

As I contemplate the emotions you must be experiencing after your mom's death, the ache within can only be eased by the assurance of Psalm 121:

"I will lift up mine eyes unto the hills,
from whence cometh my help.
My help cometh from the Lord,
which made heaven and earth.

He will not suffer thy foot to be moved:
He that keepeth thee will not slumber.
The Lord shall preserve thee from all evil:
He shall preserve thy soul.
The Lord shall preserve thy going out
and thy coming in from this time forth,
and even for evermore."

Rest in the knowledge that she is wrapped in His everlasting arms.

Sincerely yours,

TO FRIEND ON DEATH OF FATHER

Dear Earl,

Over the years we've heard much about the "Promised Land." In my heart I know your dad now knows that land as home.

He was always so good to us kids in the neighborhood. I especially remember the years he was our Little League coach. Can you imagine how much patience he must have had? Thanks for sharing him with us.

Yours,

TO COUSIN ON DEATH OF FATHER

Dear Toby,

My mother called today with the sad news of the death of your Dad.

It's hard to imagine a world without Uncle Ken. Though the memories of the hazy, lazy days of summer at the cottage in Green Lake have begun to blur, he always kept in touch with birthday cards and boxes of Florida grapefruit each Christmas.

May a lifetime of wonderful memories give strength to you and the family in the days ahead.

Fondly,

TO FRIENDS WHO LOST A CHILD

Dear Bob and Julie,

Words seem so useless at a time like this, but I had to let you know how much I care and how much I hurt with you.

Mike was the kind of son any parent would be proud of. His self-confidence and charming way were evidence of the fact that he was very much loved at home.

Be assured of my availability and eagerness to help in any way I can. Call on me, please.

Sincerely,

DEATH OF A NEWBORN

Dear Jenny and Nick,

I am stunned at the news that your baby died shortly after birth. As I shared your joy of anticipation during the past months, I now share your grief. The "whys" of life have never been answered, but at a time like this, it seems all we can say is, "Why?"

Be assured of my loving concern and availability.

Lovingly,

TO WIDOW OF FAVORITE DOCTOR

Dear Mrs. Stetson,

I was saddened to read of Dr. Stetson's death yesterday. Though you don't know me, I wanted to write to tell you how much he was appreciated by me and my husband.

The first time I saw Dr. Stetson was in 1964 when I was expecting my first child. He had just delivered one of "his babies' " babies, so I knew he'd been around awhile. Yet there was such a contagious enthusiasm about him—each baby was indeed a special event. When I had difficulty with my pregnancy, his reassurance and readiness to see me always calmed my fears. He was very kind and patient with all my questions and my nervousness.

After we moved to Plainfield, I became pregnant and my husband pleaded with me to find a local obstetrician so he wouldn't have to worry about getting me all the way to Memorial Hospital. I went to the new doctor for three visits and then I broke down in tears and told my husband that I wanted to go back to Dr. Stetson more than anything else in the world. He could see how important it was to me and said fine. It was so good to be back!

That baby is almost eleven years old now, so I haven't seen Dr. Stetson in awhile, but I'll always have fond memories of a gentle, caring doctor who treated each patient as if she were the most important one of all.

In order to be such a loving man he must have been very much loved by his family. You must be a very special person, too. I feel privileged to have known him.

Very sincerely yours,

TO BUSINESS ASSOCIATE ON DEATH OF SPOUSE

Dear Andy,

Our entire office was shocked and saddened to hear of your wife's tragic automobile accident. There is little anyone can say or do at a time like this to ease your grief, but all of us who knew Irene join me in expressing our deepest sympathy.

She was a wonderful person, and I'm sure that you and the children will be sustained in the difficult days ahead by many happy memories.

Sincerely,

TO A FRIEND WITH SERIOUS ILLNESS

Dear Jean,

Illness and pain, two of life's most dreaded commodities, have been your constant companions recently. It's comforting to know that you are in God's hands, that you trust Him totally and that He has given you such peace and strength through this ordeal. You remind me of the Apostle Paul when he wrote, "So we do not lose heart. Though our outer nature is wasting away, our inner nature is being renewed every day. For this slight momentary affliction is preparing for us an eternal weight of glory beyond all comparison." (II Corinthians 4:16,17)

The evidence of God's grace in your life during this difficult time has strengthened my faith and given me the courage to face tomorrow. I praise the Lord for giving you the ability to be a window for others to look through to see His power and strength.

Your sister in Christ,

TO A FRIEND WHO IS TERMINALLY ILL

Dear Brenda,

Last night I kept going over in my mind what you had told me about your diagnosis. After all you have gone through, it seems unfair to learn that the doctors consider your case hopeless. Your strength and calmness are a mystery to me, but I'm thankful you have such a positive attitude.

As for me, I believe hope is eternal. We hear of miracles every day. Sure, I know they don't happen to everyone, but I will continue to hope and pray that there will be a miracle in your life.

In the meantime, I will be coming to see you regularly and will not pretend or put on a happy face for your sake. You can be honest with me.

If you need a laugh, we'll reminisce over some of the crazy things we used to do. If you need to cry, my shoulder will be available. Your friendship is one of my dearest treasures.

Lovingly,

TO CO-WORKER IN HOSPITAL

Dear Kaye,

You are missed! It's awfully quiet around here without you.

I'm so glad your surgery went well. Now comes the hard part—taking it easy. This will be a whole new experience for you, the perpetual-motion machine. Please take your time. The body has a marvelous healing process, but it sometimes works more slowly than we'd like.

The others and I are splitting up your work. If we have any questions, we know where to find you!

Sincerely,

SORRY TO HEAR OF YOUR ACCIDENT

Dear Greg,

I was sorry to hear about your slipping on the ice and breaking your leg. And it's probably no consolation to have all those pretty nurses waiting in line to comfort you.

For what it's worth, you're the best stockboy our store ever had. We'll manage somehow while you're away. So don't hurry back to work till you're sure you can handle it. The job will still be here, and that's a promise.

Sincerely,

SORRY TO HEAR OF YOUR ACCIDENT

Dear Adelle,

The news of your auto accident didn't reach me till today because I was out of town. Your progress so far sounds encouraging, and I know Dr. Reynolds is tops.

I'll keep calling the hospital each day until they say I can come see you. Meanwhile, I told your mom I'd be happy to water your plants and take care of your sweet kitty. Take your time getting well. All your friends here at the apartment building send their love . . .

Especially me,

SORRY TO HEAR OF YOUR ACCIDENT

Dear Hans,

What a terrible way to spend your vacation—in a hospital bed. Your ski accident was a real bummer, especially since you are so far from home and none of the gang can pop in to cheer you up.

We're hoping when you return you'll have some words of advice to the rest of the Northwest Ski Club on how to avoid a similar mishap. We'll also want to hear your first impressions when you saw the St. Bernard approaching with a keg of brandy.

On the other hand, maybe you've decided to take up chess instead. In which case we'll simply disband, follow the leader, and form The Northwest Chess Club.

(All sign)

BOSS TO CONVALESCING SECRETARY

Dear Cathy,

I'm happy to hear that you're back home now and recovering from your surgery.

You may be interested to know that the office is in a permanent state of chaos without you. And that your grizzled old boss, who once took you for granted, now misses you terribly.

We'll manage somehow till you return, though things will be misfiled, phone calls not returned and conflicting appointments scheduled.

Effective today, dear trusted and loyal helper, your pay goes up substantially. To find out how much you're now making watch for the mail every other Friday.

Better yet, come back soon . . . HELP!

Sincerely,

TO FRIENDS GETTING A DIVORCE

Dear Gene and Marcia,

We're sending each of you a copy of this letter to let you both know how sorry we are to hear of your divorce. After 15 years of good times, helping each other through times of crisis and close friendship, this news is a shock to both of us.

We want you to know that we still think the world of both of you and hope your differences won't interfere with our friendship. Hope you both land on your feet.

Sincerely,

MOTHER TO DAUGHTER GETTING A DIVORCE

Dear Melanie,

The 500 miles that separate us seem like five million right now as you're going through this time of crisis. I was glad you called last night to tell me what has happened. As I thought about it all through the night, I had a few more thoughts I wanted to share with you.

You have assured me that the situation at this point is hopeless and the only choice is divorce. Twenty years ago I came to the same conclusion and you know as well as I the years of unhappiness and difficulty that followed. From today's perspective I'd say I was too hasty and would love to have the chance to do it differently. I know I didn't try my hardest to mend things, I just wanted what I thought was the easiest way out.

Now I see history repeating itself, and it breaks my heart. So many emotions are engulfing me . . . guilt over my performance as a parent . . . fear for your future . . . grief over the children's confusion and apprehensions . . . anger toward Gordon for not being the husband he should have been. But emotions are a waste of time and don't benefit anyone, so I've thought through a few suggestions:

1. Dry your tears, make yourself pretty and tell Gordon you'd like to have one more heart-to-heart talk.

2. Tell him you'll be willing to make some changes if he will. Tell him you love him and want him back, but not unless some changes are made.

3. Let him know what affect this is having on the children—without being maudlin or trying to fill him with guilt.

4. Tell him as you told me that you realize you've been wrong too, and that you would like to have a fresh start.

Oh, Melanie, reconciliation has to start somewhere. It will be hard for you, but do your best to forgive and let him know you are willing to forgive. I can't believe Gordon wants this divorce. Before your father died he wrote me a letter telling me he was sorry for his part in the mess before our divorce and that he was full of regret. It doesn't have to be that way for you two. Please consider my suggestions.

All my love,

SON TO PARENTS INFORMING THEM OF DIVORCE

Dear Mom and Dad,

I'm writing with bad news . . . Norma and I will soon be getting a divorce. I really don't know whether this will come as a total surprise. If it does, it's only because we live 2,000 miles away from you, and you haven't seen us together lately.

The marriage began unraveling about a year ago, shortly after we moved to the East coast. The long train commute into the city each day, coupled with the frequent 60-hour work weeks demanded by the new job, left me very little time to spend with Norma and the kids.

Too late did I realize that I couldn't have it both ways. Each of us became increasingly self-centered and less able to communicate with the other. Norma and I came independently, and almost simultaneously, to the same conclusion—to go our separate ways.

Eddie Jr. and Kristin are, predictably, quite upset. And I am shouldering a full measure of guilt. As these things go, however, the parting seems to be occurring without any hitches. We'll work out a reasonable visitation schedule, and I will probably be seeing just as much of the youngsters on alternate weekends as I did when we were living under the same roof.

Norma asked me to tell you that she hopes to remain on good terms with both of you. She'll be getting in touch soon, and personally assure you that, come what may, you are always welcome to come and see your grandchildren.

I have moved out of the house and am nowhere near settled yet in my new place. As soon as I get a phone installed, I'll call.

I'm genuinely sorry things turned out the way they did. Instead of looking back with bitterness, I am determined to pick up the pieces of my life and go on from here. Sadder but wiser, your hotshot son is now begging your understanding and prayers.

Love,

BREAKING OFF A ROMANCE

Dear John,

When you left for Germany last spring I was sure I would be content to wait for you to come back after your two-year hitch. Time changes people, I guess.

I was terribly lonely and tired of sitting at home about two months ago when Don called to invite me to a party his sister was having. We had a good time and decided to get together again. We didn't mean to have it happen, but we have fallen in love.

Now you know why I haven't answered your last two letters. The last thing I want to do is hurt you, but I can't go on leading this double life any longer. I think it will be easier for both of us if we call it quits.

Please don't be angry with Don. He didn't set out to have this come about; it just turned out that way.

You have always been good to me, John. I hope you will find a woman who will appreciate you and make you happy. Meanwhile, please forgive me.

Sincerely,

WEDDING CANCELED, GIFT RETURNED

Dear Wes and Margie,

Thank you for this lovely wedding gift. I am returning it to you because there will be no wedding.

There were problems we thought we could solve with love. But as the strain of the wedding plans set upon us, we realized our love wasn't strong enough to weather small storms, much less disasters.

We are sorry for the inconvenience to you, and appreciate your understanding.

Sincerely,

TO SON WHO HAS TO LEAVE COLLEGE

Dear Sam,

You have just encountered a major setback by being asked to leave the University of Erudition, and my heart goes out to you.

You have given it your very best and there's nothing to be ashamed of. You've always aimed high, and your mother and I encouraged you every step of the way. In hindsight, however, your high school counselor probably was right when she urged you to enroll instead in any number of universities that were just about as well regarded as U of E, but were somewhat less demanding.

In any case, you'll be home in a couple of days and we'll all be glad to see you. Sam, you have your whole life ahead of you, so before jumping into anything, take some time and unwind. The car is yours for the asking, and I'm sure you'll get used to home cooking once again.

Before deciding on which college or university to enroll in for next fall, take a close look at where you've been and where you're heading.

Some people thrive on the pressure-cooker atmosphere you experienced at U of E . . . one that constantly demands 110% of their efforts. Their need for it doesn't end with graduation. Unless one is attuned to this pace, you might expect an ulcer or a stress-induced coronary in later years. Better to find out now that this isn't your bag and pace your life accordingly.

Hang in there, pal. Come fall, you'll make a fresh beginning somewhere else. And don't consider the past year a waste. You've matured enormously and will be better off for it.

Take time out to enjoy football games and weekend parties . . . you're only young once. Keep giving it your best, and I'm sure you'll land on your feet.

With love,

9

Moving to Another House or Apartment

Most routine matters associated with moving are best handled by telephone or in person. A call can get utility service shut off at your old apartment or home and turned on at your new address. Procedures vary somewhat in different states, but the issuance of a new driver's license or a change of vehicle registration is done in person.

In an era in which freebies are practically non-existent, the post office will, on request, furnish you with an ample supply of change-of-address cards.

However, when things go wrong, a letter works best. And there are any number of unanticipated happenings which can play havoc with even the best-planned move.

Whether it's a move across country or across town, when a problem arises, your first contact should be the mover's local agent, the person who worked out the details of your move with you. If you are not satisfied with the agent's response, contact the mover's principal office. All contacts should be in writing and each letter should include your shipment number (or order number), destination, dates of move, and weight of shipment. Once you have been assigned a claim number, be sure to include it on all correspondence.

Moving companies are required by law to acknowledge claims within 30 days from their receipt, and to either pay or deny the claim or propose a compromise offer of settlement within 120 days.

The Interstate Commerce Commission regulates movers who transport goods from one state to another. Before arranging such a move, write to the ICC's National Consumer Assistance Center and ask for their free booklet which explains the rights and obligations of moving companies and consumers. If you feel the mover has been unfair or if you have questions about procedures, contact the ICC's Bureau of Operations.

Movers who transport goods within a state are licensed by a regulatory body, often called the (state) Commerce Commission. A call or letter to this agency in the state capitol will clarify the responsibilities of both the moving company and the consumer.

While neither the national nor local commission has binding authority to determine liability for a disputed claim, each is prepared to offer the consumer assistance on matters of poor service, improper rates, or denial of claims.

REQUESTING INFORMATION PRIOR TO MOVE

National Consumer Assistance Center
Interstate Commerce Commission
Washington, D.C. 20423

Dear Sir:

In four months we will be moving from Phoenix, Arizona to Gaithersberg, Maryland. This will be our first interstate move, and we would appreciate any pamphlets you could send us on our rights and responsibilities regarding the move, what to do about lost or damaged household goods, and any information you may have about specific movers.

Thank you for your assistance.

Yours truly,

MISSING ITEM CLAIM

Mr. Chad Thomas, Agent
Moving Van Lines, Ltd.
street address
city, state ZIP

Dear Mr. Thomas:

Regarding our move on May 2 to Atlanta, Georgia, order #000 000, weight 3,000 pounds—I checked the inventory carefully on the day of delivery and was dismayed to see that one box was missing.

Your men were as concerned as I was, and spent quite a bit of extra time with me trying to find the box which contained a good portion of my fine china. Mr. Barber, the driver, assured me that a tracer would be put on it. I marked the box missing on the inventory sheet and signed it.

That was 30 days ago and I still haven't heard from you. The approximate value of the contents of that box is $500. We did purchase liability insurance from you (policy #00000) and expect full payment promptly if our china is not recovered.

Yours truly,

DAMAGE CLAIM

Mr. Willard Wilcox
Vice President
Mastadon Moving Company
street address
city, state ZIP

Dear Mr. Wilcox:

According to the contract I signed with your company, a letter satisfies the legal requirement for a written claim for lost or damaged goods. Let this letter serve as such. We moved on August 18 from Los Angeles to Denver. Our order number was 0000 00; weight 4,000 pounds.

The move went smoothly for the most part, but as the men were moving our things into the house our beautiful grandfather's clock was badly damaged. While bringing it up the front steps on a dolly, the mover stumbled and fell. He lost his grip on the dolly and the clock, and both rolled down the steps and onto the sidewalk.

We have had a local clockmaker give us an estimate. He declared it a total loss and a copy of his estimate is enclosed.

As stated in the contract, we paid $25 for liability coverage up to $5,000. Please send a check for full reimbursement for the damage your workers caused.

Yours truly,

Enclosure

INCONVENIENCE OR DELAY CLAIM

Date of move:
Weight:
Destination:
Order number:

Mr. Stanley Stanner
Vice President
Truck Van Lines
street address
city, state ZIP

Dear Mr. Stanner:

We were very impressed with your agent's efficiency and attention to detail the day we signed the bill of lading when we agreed to have your company move us from Longmeadow, Massachusetts to our new home in Pompano Beach, Florida. Your agent assured us that if we chose a date during the off-peak period we would save 10% and receive more efficient service. We followed his advice and chose the second week in November.

We've since come to the conclusion that first impressions are not very reliable. We realize that the fact that the truck broke down and arrived a day late was unfortunate, but your agent's rudeness on the telephone when we called to inform him of the delay and to ask for reimbursement for our night in a motel and two meals ($115.00) was uncalled for. Particularly since the bill of lading specifically stipulated the exact date of delivery of the shipment.

Consider this letter our formal inconvenience claim. We will expect your response within 30 days, as prescribed by law.

Yours truly,

SEEKING REGULATOR'S CLARIFICATION OF BILLING DISPUTE

Name of mover:
Order number:

Interstate Commerce Commission
Bureau of Operations
Washington, D.C. 20423

Gentlemen:

Three months ago we moved from Toledo, Ohio to Charlotte, North Carolina using Vanner Van Lines. Before the men would unload our furniture at our new home, they handed us the bill and said the amount had to be paid in full before they could proceed. We paid immediately and they stamped "paid in full" across our bill of lading.

Imagine our surprise when two weeks ago we received a letter from Vanner stating that our final bill had been recalculated and we owe a balance of $161.38. My husband called and explained that our bill was paid in full. He told Vanner that any discrepancy was an error. We have since received another letter that has us enraged.

Vanner claims they have three years from the date of delivery to audit charges to ensure that correct charges are assessed. We'd appreciate a clarification from you on this statement.

They have also submitted our name to Three Star Credits Inc. which is threatening to ruin our clean credit rating.

We would appreciate your assistance as soon as possible. We aren't out to cheat the moving company, but we can't afford to pay what we don't owe either. Thank you for your help.

Sincerely yours,

DEALING WITH UNETHICAL MOVER

Claim #000 000

Mr. John Doe, President
Doe's Cartage
street address
city, state ZIP

Dear Mr. Doe:

I find it incredible that so many of my possessions could have been damaged during what should have been a routine three-mile move.

Your men were careless, and it was obvious that one (called Shorty by the others) had been drinking. The driver was in a hurry to get on to the next job and repeatedly urged me to sign the delivery receipt. I insisted that he and I take a joint inventory before I would do so.

Inspection of the goods revealed considerable damage, and I asked the driver for a claim form. He became abusive, and produced the form only when I threatened to call the police. I am enclosing the completed claim form.

It's apparent now that I should have taken more care in selecting a mover. The Better Business Bureau earlier today warned me to expect stalling with any Doe's Cartage claim. I am, however, determined to follow through on this claim until it is resolved to my satisfaction.

You'll note that a copy of this letter, along with a copy of the bill of lading and the claim form is being forwarded to the State Commerce Commission. I understand the commission regulates moving companies in this state and has the power to revoke a mover's license if improper activities are documented.

In summary, Mr. Doe, the disposition of claim 000 000 is being carefully monitored from this point forward. I'll expect prompt settlement.

Yours truly,

cc: State Commerce Commission
Enclosure

SEE YOU IN COURT

Claim #000 000

Mr. Hans Dorff
Vans, Inc.
street address
city, state ZIP

Mr. Dorff:

I am returning your "settlement" check for $360. It is totally inadequate and represents but a fraction of the actual value of the items lost when your company moved my household goods four months ago.

Evidently you haven't taken seriously my promise to bring legal action unless restitution was made in the full amount of $900. As you recall, the $900 figure was determined by an impartial appraisal. That document, along with substantiating photographs, the bill of lading and pertinent correspondence will be among the items I intend to introduce as evidence in small claims court.

Frankly, Mr. Dorff, I'm surprised that you and the driver who delivered the partial shipment can afford to spare the time to answer a summons to appear in court. I, on the other hand, am retired and can take as long as necessary to see to it that justice is served.

I intend to file a claim in small claims court next Monday morning. Unless I have a check for the entire $900 in hand before then, we'll probably be seeing a lot of each other in the weeks ahead.

_____
(signature)

STATUS REPORT TO REGULATORY AGENCY

> Re: Transylvania Movers & Cartage Co.
> Claim #00 000

(State) Commerce Commission
Mr. Graham G. Graham
Director, Consumer Affairs
street address
city, state ZIP

Dear Mr. Graham:

As you requested, I am reporting the outcome of the final phase of my exasperating experience with Transylvania Movers and Cartage Co.

The carelessness and indifference which characterized the move itself were repeated again and again as I sought compensation by filing a claim for lost and damaged household goods.

After Transylvania's final denial of responsibility, the moment of reckoning occurred yesterday. Judge Alexander Axelrod, after hearing the evidence in small claims court, ruled that Transylvania was indeed liable for the lost and damaged items.

Judge Axelrod ordered the movers to pay me $800 in compensation for the losses suffered.

A hollow victory indeed, but one I'll never regret pursuing to its conclusion. On behalf of the countless other victims of Transylvania Movers & Cartage Co. who perhaps are unable or unwilling to go to such lengths to obtain an equitable resolution, I urge you to consider suspending or revoking the license of this unethical common carrier.

Sincerely,

LETTER LEVERAGE

As mentioned earlier, the post office will provide you with change-of-address cards to send to friends, businesses and publishers. Some people, however, might prefer to keep confidential such matters as charge account numbers and insurance policy numbers, and would find a letter preferable to a post card.

Well in advance of a move you'll want to notify businesses and banks whose charge cards you hold of a change of address. If you have charge accounts with local businesses which you'll no longer be using after a long-distance move, it's a good idea to inform each of your move and ask that the account be cancelled.

Six weeks notice is required by most publishers to effect a change of address for subscribers. Be sure to enclose your present address label with your correspondence.

The sale of their former residence is often an important piece of unfinished business for people making long-distance moves. Specific written instructions to the listing real estate agent can eliminate misunderstandings.

For long-distance moves, write to arrange for utility service and garbage collection. This can be done for the price of a stamp instead of a call during business hours.

CHANGE-OF-ADDRESS NOTICE

Re: Account #0000 000

Middleton & Cavendish, Inc.
street address
city, state ZIP

Gentlemen:

On February 1, I will be moving from _____ ,
street address

_____ to _____ ,
city, state ZIP   street address

_____ .
city, state ZIP

Please change my records accordingly and send all correspondence to my new address. Thank you.

Sincerely yours,

CHANGE-OF-ADDRESS NOTICE

Firefighters' Gazette
street address
city, state ZIP

Gentlemen:
On December 1, I will be moving from _____ ,
street address

———————————————— to ————————————————— ,
      city, state ZIP   street address

———————————————————— . Please change your records accordingly
      city, state ZIP

as of that date.

    I've enclosed a label which indicates my current mailing address.

Cordially,

CHANGE-OF-ADDRESS NOTICE

Dear Mr. Harrison,

    We are heading west after ten years in Milwaukee. We will miss the Great Lakes, the rolling hills and friendly folks.
As of March 17, our new address will be:

Street address
city, state ZIP

Our auto insurance policy numbers are:

000 000
000 000

    Thank you for ten years of prompt, courteous service. We'd appreciate your recommendation as to which insurance agent we should contact once we're in our new home.

Sincerely yours,

PLEASE CANCEL MY ACCOUNT

Re: Account #000 0000

Cosmopolitan Clothiers
street address
city, state ZIP

Gentlemen:

    I will be moving out of state at the end of this month. Please cancel my charge account. Thank you.

Sincerely,

CANCELING REAL ESTATE LISTING

Dear Mr. Snorkel:

Nearly three months have passed since the "for sale" sign went up in front of our house. The one offer to purchase you forwarded to us bordered on the insulting.

This letter is your notification that when your firm's listing contract expires on September 6, we intend to engage another real estate agent.

Yours truly,

ENGAGING NEW REAL ESTATE AGENT

Dear Mrs. Howe,

In early June we moved to Seattle and listed our house at 1460 Patterson Drive for sale with Snorkel & Associates.

It remains unsold, and I have notified Lester Snorkel that I do not intend to renew the listing contract with his firm when it expires on September 6.

The house was offered for sale at $99,500, and the only offer to buy in nearly three months was for $75,000. This we considered unacceptable.

Would you please make arrangements to inspect the house and send me a letter indicating what you feel would be a realistic asking price. Also, please include a listing contract for the three-month period beginning September 7.

Sincerely yours,

THANKS TO REAL ESTATE AGENT

Dear Mr. Brooks,

My compliments to your Miss Rivers for finding a buyer for our house in so short a time.

It was with no small amount of apprehension that we handed the keys to her two weeks ago and moved to the west coast. What a relief to hear of a firm bid the very day after the open house . . . and for the asking price at that!

You may be assured that we will put in a good word for your firm when corresponding with our many friends back in Fairmont.

Cordially yours,

NOTIFYING UTILITY OF MOVE

Dear Gas Company:

On May 1, I will be moving to 2163 Cedar Street in Devonshire. Please arrange to turn on the gas the day before I arrive.

I will be using the following gas-operated equipment and appliances: range, wall oven, water heater and furnace.

The key to the house can be obtained from Jones & Jones Realtors.

Yours truly,

NOTIFYING GARBAGE COLLECTOR OF MOVE

Gentlemen:

The purpose of this letter is to arrange twice-weekly garbage pickup beginning Tuesday May 2 from my new home at 2163 Cedar Street.

It is my understanding that curbside collections will be made each Tuesday and Friday and that I will be billed $34 every three months.

Sincerely,

10

Announcements and Congratulations

LETTER LEVERAGE

When you have a happy event to announce—such as an engagement or a new arrival in the family—a letter is the perfect way to spread the news.

So versatile is the letter of announcement, it can also be used to bear the news of unhappy occurrences as well. Discretion is a must for sensitive situations. When informing friends of a divorce, for example, the writer should take care to avoid criticism of the former spouse as well as a tone of self-pity.

Professional people often send letters of announcement to their clients for any number of reasons. Moving to a new location, bringing in an associate, or retiring are a few examples. This type of correspondence can be used to help launch a new career as well.

Whether to personalize the salutation on a printed letter by inserting a name of the recipient or to address it "Dear friends/clients/patients" is a matter of personal preference.

News is only new for so long, so be sure to send your announcement promptly. Flip through the following model letters and see which one can give wings to your news.

ANNOUNCING AN ENGAGEMENT

Dear Aunt Diane and Uncle Al,

Believe it or not, it finally happened—I'm engaged! Most of the family had given up on my ever getting married. I had made many speeches on how I would never need a husband, because I was self-sufficient, and I had my future all planned.

Then, just like the storybook romances, my knight in shining armor came on the scene. His name is Todd Turner, he's 35 years old and is a broker with Green, Bean and Dean.

We met at a political convention six months ago and have been seeing each other steadily ever since. We're planning a spring wedding, and Todd and I are just beginning to make the arrangements.

As soon as we have a date set I'll let you know so you can circle your calendar and make your plane reservations. I know I can count on you.

My only regret is that Todd and I didn't meet ten years ago so Mom could've seen her dream come true. She was very proud of my achievements, but down deep she really believed no woman is complete without a man. Now I must agree she was right.

Love,

ANNOUNCING A NEW BABY

Dear Eleanor,

I have good news! On October 17, at 9:25 A.M. I gave birth to a beautiful baby girl. She was six weeks early, but is really a fighter and was big enough to come home with me. She weighed 5 pounds $11\frac{1}{2}$ ounces at birth and was 20 inches long.

We have named her Polly Lyn, and Joe and I have let her take over our lives. I wish you could see us carry on about her. We have come to know the true meaning of the old phrase "bundle of joy." She may be a small bundle to hold, but she has brought a huge bundle of joy into our hearts.

Sincerely,

ANNOUNCING A NEW BABY

Dear Martha and Ron,

As of last night we have a brand-new son! His name is Randy James, he weighs 7 pounds 8 ounces and is 22 inches long. Don says he'll be a basketball player for sure.

I was able to have a home delivery again so Don was with me, and Jill was able to see her baby brother and hold him as soon as she woke up this morning.

We are very thankful for a handsome, healthy baby. We'll send pictures in our next letter.

Lovingly,

ANNOUNCING A DIVORCE

Dear Friends:

This may come as a surprise to many of you, but after five years Carol and I were divorced recently.

I don't intend to now—or ever—elaborate upon the reasons, but I thought you should know that we have gone our separate ways.

Unlike many others who have traveled this unfortunate path before me, I do not intend to turn my back on the past and get off to a completely fresh start. Old friendships are too important for that.

I'll be in touch soon. Meanwhile, my new address and phone number are: 1600 W. Ardmore Street, 000-0000.

Best regards,

ANNOUNCING A DIVORCE

Dear_____,

I'd rather you hear it straight from me than via the grapevine—Jim and I are now divorced.

After irreconcilable differences we felt it best to go our separate ways.

I've gone back to work as a secretary at ConGlom Corp. My mom stays with Chris and Cal during the day. It's all going to take a certain period of adjustment, but I'm determined to land on my feet and get a fresh start.

The continued support and encouragement from old friends is one thing I will cherish most. I hope to get in touch as soon as the dust settles.

All my love,

RELOCATING PROFESSIONAL PRACTICE

Dear Clients:

On April 1, I will be closing my office at 1400 Dexter Street and moving to larger quarters in the Professional Building, 2250 W. Poplar Drive, Suite 205.

There is ample free parking at the new location. The office phone number will remain 000-0000.

Yours truly,

DOCTOR RETIRING

Dear Friends:

After nearly 40 years of patching up the folks of this town, I'm planning to retire and move to Florida.

Many of you know Dr. Tom Ross, who has been my associate for the past six months. Effective July 1, he will be taking over my practice. Though relatively young in years, Dr. Ross is long on experience. I have worked closely with him since the first of the year, and know him to be a competent and dedicated physician. He is on the staff of Memorial Hospital and is a member of the American Academy of Family Physicians.

Mrs. Barrett and I will take along with us many happy memories of this town and its wonderful people.

I leave you in good hands.

Sincerely yours,

PROFESSIONAL BRINGING IN AN ASSOCIATE

Dear _____ ,

I am pleased to announce that, effective November 1, Dr. Michael Grove will be joining our staff.

With my practice growing as it has, I felt that it was time to take on an associate in order to continue providing the efficient and personal care you deserve.

An extensive search was successfully concluded, and I know you will be as pleased as I am.

Dr. Grove is highly qualified and very personable. His compassion for people is as evident as his diagnostic expertise.

Feel free to call on Dr. Grove or me—day or night—any time you need to reach us.

Cordially,

ANNOUNCING A NEW BUSINESS

Dear Neighbor:

I am pleased to announce the June 15 opening of CHARLIE'S FIX-IT SHOP. If the name suggests to you that Charlie can repair just about anything, you're right.

Lawn mowers, snow blowers, small appliances, bicycles, even light welding. I'll tell you in advance how much it will cost and when the job will be completed.

So the next time something breaks down, don't throw it away. Bring it in for a free estimate to:

Charlie's Fix-It Shop
416 Frontage Road
Phone: 000-0000
Hours: 8:00 A.M.–5:00 P.M. Monday through Saturday

_____
(signature)

ANNOUNCING A NEW CAREER

Dear_____ ,

I am pleased to announce that I have recently joined the sales staff of Baxter & Bentley, Inc., the South Shore's leading realtor.

This is one fascinating business. It runs across the spectrum from finding a young couple the perfect starter home they thought they couldn't afford to helping arrange the sale of a larger home for empty-nesters. Since no two clients are alike, it provides a continuous challenge to bring buyer and seller together on terms favorable to each and, hopefully, make two friends in the process.

As you may know, Baxter & Bentley is a member of the Multiple Listing Service and has access to hundreds of listings throughout the south suburban area.

We frequently run full-page ads in community newspapers. Featured in each are large exterior photos and descriptive captions of several homes.

In addition, we're also affiliated with a national network of reputable real estate firms and can help you relocate even if you move a great distance.

Please keep Baxter & Bentley and me in mind the next time you're in the market to buy or sell a home or lot. I promise I'll leave no stone unturned to accommodate—quickly and at a realistic price.

My business card is enclosed. On it are both my office and home phone numbers. Please call any time I can be of service.

Yours truly,

REALTOR INTRODUCES NEW NEIGHBORS

Dear Mr. & Mrs. Case:

I'd like to introduce your new neighbors, Claude and Maude Bell, **who** recently bought the house at 720 Oak Street.

It was a pleasure to have been able to help them find a home in such a lovely neighborhood. It was a privilege to have represented Ed and Ellen Jasper in the sale of their home to the Bells.

The meshing of the needs of both families in this transaction didn't happen by chance. A great deal of behind-the-scenes work was involved to bring buyer and seller together.

If ever I may be of service in finding a buyer for your home, don't hesitate to call.

Yours truly,

LETTER LEVERAGE

Special events call for special recognition. When friends or loved ones reach a new plateau in life, we have an opportunity to share in their joy by sending a letter of congratulations.

No one has ever died from an overdose of encouragement, so feel free to lavishly praise the person's accomplishment. Many greeting cards will be received for the occasions described in the pages that follow, but a few who care will take the time to write a note or letter. More often than not, they are kept and re-read long after the event.

One word of caution. Even in the age of the liberated woman, remember to extend to her best wishes on her engagement or wedding. The groom is the one to be congratulated.

CONGRATULATIONS/GRADUATION

Dear Matt,

How time flies! Here you are graduating from high school and planning to attend State University in the fall. Congratulations on a job well done, and good luck to you during the next four years of school.

It's been a pleasure living next door to you and your family the past seven years. We have great confidence that your future holds many good things.

Sincerely,

CONGRATULATIONS/GRADUATION

Dear Pete,

Your grandma and I are sorry we're not going to be able to come up north to attend your high school graduation. But we're just as proud as can be of you and send our congratulations. Finishing in the top 20% of your class was quite an achievement and doubtless played a big part in your acceptance in the School of Architecture at State University next fall.

In the years to come you will probably recall the factors which led to the decision you made at 18 which will determine your life's work. From my observation point, it looks as if you've thought it out pretty well . . . certainly more thoroughly than I did at your age.

It began with basic likes and dislikes. You've always enjoyed drawing anything and everything. Way back before you started kindergarten you came up with some pretty respectable drawings of cars and airplanes.

You've never tried to camouflage your dislikes either. You seem completely turned off by three-piece suits and a business career. All well and good, but keep in mind as you do your thing that someone's successful business makes it possible to pay your fee or salary.

You frequently hear older people say "if only I knew then what I know now . . . ," and there is indeed ample time in later life to reflect over wrong decisions. But the likelihood of getting your career plans side-tracked is reduced if early-on you have a goal worth shooting for.

Soon our family will have its first architect and I know you'll be one of the best. I'm sure you'll be grateful when you're my age that you had your head on straight today.

Your proud Grandpa,

CONGRATULATIONS/GRADUATION

Dear Sarah,

Congratulations, Dr. Blake. I love the way that sounds! Now that you're graduating it seems like yesterday that you proclaimed to the world that you were going to be a doctor. At the time all those years of schooling sounded like an eternity to spend in preparation for a career.

I wish you success and fulfillment in the years ahead.

Fondly,

CONGRATULATIONS/ENGAGEMENT

Dear John and Cindy,

We are pleased as punch that you two are planning to tie the knot! Being "old-timers" ourselves, we can strongly endorse the state of matrimony.

We wish you many years of love and prosperity.

Affectionately,

CONGRATULATIONS/ENGAGEMENT

Dear Andrea,

I received the exciting news of your engagement this morning and had to sit right down and let you know how happy I am for you. Even though I haven't had a chance to meet Keith yet, I know from your letters how much you care for him.

All I can say is, any young man who loves you as much as Keith obviously does, has very good taste! Tell him your Aunt Celeste heartily approves and wishes you both happiness forever.

Love,

CONGRATULATIONS/ENGAGEMENT

Dear Don,

Good news travels fast. I heard that you and Gayle became engaged last night. Congratulations! You two are a perfect match.

Here's wishing you both a lifetime of happiness.

Fondly,

CONGRATULATIONS/WEDDING

Dear Bob and Nicole,

Your wedding was beautiful and you two were fun to watch. Your love for each other was very obvious during the ceremony, the picture taking, the fun times and the poignant moments.

We hope that the day was just a foretaste of the good things you will share during your life together. Many blessings to you.

Affectionately,

CONGRATULATIONS/WEDDING

Dear Lenore,

What a pleasant surprise to open the mail today and find your wedding invitation. I haven't kept up with news from home lately.

Will is a wonderful guy, and I know you will make him very happy. I wish you all the best, Lenore, and I am planning to come to the wedding.

Fondly,

CONGRATULATIONS/WEDDING

Dear Andy,

Your Uncle Drew and I are very proud of you, as you know. We've been two of your biggest boosters since you were a baby. Now you've increased our joy once more by bringing your lovely new bride, Jenny, into the family.

We always knew you'd pick a good one! Eternal happiness to you both.

All our love,

CONGRATULATIONS/BABY

Dear Rosemary,

How happy you must be to have a beautiful new baby girl. Now you've experienced that joy that only a new mother knows as her baby is put into her arms for the first time.

May the years ahead be filled with good health and good fortune for you and Jeff and your little Jessica.

Affectionately,

CONGRATULATIONS/BABY

Dear Barb,

Congratulations to you and Ned on the birth of your handsome son. Your mom tells me Ned is bursting his buttons!

I'm so happy for you I could cry (and I did). Take good care of that future major leaguer or president. Much happiness to you all.

Fondly,

CONGRATULATIONS/BABY

Dear Julie,

It was a real thrill to hear of the birth of the twins. Just think, your joy has been doubled by having two perfectly healthy little girls. You and Tom have some exciting years ahead of you.

I'm sure it's difficult to wait to hold them in your arms, but those three weeks will be over before you know it. They are doing so well, you may have them home before then. In the meantime, get plenty of rest. When the babies come home I'd love to help.

Affectionately,

CONGRATULATIONS/AWARD

Dear Jeremy,

Grandpa and I are so proud of you. Earning the rank of Eagle Scout is no small achievement. We know how hard you worked for it.

This experience will be valuable to you for the rest of your life. We look forward to bragging about you in the years ahead!

Love,

CONGRATULATIONS/AWARD

Dear Laurie,

The news of your music scholarship to the University made my day. No one could have been more deserving. How exciting it must be for you to realize your dream after all those years of faithful practice and proficient performance.

Your diligence combined with your innate talents indicate a dynamic future. I wish you all the best in your college years.

Fondly,

CONGRATULATIONS/AWARD

Dear Natalie,

If anyone deserves the "Secretary of the Year Award," it's you. Congratulations!

I hope your boss shows his appreciation of your talents by giving you a nice big salary increase.

Cordially yours,

CONGRATULATIONS/PROMOTION

Dear Cliff,

I see in today's paper that ConGlom Corp. has a new vice president. They've made a wise choice, and I'm sure you're going to give them their money's worth and then some.

In what's generally perceived to be a dog-eat-dog business, it's good to see a nice guy finish first for a change.

What a kick it is for Marge and me to be able to say we knew you when. Give our best to Carolyn (who must be one proud gal today).

Sincerely,

CONGRATULATIONS/PROMOTION

Dear Ruth,

It did my heart good to hear about your promotion to Vice President of the agency. I know how talented you are and how hard you've worked to attain this goal. It's been a real encouragement to me to see your efforts rewarded.

Sincere congratulations to you. Your expertise and dedication will bring out the best of everyone on your staff. They're learning from a real pro.

Sincerely yours,

11

Recommendations and Resignations

LETTER LEVERAGE

Take it as a compliment when someone asks you to write a letter of recommendation. There are any number of occasions which call for such a letter, ranging from the conventional job reference to some quite extraordinary circumstances.

Occasionally, a well-meaning friend may think he's saving you time by suggesting certain points to be covered in the letter. Gracefully decline and put things in your own words. Your letter will not only be more candid, but will also lessen the likelihood that the person you're trying to convince may receive two or more letters so similar they were obviously suggested by your friend.

A well-crafted letter to the editor appearing in a newspaper or magazine prior to an election provides a broad forum for your endorsement of a candidate. Just one such letter in print will come to the attention of more people than you could possibly contact in person during the entire campaign.

JOB RECOMMENDATION FROM A FORMER EMPLOYER

Dear Mr. Jordan:

When Tom Hawkinson handed me his resignation I was, of course, sorry to learn that our top salesman would be leaving. On the other hand, I shared his elation at having been invited to join your firm as Vice President of Sales.

In the four years Tom has been with our company, he never failed to meet his annual sales quota and often surpassed it by mid-year. This remarkable producer didn't achieve such results by accident. His thorough knowledge of our products and friendly, tactful way of dealing with customers brought impressive results.

Tom was never reluctant to put in long hours or to travel literally to the ends of the earth to obtain an order. His conscientious follow-up on customer service won the lasting allegiance of his customers. Tom's charming wife, Susan, proved a definite asset in his social contacts.

You are indeed fortunate to have landed Tom Hawkinson for this important position. I enthusiastically recommend him and believe he will more than meet your expectations.

Sincerely yours,

JOB RECOMMENDATION FROM A FORMER EMPLOYER

Dear Ms. Clendenin:

It's a pleasure for me to answer your request for a letter of recommendation for my good friend and former employee, Ted Taylor.

Ted was a part-time stock room clerk with us for $2\frac{1}{2}$ years while he was working his way through college. He was always punctual, hard working and ready to take on new responsibilities.

We have kept in touch during the five years since his graduation, and he now has a lovely wife and two small children. He has developed into a resourceful, results-oriented store manager who will, I am certain, be a great asset to your company.

Sincerely,

JOB RECOMMENDATION FROM A FORMER EMPLOYER

Dear Mrs. Anthony:

For the past four years Anna West has been my cleaning lady. She works for me one day a week and has consistently done an exceptional job.

Anna is trustworthy and has a pleasant personality. I appreciate the fact that she is a diligent worker and never discusses other clients.

Cordially,

JOB RECOMMENDATION FROM FORMER CO-WORKER

Dear Mr. Phillips:

It was my privilege to work for the better part of the 1970's with Dan Brewster. We were both employed in the sales division of Placebo Industries— Dan in sales promotion and I as a customer contact representative.

On a number of occasions we worked together in developing sales presentations which Dan would deliver to groups throughout a five-state area in the southeast. I found him to be innovative, enthusiastic and thoroughly competent, both in the behind-the-scenes preparation and in the delivery. I would go so far as to say Dan is one of the most effective meeting organizers and public speakers I've ever known.

I heartily recommend Dan for the position of Sales Promotion Manager with your firm . . . knowing that he'll not just be able to repeat past achievements, but confident that he has the ability to rapidly grow into even more challenging positions.

Yours truly,

JOB RECOMMENDATION FROM A FRIEND

Dear Ms. Davis:

I am writing in response to your letter requesting a reference for Gloria Roberts who has applied for a job with your company.

Gloria and I were roommates in college and have remained close friends in the four years since graduation. She was a conscientious student, graduating in the top 20% of our class. Gloria held various positions of responsibility with the Inter-Sorority Council during those years and was respected by all who worked with her. Her keen sense of organization and unlimited energy inevitably led to success in each endeavor. Her career progress in the years since has been as impressive as we all expected.

Her dedication to the job at hand carries through in her personal relationships as well. I highly value her friendship, knowing she will never let me down.

I am both pleased and honored to have been asked to recommend Gloria Roberts, and I think she is very worthy of your serious consideration.

Cordially yours,

TEACHER RECOMMENDING STUDENT FOR SCHOLARSHIP

Dear Mr. Powell:

As an English teacher at Pendleton High School who has known Linda Grey for three years, I can highly recommend this remarkable young woman for a scholarship to the University of Erudition.

Linda was in my English class this year and maintained an A− average. This is the third year I have worked with her on the school newspaper, and I have been very impressed with her creative talents and attention to detail.

I have seen Linda grow from an eager learner when she was new on the newspaper to a capable special features editor this year. She has demonstrated superb leadership qualities by helping younger staff members develop their journalistic skills.

Linda Grey will be a highly-motivated college student and an asset to the company that hires her upon graduation. She deserves your consideration for a scholarship.

Yours truly,

RECOMMENDING CHILD FOR PRIVATE SCHOOL

Dear Madam:

For two years Bailey Black was in my Sunday School class and during that time we became good friends. Bailey is all boy on the baseball diamond and the soccer field, but also a serious student while in class.

His attentive behavior in class and good sportsmanship at play are vital evidence of the loving home he comes from. He receives a lot of support balanced with prudent discipline. As the oldest of four children, he handles responsibility well.

I'm certain Bailey will adapt to his new school and make friends quickly. My only regret is that he and his family have moved so far away. I will miss watching him grow up to be the fine young man I know he will be.

Sincerely yours,

RECOMMENDATION FROM FORMER LANDLORD

To whom it may concern:

I am the owner of an apartment building at 5840-46 W. Claxton Avenue in Fairview.

For the past three years Oscar Hansen has rented a one-bedroom unit in my building. He recently informed me that he would not be renewing his lease because he now requires larger living quarters.

Mr. Hansen has always been prompt in paying his rent, is well-mannered and highly thought of by my other tenants. I will miss him.

Sincerely yours,

CLUB MEMBER RECOMMENDING FRIEND

Dear Board Members:

I would like to place before you the name of my long-time friend, George White, for consideration for membership. George and I are neighbors and co-workers, so I know him quite well.

His credentials are impressive as you can see on the attached sheet. But just as important is George's dynamic personality. He's not afraid to make commitments as evidenced by his extensive involvement in community affairs. He's a dedicated family man as well.

I believe our club would benefit by his membership.

Sincerely yours,

Encl.

LETTER OF MITIGATION

Dear Judge Green:

I was shocked and saddened to learn of the recent conviction of my close friend, John Martin, on one count of mail fraud. I understand you have set September 20th as the date for sentencing, and hope this letter reaches you in time to offer in mitigation a few observations about an otherwise exemplary life which was marred by a single event.

Mr. Martin and I have for many years been neighbors and members of the Grace Christian Church in Fairview. He has given generously of his time and talents to the community, serving on the Fairview Board of Education and, most recently, serving two terms as Village Trustee.

As president and founder of Martin Distributors, Inc. he is not only Fairview's leading employer, but an entrepreneur who is respected by competitors and associates alike. He is regarded by his hundreds of employees as a fair, honest and generous man.

As past chairman of the Fairview Annual Charity Drive, he demonstrated his concern for the less fortunate by tirelessly working to help the community understand and respond to unmet needs.

Mr. Martin answered the call of his country during the Korean conflict and served with distinction, rising to the rank of captain.

It has been my privilege also to know John's wife, Cynthia, and their three sons and two daughters. All five children give evidence of an upbringing in a home that stresses devotion to their God, their country and each other.

I am certainly not attempting to minimize the seriousness of his offense, but I believe that a look at all sides of John Martin will reveal a man whose many fine qualities overshadow his one transgression.

Respectfully,

LETTER TO EDITOR RECOMMENDING CANDIDATE

Dear Editor:

As citizens of Fairview, you will be making a number of important choices when you go to the polls next Tuesday. Among them will be the selection of our next mayor.

I believe Lee Billingsby is well qualified to serve in this important post for the next four years. His achievements as park district commissioner and, more recently, as councilman are solid evidence of his ability to assume added responsibilities.

In the next few years decisions will be made on matters that will affect our village for generations. Influential outsiders are already petitioning the planning commission for zoning changes which will permit an industrial park on the southeast part of town.

Lee Billingsby is on record as being committed to preserving the essential residential character of our community. A vote for his opponent, while not an intentional endorsement of smokestacks, could in time prove to be just that.

I urge every voter in Fairview to look closely at all the facts before heading for the polling place on Tuesday.

_____

(signature)

LETTER TO EDITOR RECOMMENDING CANDIDATE

Dear Editor:

Lois James, candidate for State Senator of the seventh district, has my endorsement. For the past four years she has done an excellent job as County Clerk, and has helped restore public trust in that office.

Lois' goals and priorities are made clear in her speeches and are summarized in a printed piece entitled, "James Names the Issues." Her commitment to the Education Act and the Metropolitan Transportation Bill indicates that her priorities are in tune with the long-term interests of her constituency.

A vote for Mrs. James is a vote for honesty, integrity and progress in state government.

_____

(signature)

LETTER LEVERAGE

If first impressions count for a lot, so, too, do final ones. A brief letter of resignation, concluding a certain phase of your life, enables you to bow out with class.

When you've made the decision to resign from a job, arrange to see your boss privately and tell him why you're leaving. Give him your letter of resignation. It should be congenial, should mention briefly that you've enjoyed your association with the firm, and state the date of your departure.

Even when you're leaving a job under less than ideal conditions, resist the temptation to sign off with a vengeance. The last item to go into your employment file will be your letter of resignation. That means it will be the first thing to be picked up later—perhaps years later—by someone you may never have met who's being asked to furnish a job reference.

When departing from a volunteer post or an elected position under amicable conditions, a gracious letter of resignation appropriately caps your term of service.

The one time that a blistering letter of resignation can accomplish anything is when it serves to point out the futility of continuing with the status quo. It also affords you the opportunity to step down from an intolerable situation with your dignity intact.

RESIGNATION FROM JOB

Dear Mr. Harper:

This letter is to notify you that I will be resigning my position with the company on June 20, two weeks from today.

It has been a pleasure to have worked with you and the rest of the staff in the purchasing department these past four years. I believe I have gained valuable experience which will serve me well in the years to come.

I will, of course, be happy to assist with training my replacement in the time remaining.

Sincerely,

RESIGNATION FROM JOB

Dear Mrs. Quinn:

Please be advised of my intention to resign from the company, effective January 31.

I have enjoyed my five years here, but succumbed to "an offer I couldn't refuse." I will always appreciate having had the opportunity to earn my degree at night school through the company-subsidized tuition plan.

I wish you and all the rest of my co-workers the very best in the years to come.

Sincerely yours,

RESIGNATION FROM JOB

Dear Mr. White:

This letter of resignation, effective June 19, is written with sadness over leaving, but also with joy over the circumstances.

The past five years at White & Associates have been rewarding as I worked my way up from a job in the steno pool to that of secretary to the vice president. I will always remember my years here with affection.

My sad/joyful parting is due to the fact that my husband and I have two exciting events approaching. We are moving to San Antonio, Texas where he will assume added responsibilities with his corporation, and sometime around Thanksgiving, we will become parents for the first time.

Thank you for your confidence in me and for the pleasant, yet challenging atmosphere at White & Associates.

Sincerely yours,

RESIGNATION FROM JOB

Dear Mr. Whalen:

This is to inform you that it is my intention to take an early retirement, effective March 31.

I wish to apply my four weeks of unused vacation time for this calendar year to the period following March 3, my last working day.

Yours truly,

RESIGNATION FROM PTA BOARD

Dear Board Members:

It is difficult for me to write this letter of resignation because we have together accomplished so much during my term as PTA president for this school year. In four weeks my husband and I will be packing up our home and children and moving to Virginia Beach, Virginia. It is an exciting move for him in his career, yet it is with sadness that we leave behind so many dear friends.

Thank you all for your cooperation and hard work. It has been a pleasure to work with you. I hope we find as cohesive a group of parents in our new school.

Fondly,

RESIGNATION FROM VOLUNTEER POSITION

Dear Board Members:

With this letter I ask you to accept my resignation from the Memorial Hospital Auxiliary Board. I wish this resignation to take effect two weeks from today, March 29.

I've been offered an attractive position with a firm in Tulsa, Oklahoma and will be assuming my duties there three weeks from today. My time serving with you at Memorial Hospital has been one of the highlights of our years in Fairview.

I'm sure the hospital will continue to grow and serve the community with your able guidance.

Sincerely yours,

RESIGNATION FROM CHURCH BOARD

Dear Deacon Board:

Please accept this letter of resignation, effective immediately. As many of you know, my wife has been diagnosed as having a brain tumor. Surgery is scheduled for the end of the week and the outlook is uncertain at best.

In the period ahead, Laura and the children will be my main concern. It would not be fair to the Deacon Board for me to continue, as I would have to neglect my duties for an unknown length of time.

I have thoroughly enjoyed my time on the board and hope to be able to serve again sometime in the future.

Sincerely yours,

RESIGNATION FROM APPOINTED POSITION

Dear Mayor Hoffman:

I have thoroughly enjoyed the year I have spent on the Village Planning Commission and regret having to write this letter of resignation.

My job situation has changed and added responsibilities have lead to frequent overseas trips. It wouldn't be fair to the Board for me to continue when I won't be available much of the time.

It's been a pleasure working with you.

Cordially,

RESIGNATION FROM ELECTED POSITION

Dear Board Members:

With regret I submit my letter of resignation as Park District Trustee. I would like this resignation to become effective within 30 days or as soon as a replacement is found, whichever comes first.

Personal problems compel me to take this step. For the next six months to a year I would be unable to give the job the time and attention it deserves.

I will be forever grateful for having had the opportunity to work with such a dedicated group of people. Our long hours of hard work brought meaningful results which made the effort very worthwhile.

Thank you for your understanding.

Sincerely,

WHEN THE BOARD SPLINTERS

Dear Board Members:

When I accepted the position of PTA Ways and Means Chairman I was eager to get to work and do the best job I could. Since then I have met with nothing but frustration.

As a result, you have my resignation effective immediately. After my experience with the Book Sale where I did 90% of the work ahead of time and then had half my volunteers not show up (including board members), I decided that enough is enough. When all of you decide to get together and work as a team you'll be dynamite, but leave me out till then.

Yours truly,

COOPERATE, DON'T PROCRASTINATE

To Members of the Fairview Town Council:

As a lifelong big city resident who was not unaware of its frequently tainted politics, I looked upon Fairview as a breath of fresh air when I moved here with my family eight years ago.

Input from citizens was sought and heeded by the Mayor and Town Council. Elected officials gave generously of their time without pay. And never has there even been a hint of a dishonest dollar changing hands.

Reform, as commonly defined, was not my object when I successfully campaigned for a seat on the Council two years ago. Instead, I sought to make a contribution to effective government by bringing to the Council special expertise on cost control.

It would be an understatement to say that these two years have been disappointing. Pettiness abounds at the interminable committee meetings which usually end inconclusively after midnight.

The endless rehashing of minor points and the near universal fascination with the irrelevant waste countless hours. Not one of us could function in our principal lines of work if we spent most of the time between nine and five arguing about inconsequential matters.

Last night's three-hour meeting, to discuss for the fourth time whether to amend the village ordinance on leashing dogs in the park, was my last. I have decided, in order to preserve what remains of my sanity, to resign from the Town Council, effective immediately.

I wish I could say in departing that it has been a genuine pleasure to have worked with you all, but that wouldn't be truthful. Sadder but wiser, I conclude my elected term a year before its expiration. And wish the best of luck—and patience—to whomever is appointed as my successor.

_____
(signature)

Part II

Letters Covering

Special Situations

12

Car-Ache Remedies

It's been said that America's love affair with the automobile peaked in the era of tail fins, glitzy chrome and cheap gasoline. In subsequent years cars have become increasingly expensive, complex and temperamental.

Not only don't they build 'em like they used to; they often can't fix 'em when things go wrong. But don't despair—frequently a letter can bring results. Especially when encountering problems with a new car under warranty.

There are three escalating levels of contact for customer complaints: the dealer who sold the car, the local district office which acts as a liaison between the manufacturer and the customer, and finally the division office of the manufacturer at corporate headquarters. Always address your letter to the person in charge by name and title. It will be opened faster than one addressed to the Customer Relations Department. It just takes a phone call to the switchboard to determine who's who at the dealer, district office or division office.

In each case your letter will very likely be the first the recipient has heard about your problem. So state the situation calmly and concisely, and indicate what corrective measures were attempted and when. Save all repair orders and receipts. Keep a record of all conversations and copies of all correspondence.

If the service department of the dealership which sold you the car can't or won't perform warranty work satisfactorily, don't waste your time complaining to the service manager. Instead, write to the owner or general manager. Most reputable establishments value customer goodwill and would like to sell you another car some day. If you mention that the dealer's good reputation was a factor in your decision to do business there in the first place, the boss will often make an extra effort to accommodate a reasonable request.

If you don't get satisfactory results from the dealer, contact the manufacturer's district office. Its location is listed in the telephone directory, and often in the owner's manual that came with the car. The matter will probably be referred to a district representative who will set up an appointment to inspect your car at the dealer's service department.

If the combined efforts of the dealer and the district office still aren't enough to straighten things out, write the division office of the manufacturer. Too often such a letter, unless targeted to the right person, is referred right back to the district office for handling. So be sure to send it directly to the vice president in charge of the division. To ensure that it gets his attention, send a copy to the president.

TO GENERAL MANAGER OF DEALERSHIP

Mr. Hiram Moat
General Manager
Uptown Motors
street address
city, state ZIP

Dear Mr. Moat:

The need for reliable, economical transportation led me to Uptown Motors where two months ago I purchased a new 4-cylinder Pelican hatchback.

The car has proved to be neither reliable nor economical, and I think it's time to bring to your attention one of the car's more prominent defects: the automatic transmission sticks in low; doesn't shift until 45 mph, then jumps into high gear. This causes the motor to race at too many RPM's, resulting in excessive motor wear and terrible gas mileage (about 10 miles per gallon).

I have brought the Pelican in five times and explained what is wrong to your service manager. And five times I have had the car returned to me in the same condition. On each occasion I emphasized that all is well on cold starts, and that the delayed shifting occurs only after the car has been running for a while.

The scenario is the same each time—the service manager writes up a ticket, hangs a number on the windshield and the car is driven onto the back lot. Presumably, several hours later a mechanic starts up the car, takes it around the block and pronounces it okay.

I'm certainly no automotive expert, but it should be obvious to anyone that in order to even understand the problem the car must be allowed to warm up. I've asked the service manager to take my car home with him overnight and see for himself, but he says that's impossible.

No one at Uptown Motors takes the time to correct the problem because no one cares. I'll never understand what could be more important to a dealer's service department than to service the cars that particular dealer sells. But follow-up care is viewed as nuisance warranty work and given a low priority.

Meanwhile I'm stuck with a gas-guzzling, high-revving car that falls far short of expectations.

I'm hoping, Mr. Moat, that you'll agree that something should be done. And that you'll be able to convince your people to take an interest in restoring my car to normal operating conditions.

Sincerely,

TO MANUFACTURER'S DISTRICT OFFICE

Mr. Albert Hawkins
District Office Manager
Pelican Division
MegaMotors, Inc.
street address
city, state ZIP

Dear Mr. Hawkins:

I'm enclosing a copy of a letter I sent two weeks ago to Hiram Moat, General Manager of Uptown Motors. I didn't even receive the courtesy of a response, which confirms my suspicions that no one there cares one bit about the customer once they have his money.

This new Pelican, touted in your multi-million dollar advertising campaign as a fuel-efficient car, delivers just 10 miles per gallon of gas. Its four-cylinder engine is straining at a much higher rate of RPM's than is necessary. All because no one in the service department at Uptown Motors is willing to take the time to road test the car to determine the problem.

This may well be an isolated instance, and not representative of the attitude of other Pelican dealers or the manufacturer. But three months of getting the run-around at Uptown Motors is enough.

I would appreciate it if someone on your staff would contact me and arrange to inspect my car at Uptown Motors or any other authorized Pelican dealer.

Yours truly,

Enclosure

CERTIFIED LETTER TO OFFICER
AT CORPORATE HEADQUARTERS

Mr. Kyle McAllister
Vice President
Pelican Division
MegaMotors, Inc.
street address
city, state ZIP

Dear Mr. McAllister:

    In the not too distant future, when time permits and my temper subsides, I intend to send to your chairman and the board of directors a rather lengthy account explaining why my new Pelican is the last MegaMotors product I'll ever own.

    The Pelican was carelessly built and is being poorly serviced. Equal measures of indifference and incompetence characterize the operations of both the dealer who sold me the car and the district office to which I appealed in desperation for resolution of a lengthening list of problems.

    The enclosed sheet summarizes the difficulties I've encountered with the car. The date and odometer reading of each of seven trips back to the dealer are indicated, along with my specific complaints on each occasion, what was done to try to correct the problem, and the result. Copies of each repair order are also enclosed.

    On the last two occasions a representative from the local Pelican office was present. On only one point did everyone agree—this 4-cylinder car should be getting considerably more than 10 miles per gallon of gas.

    I have wasted a lot of time with these people, Mr. McAllister, and my patience is wearing thin. Unless prompt steps are taken to correct the car's many defects—or the purchase price refunded in full—I will have no choice but to bring before a court of law your company's refusal to honor the warranty.

                            Yours truly,

cc: President, MegaMotors, Inc.
Enclosures

TO OWNER OF CAR DEALERSHIP

Mr. Robert Ballantine, President
Monsoon Motors
street address
city, state ZIP

Dear Mr. Ballantine:

Of the four Penguin dealers in this city, two are closer to my home than is Monsoon Motors. So it wasn't by accident that I traveled across town to purchase my new car from you three months ago. The recommendation of several of your satisfied customers made the distance a secondary consideration. In hindsight, it appears to have been a mistake. I am dissatisfied with both the Penguin and your service department's to-date futile attempts to get it running properly.

Five trips to your shop have failed to correct the Penguin's difficult starting, rough idling and engine stalling. None of your people seem to know what to do about it, and appear content to let it remain my problem.

Art Masterson, one of my neighbors who steered me to Monsoon Motors in the first place, suggested I get in touch with you personally before taking the matter up with the Penguin district office.

If in these hurried times there still exist some businessmen who place a value on customer goodwill, here is one last chance to recapture mine. Should you succeed in convincing your service manager that correcting the problems of the car you sold me is a serious matter, there may yet be hope.

Sincerely yours,

TO MANUFACTURER'S DISTRICT OFFICE

Mr. Oliver Richter
District Office Manager
Penguin Division
MegaMotors, Inc.
street address
city, state ZIP

Dear Mr. Richter:

Four frustrating, anguished months have passed since I purchased a new Penguin from Monsoon Motors in Boardville. The car didn't run properly from the beginning and after six trips back to the service department it is still hard to start, chugs erratically while idling and frequently stalls.

What began as a mere annoyance has become a potentially life-threatening problem. One day last week the Penguin's engine sputtered and died on an exit ramp off Highway 56. As my family watched in horror, cars sped around our disabled vehicle. Thirty minutes passed before a tow truck brought us to Sunshine Motors, the nearest Penguin dealer.

There it remained for two days. I was assured it was now running fine and it was . . . until yesterday. At this writing I have a totally unreliable four-month-old car, still under warranty, sitting in my garage.

What do you suggest? The solution is evidently beyond the scope of both these Penguin dealers.

Yours truly,

CERTIFIED LETTER TO OFFICER AT CORPORATE HEADQUARTERS

Mr. Wendell Reeves
Vice President
Penguin Division
MegaMotors, Inc.
street address
city, state ZIP

Dear Mr. Reeves:

The mechanical difficulties encountered with my new Penguin since its purchase last May 17 seem almost beyond belief. Eight trips back to the dealer's service department have accomplished nothing.

Regional office representatives have recently met with the dealer, Monsoon Motors. Despite numerous attempts to correct the problem, the car continues to operate defectively.

Most recently Mr. Richter of your regional office authorized special warranty work in an attempt to correct repeated instances of wildly gyrating engine speeds and frequent stalling.

After my Penguin had been in the shop for three days, I was finally assured by Mr. Richter that all was well. On the way home that night it stopped running and wouldn't start. I had the disabled car towed home and pushed it into my garage where it remains today.

The fact that the mechanical problems seem to be such that they can't be solved by the alleged repairs already made leaves me with grave doubts about the future performance of an automobile that has proved so troublesome to date.

I don't think it unreasonable to expect satisfactory service from an automobile representing so sizeable an investment and reputed to be a precision machine. Since all attempts to get it to run properly have failed and the matter has been shrugged off by apparently disinterested service personnel, I am appealing to you as chief executive of the Penguin Division to rectify this situation.

Yours truly,

cc: President, MegaMotors, Inc.

LETTER LEVERAGE

An often-overlooked ally of the beleagured car-ache victim is the local Better Business Bureau. Incorrectly perceived by many to be puppets of the firms who help fund them, many BBBs have really gone out of their way in recent years to promote higher standards of business ethics.

A call or letter to the BBB at any stage of the dealer-district office-manufacturer complaint process will set things in motion. There's no need to get into all the specifics at this point. A form will come by return mail. The consumer is asked to describe the nature of the complaint and to indicate what adjustment he'd consider fair. Copies are sent to the company and the BBB.

The Bureau will often attempt to mediate disputes. If, for instance, you're getting nowhere with the local district office, the Bureau will furnish you with the name of a key person to contact at that office who is accustomed to dealing with such referrals. You are asked to notify the BBB when the problem has been resolved or an adjustment promised.

If mediation efforts fail, you or the participating business can request the BBB to take the matter to arbitration. The decision of the arbitrator, a volunteer specially selected and trained by the Bureau, is binding on both parties.

FILING A COMPLAINT WITH BETTER BUSINESS BUREAU

Gentlemen:

I have had nothing but trouble with the new Pachyderm station wagon I purchased six months ago from Blake Motors.

The dealer's service department has failed to correct its many defects, and the local district office hasn't helped a bit.

Please send me a complaint form and the name of the person in the Pachyderm district office whom I should contact.

Sincerely,

REPORT TO BETTER BUSINESS BUREAU ON MEDIATION

Re: Complaint #00 0000

Gentlemen:

As you requested, I am writing to inform you of the results of my dispute with Blake Motors and the Pachyderm district office.

Eric Svenson, to whom you referred me at the district office, was very helpful. He set up an appointment with Blake's service manager and together they went over my long list of complaints. The next day I picked up the car and everything had been fixed to my satisfaction.

Many thanks for your assistance in helping resolve this matter.

Sincerely yours,

REQUESTING ARBITRATION THROUGH
BETTER BUSINESS BUREAU

Re: Complaint #00 0000

Gentlemen:

As you requested, I am writing to inform you of the results of my dispute with Blake Motors and the Pachyderm district office.

Sven Ericson, your contact at the district office, set up an appointment with Blake's service manager and together they went over my long list of complaints. Unfortunately, we are still as far apart as ever on the question of how far the manufacturer's responsibility extends.

A few perfunctory adjustments were made (see enclosed copy of repair order), but they refused to repair or replace the power steering unit under the terms of the warranty. They continue to maintain that through negligence I had failed to maintain the proper fluid level in the pump reservoir. I showed them receipts proving that periodic maintenance, as prescribed in the owner's manual, had indeed been performed by the dealer.

It is my understanding that MegaMotors, Inc., manufacturer of the Pachyderm, is committed to arbitrate any complaints which can't be settled through the Better Business Bureau's mediation efforts.

I am willing to go to arbitration on the disputed issues, and to abide by the decision. Please send me the agreement form and advise me of the time and place of the arbitration hearing.

Cordially,

Enclosure

LETTER LEVERAGE

When disputes arise, the average car owner is usually no match for people who make a living selling or fixing cars, day in and day out. They're the ones who ultimately determine, after engaging in ritualistic negotiations, what price you'll pay for a new or used car. They decide how much to charge for repairs, and to what extent they'll honor the warranty.

In short, the cards are often stacked in favor of these "experts." And abuses abound. But the consumer can play hard ball, too.

A timely letter can focus on an unethical adversary's weak spot when he knows that you know he's operating on the fringe of the law—or beyond.

The suggestion of legal action never fails to get his attention. And the threat to picket his place of business is always taken seriously. Either could be a bluff—only the letter writer knows for sure—but often the threat alone brings prompt action. If push comes to shove and you do picket, remember to stay off his property and don't interfere with people coming and going.

Should you ever be victimized by clearly illegal tactics, don't hesitate to report the incident to law enforcement authorities.

PREMATURE RUSTING . . . AND EXTENDED WARRANTY

Mr. Wendell Reeves
Vice President
Penguin Division
MegaMotors, Inc.
street address
city, state ZIP

Dear Mr. Reeves:

The pride I once took in my Penguin has eroded right along with the car's body. The ravages of rust have left my four-year-old sedan with rocker panels and fenders that resemble Swiss cheese.

In dismay I returned to Peregrine Motors, where I purchased the car and asked the service manager what could be done about this. He replied that nothing could be done since the warranty has expired, and added that rust perforation is common with this particular model. The service manager advised against cosmetic repairs and repainting, because the rust would soon reappear worse than ever.

In recent weeks I've heard from a number of sources that Penguin is quietly authorizing the replacement of badly-rusted parts at no charge in some cases, even though the warranty is up. Confirming this in a column in last Sunday's Henderson Herald, auto editor Clay Carson wrote that, "if Penguin owners complain long enough and loudly enough, dealers will repair or replace the rusted parts and pass along the costs to the manufacturer, even though the warranty has expired."

Out of respect for your time, and because I abhor long and loud confrontations, I'll mention this matter only once before turning it over in ten days to Lance MacFarland of the law firm of Evers, MacFarland and Parsons. If secret warranty extensions for certain favored customers exist, I'll soon know about it.

It is not the purpose of this letter to dispute the ethics of your company's decision to make repairs on some carelessly manufactured cars and refusing to do so on others. Rather, it is to ensure that the components of my own car damaged from premature rusting are replaced—promptly and at no charge.

Yours truly,

THREAT TO PICKET A DEALER'S SHOWROOM

Dear Mr. Walters:

I am enclosing a color photograph of my new Clipper which I bought six months ago from Wally's Motors. As you can see, I've rigged up a roof rack which holds a six-foot long fiberboard lemon.

Can you imagine the impact on your weekend floor traffic when I park this car on the street right in front of your entrance? My wife and I will be on hand to distribute to passersby mimeographed sheets detailing our experiences with this lemon and the incompetence and indifference of your mechanics.

Fourteen trips to your service department have failed to correct the defects listed on the attached sheet. And you, Mr. Walters, have never returned my calls.

If I finally have your attention, and if you wish to avoid this curbside demonstration—which will begin a week from Saturday and continue until the problems are corrected—have your service manager call me and set up an appointment.

I'll expect you and a regional representative from Clipper to be present.

_____
(signature)

Enclosure

CERTIFIED LETTER TO USED CAR SALESMAN

Mr. Waldo Clark
Waldo's Motor Sales
street address
city, state ZIP

Mr. Clark:

I have proof that you deliberately misrepresented the mileage on the three-year-old Panther sedan that I purchased from you earlier this month. I intend to report this violation of the anti-rollback provision of the Motor Vehicle Information and Cost Savings Act to the federal authorities unless you return my entire purchase price of $3,000 by Friday, April 10.

Within a matter of days the transmission and brakes gave indications of serious trouble—hardly what one would expect of a car with just 23,000 miles of use.

I was able to learn the name of the previous owner, Howard Miller of Hartford, and obtain from him an affidavit stating that the car had 60,000 miles on the odometer when he sold it to you on February 28. I'm enclosing a copy of this affidavit. In addition, Mr. Miller has provided me with service records which will substantiate my charge if you choose to contest the matter.

You have cheated the wrong person this time, Mr. Clark, and I am prepared to go to whatever lengths are necessary to make you pay for it. I will do so unless you make arrangements to pick up the defective car and see to it that I have in hand a certified check for $3,000 by next Friday.

_____
(signature)

Enclosure

REPORTING EXTORTION TO THE AUTHORITIES

Mr. David Fosdick
County District Attorney
street address
city, state ZIP

Dear Mr. Fosdick:

I don't know the legal definition of extortion in this state, but there's no doubt that I have been victimized.

On June 20, while driving north on Route 15, a car coming in the opposite direction crossed the center line, sideswiped my car and kept on going. In minutes a tow truck appeared and offered to remove my damaged car from the highway. While uninjured, I was highly distressed and signed what the driver told me was a form authorizing the tow.

I was later to learn that what I signed was really an authorization for Ace Garage of Finchburg to do the repairs. The next day I stopped by Ace Garage to pay them and arrange to have the car brought to the garage of my choice. To my astonishment, Joe Cardelli, owner of Ace, showed me the form I had signed, now with itemized repair work totalling $1,800 included. He demanded immediate payment of half that amount before work would begin.

I protested that I hadn't even completed my insurance accident report, and Mr. Cardelli became belligerent. He said that I had committed a crime by leaving the scene of the accident before police arrived and threatened to have me sent to jail.

It's quite obvious now that I should have called the police immediately and not signed the "towing" form. But when predators such as Ace get to accident victims while they're still dazed, anything can happen.

The situation now appears hopeless. I refuse to pay Ace any sum in excess of the towing charge and they won't release my car. Furthermore, I'm told there will be a $20 per day storage charge.

Can you help?

Sincerely yours,

REPORTING FRAUDULENT SALES TACTICS

Office of States Attorney
Consumer Fraud Division
street address
city, state ZIP

Gentlemen:

I'm writing to report a flagrant violation of the Installment Sales Act. Enclosed is an ad which appeared last Sunday in the Huntsville Herald.

You'll notice that Hawk Motors is offering a brand new Parrot sedan for a down payment of just $200.

This sounded too good to be true, and indeed it was. Once in Hawk's showroom, I was unable to learn from the salesman the annual percentage rate of the loan or the length of time for repaying it.

"Just sign here, gimme a check for $200 and let us worry about all the details," urged Max Montegue, Sales Manager. After a few quick calculations I determined that the financing charges exceeded 40 per cent and beat a hasty retreat.

It would appear that Hawk Motors is engaging in deceptive trade practices—as defined by the state—by hyping a small down payment in their ad while omitting any mention of the full price of the car, the financing rate, and the number of payments.

I hope you take appropriate action to put a stop to this illegal practice.

Sincerely,

Enclosure

LETTER LEVERAGE

Few things unhinge automotive executives as much as a government-ordered recall to make no-charge corrections and adjustments on cars already sold.

If you're having a safety-related problem—even after the expiration of the warranty period—you'll get prompt action by writing a letter to the manufacturer's vice president of Product Development. This division is very responsive to feedback from owners, and eager to correct small problems before they become big ones.

Top auto executives often publicly express astonishment when informed of unethical practices in their dealer network. How anyone so naive could have gone so far is questionable, but if you can enlighten one such corporate chieftain with a first-hand account, it's worth the time and effort.

Even dealers may not be aware of everything that goes on behind the scenes. Small accessories and items in the glove compartment sometimes have a way of disappearing while a car is entrusted to their care. A letter to the boss will usually bring prompt restitution.

A SAFETY-RELATED INQUIRY

Mr. Ivan Mueller
Vice President, Product Development
Fireball Division
MegaMotors, Inc.
street address
city, state ZIP

Dear Mr. Mueller:

I am writing to inform you of a potentially dangerous defect in my otherwise satisfactory 1982 Fireball coupe. On several occasions the gas pedal has stuck to the floorboard while the car was in motion. In each case my wife or I was able to pry it back up with the side of the shoe and there were no unfortunate consequences.

While the car was still under warranty I mentioned the problem to a service writer at Bayshore Motors. He said that because of its design, correction was impossible, and that in order to avoid a recurrence I must remember to depress the bottom part of the accelerator, not the top.

All well and good—if this becomes a habit. My primary concern, however, is that when my teenage son begins driving next year he may not always remember to take such an unusual precaution to avoid an accident.

Can't something be done?

Yours truly,

CAN DESIGN FLAW BE CORRECTED?

Mr. Elliott Cartier
Vice President, Product Development
Flamingo Division
MegaMotors, Inc.
street address
city, state ZIP

Dear Mr. Cartier:

My new Flamingo sedan is the best car I've ever owned. What few minor adjustments were required—with one exception—were performed promptly and satisfactorily by the dealer.

There is, however, a lingering problem which at first glance may appear trivial. But since I am among the small percentage of Americans who buckle up, it continues to annoy.

The three seat belts in the back as well as the belt in the center of the front seat are fine. But the belts in the driver's seat and the right front passenger seat are suffocating to say the least. Designed like a slip-knot to constrict relentlessly with the slightest movement, I find I must release the belt, let it wind back to the starting position and adjust it every few miles. This discomfort and inconvenience discourage use of the belts and certainly contradict Flamingo's professed concern for safety.

Because the left and right front seat belts were so designed and are beyond correction under the terms of the warranty, I offered to pay the dealer to convert them so they would operate as the other four belts, but was told this was impossible.

Any suggestions?

Yours truly,

GREEDY DEALER BLOWS SALE

Mr. W. W. Kane
Vice President
Astral Division
MegaMotors, Inc.
street address
city, state ZIP

Dear Mr. Kane:

I am writing to report an incident in which one of your dealers attempted to cheat me out of $400.

Three months ago, after placing a deposit, I obtained a signed contract from Evergreen Motors in Brownsville to deliver a new Astral sedan for $10,400 plus tax. No trade-in was involved.

Yesterday I received word that the car was in and that I could pick it up. To my astonishment, I was told that the price would now be $10,800 plus tax because the factory had increased the price on Astrals between the time I placed the order and the time of delivery.

I had read about the increase, but pointed out to the dealer that he had no right to jack up the price at delivery. I told him I knew the manufacturer's guaranteed price policy locks in the agreed-upon figure to the consumer and reimburses the dealer for each car ordered before the increase. He denied this was the case, and said in effect, "Take it or leave it."

I realize dealers are independent businesses and that the manufacturer isn't responsible for the ways in which they market your product. But it seems unethical at best for them to cash in on your reimbursement policy and, at the same time, try to wring out additional dollars from the customer after voiding his contract.

After heated words, Evergreen Motors returned my deposit, and I left— determined to make my old car last as long as possible.

Here's one potential customer you've lost forever . . . unless you can somehow enforce a minimum standard of fair-play in your dealer network.

Yours truly,

GOOD JOB SPOILED BY STICKY FINGERS

Mr. Nick Hubbard, President
Hubbard Piranha, Inc.
street address
city, state ZIP

Dear Mr. Hubbard,

Yesterday I finally picked up my Piranha convertible after extensive body work had been performed by your people following an accident two months ago. The car looks as good as new, and I am quite satisfied with the overall results.

On the other hand, I felt it inexcusable to find that many small items had disappeared during the lengthy period in which the car remained in your shop. They include:

—floor mats
—black gear shift knob (replaced at my insistence before accepting the car but with a chrome one)
—cigarette lighter
—chrome knob for adjusting left seat
—right rubber bumper for convertible top (now on back order from your parts department)

Whether the souvenir hunters were your employees or—as it was suggested—Piranha owner's club members who "have the run of the place on Wednesday nights," something is clearly wrong. And I would be reluctant to do business again with Hubbard Piranha unless the above items are replaced.

Yours truly,

LETTER LEVERAGE

The point of purchase for most automotive needs is light-years removed from the sedate corporate headquarters of the multi-billion dollar companies behind it all.

What's more, the company's franchised dealers and their employees along with the person selling in the automotive section of a large retail store often bear little resemblance to the polite, competent and concerned actor you see on television promoting the product.

After the dust has settled and further discussion across the counter seems pointless, go home and forget about it—till the next day. Then reconstruct the details of the incident and send a letter to the appropriate officer of the company that manufactured or sold the product.

The best you could hope for would be a complete refund, and that is not as far-fetched as it may seem if you strike a responsive chord.

The least you should expect is a written apology. In either case, it is some consolation to know that you've rattled the cage of your tormentor. For it is a fact in American business that the buck doesn't stop at the top. When the person at the top becomes annoyed, the reverberations echo down the line and become deafening at the source.

For good measure, take the time to inform legislators sitting on relevant committees of your experience.

SERVICE STATION RIPOFF

Mr. Ralph Hutter
Vice President, Marketing
Viscid Oil Company
street address
city, state ZIP

Dear Mr. Hutter,

I want to register my outrage at a modern-day version of highway robbery being perpetrated by the operator of one of your "service" stations.

Enroute from Florida last Friday, I stopped for gas at a Viscid station in northern Georgia along Interstate 00 at Route 000. Seconds after the attendant offered to check the oil, he reported that I had "big trouble."

He pointed out splotches of oil all over the engine and urgently advised against my going any farther until he could put the car up to take a look. I was informed that it needed a new oil pump. I asked the location of the nearest Panther dealer and was told it was 30 miles away.

Your man said he had in stock the pump I needed, and that for $145— parts and labor—I could be on my way. Knowing practically nothing about the mechanical operation of a car, I reluctantly agreed although I was more than a little suspicious.

After the job was completed and I had paid the bill, I asked to have back the old oil pump. He said it had already gone into the compactor. Only after my repeated insistence was I even given a receipt.

When I arrived home, I mentioned this incident to the mechanic at a gas station I frequent. He said I had been the victim of a fraudulent scheme in which oil is squirted on the engine to make it appear as if something is leaking. When we looked under the car, the mechanic assured me that the oil pump was the same one that came with the car three years and 30,000 miles ago.

I don't know whether the Viscid station where I was cheated is company-operated or one of your franchised dealers. Either way, I hold your firm accountable for not enforcing a minimum standard of ethics.

I have enclosed a copy of the receipt as evidence of this unconscionable gouging. And I expect a prompt refund of the $145. Your failure to do so by the end of this month will unleash a torrent of publicity about this unsavory. incident as the story is told and retold to:

—Action Line columns in newspapers

—The Georgia Attorney General's office

—State of Georgia Bureau of Consumer Fraud

—Auto clubs and car magazines

—Travel guides

Yours truly,

Enclosure

COMPLAINT TO TIRE BUYER OF RETAIL STORE CHAIN

Mr. Dwayne Dutton
Buyer, Automotive Division
Smith & Jones Co.
street address
city, state ZIP

Dear Mr. Dutton:

Since experiencing a near-disaster last Saturday, I have had good reason to regard the Smith & Jones tire as a potentially dangerous product. An item I'll never buy again . . . and one which I shall urge my friends to avoid.

My wife was driving with two of my children in our car when one of the five Smith & Jones tires I purchased recently (see enclosed receipts) had a blowout just south of the Newberry Oasis on Interstate 40. The tire left the rim completely causing loss of control. The car then slammed into an abutment and spun around coming to a stop on the shoulder. No one was hurt, though the car did sustain an estimated $500 damage.

I called Mr. Austin of the Briarcliff store and arranged to meet with him and Mr. Gleason at the auto service department in an attempt to learn the cause of the blowout. An inspection of the tire revealed two large holes in the inner side of the casing, but no puncture of the tread. They concluded that the tire must have hit something and ruled out any chance of a defective casing. I know otherwise because I was traveling in the same center lane about 100 feet ahead in my other car.

"When you sell as many tires as we do, mishaps of this kind occur 45 to 50 times a year. And it's almost always from hitting something," I was told. I came asking for nothing but a plausible explanation. And I left deeply concerned about the reliability of the remaining Smith & Jones tires on this car.

I've had the blown-out tire replaced elsewhere. There I learned that structural failure was unquestionably the cause . . . possibly coupled with over-inflation.

On behalf of the 45 to 50 unfortunates who don't survive to register a complaint, I do so now—not in expectation of an adjustment of any kind, or even a reply—but hopefully to prompt an increased sense of responsibility on the part of Smith & Jones in matters where people's lives are at stake.

Yours truly,

cc: J. L. Edwards, Vice President of Merchandising
Enclosures

INFORMING LEGISLATOR OF YOUR EXPERIENCE

Representative Jeremiah Wilmot
U. S. House of Representatives
Washington, D.C. 20515

Dear Mr. Wilmot:

I read of your subcommittee's investigation into unsafe auto tires and want to assure you that Hawthorn is not the only negligent manufacturer.

The enclosed copy of a letter I sent earlier this year is, I think, self-explanatory. The response from Smith & Jones was predictably defensive and entirely unsatisfactory.

Keep after 'em!

Sincerely yours,

Enclosure

COMPLAINT TO PRESIDENT OF MOTOR CLUB

Dear Mr. Emerson:

For many years I have carried a Rainbow Motor Club card in my wallet, secure in the knowledge that help was close at hand if needed.

Yesterday, for the first time, I needed help. I phoned from a gas station two blocks from where my car had overheated and come to a stop. When no Rainbow truck materialized after an hour, I called again. I declined the gas station owner's offer to send his own truck over.

Another hour and a half passed before your man arrived. He said a broken fan belt had to be replaced but he didn't have that size in his truck. So I was towed two blocks to the now-familiar gas station where the new belt was installed.

I wound up wasting the better part of an afternoon and spending just about as much as someone not carrying the coveted gold card. And I wondered how long I'd have to wait to have my battery jumped on a subzero day when half the cars in town won't start.

All in all, Mr. Emerson, I'm disappointed in what I'm getting for my $40 annual membership and do not intend to renew it next year.

Yours truly,

13

Contacting Government Officials

Elected officials at every level of government must stay attuned to the public mood if they expect to be *re-elected*. A message stating the views of a constituent is rarely ignored.

Phone calls, telegrams and letters on any issue are tallied pro and con and the official apprised of the response. The concise, well-written letter remains the most effective way to get through the layers of staff assistants to the governor, congressman or even the president himself.

Of course, each piece of correspondence is screened initially by assistants. The printed form letter or coupon which readers are urged to clip from a newspaper, sign, and send are simply noted. But the message that comes through the loudest is one in which the writer has taken time to compose his thoughts in a carefully thought-out letter. Numerous government officials have indicated that this kind of letter most closely approximates the pulse of the typical voter. And many have instructed staff assistants to cull from their overstuffed mailbags for their personal review a representative sample of letters indicating how Americans really feel about an issue.

The tone of your letter should be restrained, even if you're outraged. The official should be addressed respectfully even if you consider him a fool. It's all right to come to the point circuitously if you're injecting an element of human interest describing how a matter affects you, your family and friends.

Give your elected representative the benefit of any constructive ideas you have. Let him know conclusively whether you support his stand or not. If not, state why he should consider changing his position.

State legislators have considerably smaller office staffs to handle the mail than do U.S. congressmen, so it may take a bit longer to get a reply. But with their proportionately smaller volume of mail, your letter assumes greater importance. In fact, a letter from a constituent is often presented as evidence in committee meetings.

Finally, try to confine your letter to just one subject. And be sure to include your name and complete address on the letter as well as the envelope.

Here are the correct forms of address and salutations for the following government officials:

The President of the United States	The President The White House Washington, D.C. 20500 (Dear Mr. President:)
A United States Senator	The Honorable John R. Thomas United States Senate Washington, D.C. 20510 (Dear Senator Thomas:)
A United States Representative	The Honorable Arthur J. James House of Representatives Washington, D.C. 20515 (Dear Mr. James:)
The Governor	The Honorable Martin A. Anthony Governor of_____(state)_____ city, state ZIP (Dear Governor Anthony:)
A State Senator	The Honorable Michael L. Bell The State Senate city, state ZIP (Dear Senator Bell:)
A State Representative, Assemblyman or Delegate	The Honorable Wayne R. Russell House of Representatives city, state ZIP (Dear Mr. Russell:)
The Mayor of a city	The Honorable Karen E. Fuller Mayor of _____(city)_____ city, state ZIP (Dear Mayor Fuller:)
An Alderman	Alderman Charles B. Lester City Hall city, state ZIP (Dear Mr. Lester:)

URGING PRESIDENT TO RESTORE SOCIAL SECURITY INCREASES

The President
The White House
Washington, D.C. 20500

Dear Mr. President:

It was upsetting to hear of your plan to freeze Social Security benefits at their present level for the next 12 months. If preceding administrations and your own had been able to bring inflation under control, I would gladly support your proposal. Regrettably, that's not the case. I don't think senior citizens should be asked to shoulder a major part of the burden that follows decades of fiscal mismanagement.

The scheduled increase in benefits is not extravagant. At best, it will simply allow many of us to continue at a bare-bones level. This hardly seems unreasonable when you realize that my generation worked hard, paid its taxes and responded by the millions to the call to arms.

I urge you to keep pruning wasteful and unnecessary government expenditures, but to uphold the integrity of the Social Security system which so many of us faithfully funded during our working years.

Very truly yours,

A CONTRARY OPINION ON SOCIAL SECURITY

The President
The White House
Washington, D.C. 20500

Dear Mr. President:

Just about everyone agrees—something will have to be done about Social Security. The elderly clamor for ever higher and higher payments, even though millions of them are reaping benefits far out of proportion to their contributions. Younger workers despair of ever collecting anything from a system continually teetering on the brink of bankruptcy.

I am one of the latter group, and I believe Social Security should be made voluntary. At 34 years of age I have already in my short working career contributed—or to put it more accurately, been assessed—nearly $20,000. And I don't expect to see any of it coming back when I retire. I would gladly forfeit the entire amount I've put in to date for the opportunity to withdraw irrevocably from the scheme. So, too, would many other working people if given the choice.

Since we're not a cohesive group of millions of one-issue voters as are many of the current recipients, it could well be politically risky to support us and our position. But the bold initiative of putting Social Security on a voluntary basis would be seen by thinking people of all ages as a courageous stand.

Beneficiaries and contributors alike would realize that their president does not intend to stand by and watch the system collapse of its own weight. To do otherwise will simply defer for a short while the ultimate day of reckoning.

Very respectfully yours,

CONTACTING HOUSE COMMITTEE ON PENDING BILL

Committee on Public Works and Transportation
2165 Rayburn House Office Building
Washington, D.C. 20515

Dear Sirs:

I am quite concerned about recent attempts (Bill Nos. HR0000 and HR0000) to rescind the national 55-mph speed limit, and urge you to use your influence to see to it that this life-saving, fuel-saving measure remains the law of the land.

Two irrefutable pieces of evidence have emerged since the adoption by all states of the uniform speed limit.

First, traffic fatalities have been substantially reduced. Yet, for reasons I can't fathom, some are urging repeal of the 55-mph speed limit. But there's no repealing the law of physics—when two objects collide, something's got to give. And it's obvious that a collision at a lower speed is less likely to result in death or serious injury.

Secondly, it has been proved that less fuel is consumed at 55 mph than at higher highway speeds. It is generally agreed that the less fuel America must import, the better. To wipe out the easiest and most efficient fuel conservation measure yet devised would be foolish.

We have made a start toward lessening America's dependence on foreign oil. Let's not turn back now.

Very truly yours,

AN APPEAL TO U.S. SENATOR TO CHANGE A LAW

The Honorable W. R. Ladd
United States Senate
Washington, D.C. 20510

Dear Senator Ladd:

I urge you to vote to rescind the national 55-mph speed limit. If ever there were a matter best left to individual states, this is it.

Fifty-five may be appropriate on the congested highways of heavily populated areas, but makes no sense at all in the wide-open spaces. To have a uniform speed limit for the entire country without regard for the widely varying conditions in each state is absurd.

The wasted time and lower level of productivity caused by unrealistically low highway speeds more than offsets any perceived fuel conservation measures. In addition, there are hundreds, perhaps thousands, of routes which had a very low incidence of accidents prior to the enactment in 1975 of the 55-mph limit. There is little reason to believe that if reasonable speed limits were restored to these remote places that accidents would increase.

It's too late to recover the countless millions of hours people have wasted since 1975 behind the wheel of meandering cars plodding slowly along four-lane Interstates or on desolate country highways. But there's a new spirit in the land to undo the mistake and repeal the national 55-mph speed limit.

Please give this matter your consideration. I'm sure you'll come to the conclusion that "55" is an idea whose time has passed.

Sincerely yours,

ASKING GOVERNOR TO CHANGE STATE HOLIDAY

Dear Governor Wells:

We have been residents of this state for five years, and would really like to see it get in step with the rest of the nation on one matter. Unlike any other state we've lived in, the schools here are closed on Abraham Lincoln's birthday, but open on Presidents' Day. As a result, my children are home on one day and my husband on the other.

This is most inconvenient for people with families. For all practical purposes, we end up with two wasted holidays. Revenue could be increased in the state by celebrating both on the federal holiday—Presidents' Day—because entire families could be taking advantage of local recreational facilities.

Very sincerely yours,

PROTESTING FUND CUTBACKS TO STATE SENATOR

Dear Senator Edelmar:

As the parent of a hearing-impaired child, I was disturbed to learn of recent attempts to cut back on state funding for the Grove Development Center.

It is doubtless true that there is some fat in the state budget that could be trimmed. But there certainly isn't anything frivolous about the Center. The competent and dedicated staff there has gone a long way toward preparing my 11-year-old daughter to cope with her handicap and lead a productive, near-normal life. It would be tragic to ignore the special needs of such children.

I urge your vote against Bill #214 or any other piece of legislation which would seek to undermine the Grove Development Center.

Sincerely yours,

ALERTING CITY HALL TO DANGEROUS STREET CONDITIONS

Dear Mayor Fleming:

My 14-year-old son recently began collecting hub caps. Each day a half-dozen or so come flying off wheels as cars are jolted by the crater-like potholes in the street in front of my house.

In fact, the entire 1400 block of Paxton Avenue resembles a war zone. I called the Department of Public Streets three weeks ago and heard the usual excuses about how busy the repair crews are.

It's just a matter of time before these worsening conditions cause a driver to lose control of his car entirely. Before this negligence results in a serious accident, I urge you to direct the street department to at least put up temporary SLOW/CAUTION signs until repairs or resurfacing can be scheduled.

Sincerely yours,

PROPOSING NEW ORDINANCE FOR VILLAGE

Dear Mayor Price:

Last night I answered the doorbell and was confronted by a large, menacing teenager selling magazine subscriptions. He wouldn't take "no" for an answer and literally put his foot in the door so I couldn't close it.

The youth loudly announced that the only way some of my neighbors had been able to get rid of him was to order some magazines. I responded just as loudly—and somewhat hysterically—that if he didn't leave I'd call the police. He finally got the hint.

The police told me there is no ordinance in our village prohibiting such solicitations, and that it's not at all uncommon for these uninvited individuals to go to any lengths to sell their merchandise.

I think it's time that you and the village trustees consider enacting such an ordinance. Either require door-to-door solicitors to register with the police and meet prescribed standards, or prohibit such intrusions entirely.

I will eagerly await your response.

Sincerely yours,

COMPLAINT TO MAYOR OF NEIGHBORING CITY

Dear Mayor Cook:

I've noticed that again this year, the Park District of Tanglewood Bluffs has posted a sign at each of their public beaches that reads, "Parking Permitted with Tanglewood Bluffs Beach Stickers Only . . . Violators will be Prosecuted."

In past years we Dinsmore residents could obtain from the Park District of Tanglewood Bluffs—free for the asking—a sticker that permitted parking in the public areas along the lakefront. In return, Dinsmore extended reciprocal privileges to Tanglewood Bluffs residents who wanted to use our town's swimming pool.

I was astonished to learn that this year, for the first time, if you live in Dinsmore you'll have to pay $50 for a beach sticker.

It comes as no surprise that all municipal governments are under budgetary constraints and seeking new means of revenue, but this heavy-handed approach to selling for an exhorbitant price a sticker that was free until this year will not go unnoticed.

I don't believe you and the Councilmen intended this step as part of an overall scheme to deliberately discriminate against Dinsmore. Instead I view it as an ill-advised attempt to fatten the city's coffers—one that will backfire if it begins to hurt in the pocketbook.

Obviously, since I don't live in Tanglewood Bluffs, I can't express my displeasure on election day. But I have decided that from now on I will refrain from spending one more cent in Tanglewood Bluffs. And I will urge my friends and neighbors to do likewise.

I will miss its many fine shops and restaurants. But until the privilege of using the public beaches in Tanglewood Bluffs is restored to Dinsmore residents, I can surely find a more hospitable town in which to spend my money.

Yours truly,

cc: Councilmen

COMPLAINT TO ALDERMAN ON GARBAGE COLLECTION

Dear Mr. Becker:

Of all the municipal services provided to citizens in a large city I should think garbage collection would be the easiest to perform efficiently. Unlike the heavy and unexpected snowfalls which stretch thin a city's street plowing crew and equipment, the routine of picking up garbage seems predictable and easy to schedule.

Why, then, are the streets and alleys in the 52nd Ward always cluttered with overflowing cans of garbage and trash? Why is it the exception rather than the rule to have the trucks come by on scheduled pickup days?

My friends in other parts of the city don't have this problem. Several have suggested that you may be at odds with the Commissioner of Sanitation and that giving a low priority to garbage collection in our ward is his means of paying you back.

If there's even a bit of truth to this, I suggest that you mend fences with him at once. If you have your own theory why the ward you represent in the City Council is so neglected, I'd like to hear it.

Meanwhile we continue to be taxed at ever higher rates. We deserve better, Alderman Becker, and I expect to see a noticeable improvement soon.

If not, count on my participation in a grassroots effort prior to next year's election to see that the 52nd Ward gets better representation.

                                        Sincerely yours,

REQUESTING AN ABSENTEE BALLOT

Absentee Department
City Hall
street address
city, state ZIP

Gentlemen:

Please send me an absentee ballot for the mayoral election to be held on April 8th. I will be out of town that week.

                                        Yours truly,
                                        (signature)

                                        name
                                        street address
                                        city, state ZIP

LETTER LEVERAGE

Dealing with the intricacies of federal and state governmental agencies can at times drive even the most sophisticated citizen up a wall. That's when it's time to remember that you have a number of influential friends in your corner, and that a letter to a U.S. congressman or state legislator representing your district can work wonders.

Because their staff members deal regularly with the bureaucratic maze, they know exactly whom to contact to get through the red tape. In an ideal world all citizens would receive prompt, courteous assistance in dealing with civil servants; in real-life situations, clout goes a long way.

So don't hesitate to ask for assistance when you run into a dead end. Be sure, however, that a specific request goes to the person in a position to handle it. U.S. congressmen are able to intervene on your behalf in federal matters, while the help of state legislators can often be brought to bear on state and local issues.

A little-known privilege of some state legislators is their ability to designate one or more scholarships to state-supported universities each year. The request for consideration should come from the student rather than the parents. There's nothing unethical about sending a similar letter to the state senator and the state representatives for your district. But be sure to let the others know when a scholarship has been awarded.

ASKING U.S. CONGRESSMAN FOR HELP
IN OBTAINING SOCIAL SECURITY PAYMENTS

The Honorable Calvin G. Spencer
House of Representatives
Washington, D.C. 20515

Dear Mr. Spencer:

I haven't received any Social Security checks in the four months since I moved, and my situation is becoming more desperate by the day.

Six weeks before moving, I notified the local Social Security office by sending in a change-of-address form and two weeks later followed up with a confirming phone call. I might as well have been talking to a tree.

At least a dozen phone inquiries and two letters since the move have failed to pry loose either my checks or even a plausible explanation for their delay.

While I'm one of your newer constituents, friends in the 14th Congressional District tell me that a word from you can work wonders in the labyrinth of the Department of Health and Human Services. That's the kind of help I need at this point.

—My Social Security number is 000-00-000

—My former address was _____

—My new address (since Feb. 15) is _____

—My phone number is 000-0000

I'd appreciate anything you could do to straighten out this matter.

Sincerely yours,

ASKING U.S. SENATOR FOR HELP IN SECURING A GOVERNMENT JOB

The Honorable Leon J. Voss
United States Senate
Washington, D.C. 20510

Dear Senator Voss:

Two years ago I was Eagle County Coordinator of the Vets for Voss. I'd like to think that the efforts of our group helped contribute to your successful campaign for the Senate.

In the ensuing period you have more than lived up to our expectations, especially in the area of standing solidly behind Veteran's benefits. Fortune has not smiled on me in the same period, and I am turning to you for help at this point.

As you may recall, I am a Vietnam veteran with a 50% service-connected disability. This has not, in itself, kept me from being able to hold a job—until lately.

I haven't been able to find employment in the four months since being laid off by Abbott Industries. The overall economic situation hasn't helped, but I've gotten the impression that—everything else being equal—a prospective employer would just as soon not hire a partially-disabled vet.

I've been thinking it over and believe it's not too late to begin building a meaningful career as an employee of the federal government. Would you please take a few minutes to look over the resumé which I have enclosed?

If anything with any of the governmental agencies in this area should be or become available, I'd be forever grateful if you could put in a word on my behalf.

Sincerely yours,

Enclosure

REQUESTING U.S. SENATOR'S INTERVENTION WITH VA

The Honorable Alan F. Baldwin
United States Senate
Washington, D.C. 20510

Dear Senator Baldwin:

Since becoming a widow four months ago I have been following the written instructions my husband left me regarding the financial future for me and my four children.

He said I should call the Veterans Administration since he was sure the children and I would be entitled to benefits because he was a veteran of the Korean conflict. When I called, the man to whom I spoke said, "We'll send you a copy of 'Federal Benefits for Veterans and Dependents,' that will answer all your questions."

I have received the 78-page booklet and read it through, but I still don't understand what, if anything, we are eligible for or how to obtain it. Could you please inform me if I am entitled to widow's benefits or if my children will be able to receive any educational assistance?

My husband, Claude R. Atwel served in the U.S. Army from mid-February, 1952 through the end of June, 1954. His army serial number was U.S.00000000; his Social Security number was 000-00-0000. Date of birth—September 9, 1932; date of death—January 12, 1983. A copy of his honorable discharge is enclosed.

There are many difficult matters for me to tend to these days and your assistance in simplifying this one would be a real blessing to me. Thank you.

Very truly yours,

ASKING STATE SENATOR FOR HELP IN OBTAINING PUBLIC AID

The Honorable Jonathan H. Cutter
The State Senate
city, state ZIP

Dear Mr. Cutter:

You have been the senator representing my district for many years and more often than not I have agreed with your votes on various issues. I believe you are responsive to the needs of your constituency.

Two months ago my husband deserted me and my three children. He cleaned out our bank accounts and left me destitute. I have applied for public aid to hold us over till next fall when my youngest child will enter first grade. My doctor has advised against my going to work before then if at all possible because the children are suffering terribly from the trauma of desertion.

The emotional problems we are undergoing could be greatly alleviated with food in our stomachs. There seems to be a tangle of red tape in the Welfare Department that is holding up action on our case. Would you please look into this? My phone calls have gotten me nowhere, and at the end of this month I will no longer have phone service.

Sincerely yours,

REQUESTING SCHOLARSHIP FROM STATE SENATOR

Dear Senator Forrester:

This June I will graduate from Mount Vernon High School. I have been accepted into the School of Architecture at the University of Illinois and have enrolled for the fall semester.

I would very much appreciate your consideration when it comes time to award a state university scholarship to a resident of the 22nd District. My credentials include the following:

— Top 15% of graduating class. ACT score—26. SAT score—500 verbal, 610 math

— Elected to Student Council—3 years, vice president in Senior year

— Reporter for the school newspaper

— Member of the Mount Vernon High debating team

— Listing in this year's Who's Who Among American High School Students

— Successful completion of a college-credit course at The Art Institute of Chicago

—U.S. Achievement Academy Physical Education Award

—Letters for the freshman, sophomore, varsity baseball teams

—Winner of Best-of-Show Art Award, Lake County Fair, 1982

I intend to pay for my education in large part out of savings from past summers of cutting lawns for dozens of my neighbors. My younger brothers will doubtless inherit the equipment and the customers if I succeed in obtaining an internship with an architectural firm in future summers.

One way or another, I'll be an architect someday, though some help along the way would certainly make the going a lot smoother. If no scholarship is available at this time, please put me on the waiting list.

Thank you in advance, Senator Forrester, for your consideration.

Sincerely yours,

name
Social Security #000-00-0000

LETTER LEVERAGE

Determining the value of property for tax purposes is not as easy as it once was. It is said that in early Roman times, the tax collector would ask a citizen to determine fair value. And usually it was that figure on which taxes were based. There was one provision, though, which kept most property owners honest. If the tax collector felt that the appraisal was too low, he had the option of acquiring it himself for that amount.

Today the arrival of a real estate tax bill usually provokes an anguished howl. But if your objection is just that taxes are "too high," you might as well just bite the bullet and ante up.

On the other hand, if you can cite specific reasons why you believe the assessor's estimated market value (on which the tax is determined) is higher than it should be, there stands a chance of a downward revision. But act as soon as you receive a notice of assessment change rather than wait until you get the tax bill.

Procedures for protesting assessments vary within each state and county, but usually involve filling out a form or appearing in person at a hearing. Occasionally a letter can do the job if you've done your homework first.

To file a complaint that is most likely to succeed, provide evidence that comparable residences in your area are either assessed at a lower rate than yours, or that they have recently sold for a lower price than your estimated market value.

Such figures are a matter of public record and aren't hard to obtain. Many newspapers publish an annual list showing how much your neighbor pays in real estate tax. A similar list is also available for inspection in the assessor's office.

Real estate transfers are listed in many trade publications and show, by county, the address, legal description, names of buyer and seller, sale price and date of recording.

HOW TO CONVINCE THE ASSESSOR HE OVER-ESTIMATED THE VALUE OF YOUR HOME

Mr. Richard R. Kelly
Supervisor of Assessments
street address
city, state ZIP

Property location: 657 Apple Tree Lane
Index number: 123-456-789

Dear Mr. Kelly:

I had hoped to be able to come down to your office during the annual protest period for a hearing with an appraiser on my residential real estate taxes. But my failing health makes such a trip out of the question, so I will attempt instead to include all pertinent information along with the grounds for my protest in this letter.

Using for comparison purposes the published list of assessed valuation for homes of similar size, age and construction within four blocks of my own, I submit the following:

Address	Owner	Assessed Value of Land	Assessed Value of Building

(List information on your own home first, then three or more comparable homes with lower assessments.)

The conclusion is obvious; either I am paying too much in real estate taxes or they are paying too little.

If further proof of the former is needed, I cite below three examples of nearby homes similar to mine which in the past six months were sold for considerably less than the appraised market value of mine. The source of the information below is the published list of real estate transfers.

Address	Date Sold	Sale Price

(List information on three comparable homes.)

Our family has always been proud of our home, but in this instance we're not flattered by your more-than-generous estimate of its value.

I would appreciate your sending an appraiser to take a closer look— inside as well as out, if he'd like. I'm convinced that a re-inspection of any of the comparable homes listed above will prove my point.

After the assessor has made his report, please let me know the findings.

Yours truly,

ASKING ASSESSOR FOR A RE-APPRAISAL
BEFORE INITIATING APPEALS

Mr. Bernard Pritikin
Director of Assessments
street address
city, state ZIP   Property location: 657 Apple Tree Lane
                                                  Index number: 123-456-789

Dear Mr. Pritikin:

I am writing to protest the huge increase in the assessed valuation of my home. In the ten years I have lived at this address, my real estate taxes have nearly tripled. By contrast, enrollment in the local schools (the largest beneficiary of property tax dollars) has dropped by 20% in the past decade.

According to the Notice of Proposed Assessment Valuation, I have until the end of the month in which to file a complaint with the County Board of Review. And this I will do unless I hear from your office within seven days.

I am prepared to appear at a hearing before the Board of Review and present evidence that homes of comparable size, age and construction in my neighborhood are assessed at a considerably lower level than is mine. I will also cite examples of similar homes which have been sold in the past year for less than the perceived market value of my own.

In the unlikely event that the County Board of Review upholds your original assessment, I will initiate a further complaint with the State Property Tax Appeal Board.

You must agree, Mr. Pritikin, that a typical taxpayer would hardly go to these extremes unless he felt he had sufficient grounds. If there's even the slightest possibility that an error may have occurred in determining my assessed valuation, please have someone on your appraisal staff get in touch with me within seven days. It would certainly save us all a lot of time and trouble.

Yours truly,

14

Write Your Ticket to a Better Job

A well-prepared resumé is essential when you're applying for a job. Many excellent books on this subject show how to present all the necessary elements in a concise, organized format.

Equally important is the accompanying cover letter. Unlike the printed resumé, the cover letter can be customized to fit each particular situation.

For example, if an ad seeks a financial analyst with a strong background in computer systems, give prominent emphasis in your response to your extensive experience in data retrieval and computer applications. When you're answering an ad for a secretary/receptionist in a doctor's office, cite your strong organizational abilities that will help maintain patient records.

A cover letter serves only one purpose, and that is to obtain an interview. In its singular job of selling the writer, it should showcase the applicant by accentuating the positive. Focus on the skills you can bring to the job, not on how the position could be another building block in your own career development.

Since a cover letter should not exceed one single-spaced typewritten page, you have no room for such fluff as, "health: excellent" or "references available on request." Nor should you make any negative mention of present or past employers.

Whenever possible, send your cover letter and resumé to a specific person. This is especially important when you're writing an unsolicited letter of application. The name and title of the individual you want to contact in such a letter can be found in trade and professional directories.

Occasionally an unsolicited letter hits pay dirt when a company has an obvious and unfilled need, and you just happen along at the right time in the right place with the right idea.

For many years it was considered appropriate to begin a letter with "Dear Sir" or "Gentlemen" when responding to a blind ad. Today, there's a good chance your letter will be read by a woman, who may take exception to those salutations.

Instead, skip the greeting altogether and begin the letter two spaces beneath the inside address. Or, if you prefer, use a neutered salutation with the probable title of the person who will receive it:

Dear Sales Manager, or
Dear Personnel Director

COVER LETTER ACCOMPANYING RESUMÉ

Mr. L. Wesley Clark
Marketing Director
All American Industries
street address
city, state ZIP

Dear Mr. Clark:

The opportunity to join an on-the-go company in the rapidly growing athletic and leisure-time industry intrigues me. In the hope that an association with your firm will be mutually beneficial, I enclose my resumé.

As with any capsulized version of ten years of successful selling experience, it reveals little more than does the tip of an iceberg. I'm convinced, however, that the submerged element of motivation and moxie will become apparent after our first meeting.

At that time, I will be happy to elaborate upon certain qualifications—not to be found on the printed form—that I hope will lead you to the conclusion that I'm your man. For example, as a lifelong resident of the Chicago area, I know the 4-state territory of Minnesota, Wisconsin, Iowa and Illinois like my own backyard. And as an avid handball player, golfer and fisherman your product line is already familiar to me.

Whatever challenges may come along in the years ahead I am, in a word, "hungry." Hungry for achievement, for high earnings, for a chance to make a meaningful contribution. I hope we can get together soon.

Yours truly,

Enclosure

COVER LETTER ACCOMPANYING RESUMÉ

Mr. P. M. Simmons, Vice President
Corporate Communications
Trans-Coastal Power Co.
street address
city, state ZIP

Dear Mr. Simmons:

Eleven years of increasing responsibilities with Albino Petroleum, Inc., a thorough background in every phase of financial writing and public relations and uncommon enthusiasm are what I hope to bring to Trans-Coastal Power Co.

As your new Director of Public Affairs, I would welcome the chance to expand on abilities I have and to quickly develop new ones.

The annual report and quarterly reports of a company—once considered rather staid documents—can and should reflect a contemporary corporation's achievements and goals.

Likewise, press releases and speeches by corporate officers should combine candor with imagination—so essential in light of the sensitive regulatory climate prevailing today.

Here, and in countless other ways, I can help. For example, I believe that Trans-Coastal is not widely perceived by the investment community to be the innovative, fast-growing company it is. To correct this, and in the process attempt to bring the price-earnings ratio of the company's stock into a more realistic range, I would recommend establishing an ongoing investor relations program.

With an advertising campaign directed at the financial community and a full schedule of presentations before security analysts, it shouldn't take long before the underlying value of Trans-Coastal is widely understood.

My resumé is enclosed. I would appreciate the opportunity to meet with you at any time you find convenient.

Sincerely,

Enclosure

COVER LETTER ACCOMPANYING RESUMÉ

Dr. Dwight Dawson, Chairman
Department of Speech
Hillside College
street address
city, state ZIP

Dear Dr. Dawson:

   I am a Ph.D. candidate in speech pathology at the University of Erudition and expect to graduate in May. I believe my two years of teaching speech science courses and my experience in clinic supervision qualify me for consideration for the position you advertised in the December Job Information Directory for an Assistant Professor in speech pathology.

   My college teaching background has included a variety of speech science courses. I have taught introductory speech science in a community college and acoustics and phonetics in two universities. Student evaluations of my courses and techniques have affirmed my effectiveness as a dedicated teacher.

   My previous supervision experience includes two years at the University of Erudition Clinic and one year at the Hayes-Whittaker Clinic. My areas of specialization are stutterers and laryngectomy patients.

   After you have reviewed the enclosed curriculum vitae, I would appreciate an opportunity to discuss how I may contribute to your department. Please call me at 000-0000 so that we may set an interview date.

                              Yours truly,

Enclosure

COVER LETTER ACCOMPANYING RESUMÉ

Box 525
c/o The Daily News
street address
city, state ZIP

Dear Personnel Director:

   Five years' experience as secretary to the president of an international corporation tops the list of credentials I believe will qualify me for your executive secretarial position. In fact, the job described in your ad in today's Daily News sounds tailor-made to my abilities and experience.

   My duties as an executive secretary have included the routine obligations plus extensive experience in communicating with and travelling to foreign countries. I have learned to be assertive yet diplomatic, especially in sensitive situations.

The attached resumé details my business and academic background.

I look forward to hearing from you. I can be reached at 000-0000 during workdays; at 000-0000 evenings and weekends.

Sincerely,

Enclosure

COVER LETTER ACCOMPANYING RESUMÉ

Box 325
c/o The Claxton Clarion
street address
city, state ZIP

The background and requirements outlined in your ad in Sunday's Claxton Clarion for a Director of Manufacturing appear to mesh almost exactly with my own.

For the past three years I have been Assistant Manager of Manufacturing for The Cactus Corporation. In that position I have coordinated manufacturing and production activity to meet schedules within quality and cost objectives.

My extensive experience in purchasing, materials management and all facets of factory management should prove useful to a firm that places a high priority on versatility and results. My ability to relate to all levels within the company—from the assembly line worker through upper-level management—has proved invaluable.

I have enclosed my resumé and salary history, and will be happy to elaborate upon any of these points.

Sincerely,

Enclosure

COVER LETTER ACCOMPANYING RESUMÉ

Manager of Professional Recruitment
Abracadabra, Inc.
street address
city, state ZIP

Your ad in Sunday's Gazette for a tax accountant intrigued me because it offered a free rein in taking on responsibility for total tax compliance.

My four years experience in corporate tax compliance dealt primarily with federal returns. I have had exposure to computerized and M.I.S. tax data and am familiar with international and DISC returns.

I have a reputation as a highly organized, self-reliant person who functions well without supervision. The intricacies of IRS procedures hold few surprises.

My resumé is enclosed. I look forward to meeting you and discussing this opportunity in detail. Please call me at 000-0000.

                                        Sincerely,

Enclosure

COVER LETTER ACCOMPANYING RESUMÉ

Mr. J. S. Graham, Superintendent
Auditing Department
Megabux Corp.
street address
city, state ZIP

Dear Mr. Graham:

One of your employees, my good friend, Lee Furnham, informed me that you will soon have an opening in your auditing department. He encouraged me to contact you so that you could look over my resumé, which I have enclosed.

The reputation of Megabux as a fast-growing, innovative company appeals to me. In addition, Lee has spoken highly of your firm's policy of promotion from within.

I am not applying with the intention of coasting along in an easy nine-to-five job. I would expect Megabux to utilize me to the limits of my abilities. Only then will you—and I—know how much can be accomplished.

I'd be happy to stop in at your convenience to discuss my potential contributions to your company. My phone number is 000-0000.

                                        Sincerely,

Enclosure

A CUSTOMIZED COVER LETTER

Ms. Sue Shafer
Vice President, Public Relations
Excaliber Co.
street address
city, state ZIP

Dear Ms. Shafer:

There are many definitions for:

Community Relations

As generally perceived by the public	Corporate glad handers, exuding pomposity, and stuffed with endless banquets.
As it is often practiced	Hard-working, well-intentioned people trying too hard to please everyone, and often not seeing the forest for the trees.
As I think it should be	An opportunity to put out brushfires before they get out of control; to help create an image of a company meeting the needs of today and anticipating the challenges of tomorrow.

There would be no real need to consider hiring a community relations specialist if your company had no competition, no stockholders and no problem with governmental regulations.

On the other hand . . . perhaps the diverse skills of a not-so-old pro could prove useful. One who is proficient in oral and written communications, capable of quickly developing and implementing programs addressed to specific needs, and blessed with an all-around sense of how to get things done.

Please take a minute to read the enclosed resumé. Then call me at 000-0000 (evenings) to set up a meeting at a time convenient to you.

Yours truly,

Enclosure

LETTER LEVERAGE

On rare occasions a letter of application can be sent without an accompanying resumé. This is acceptable for someone seeking a first job, or for an applicant returning to the work force after many years.

The college freshman hoping to set up a summer job months in advance hasn't yet the credentials to include in an impressive resumé. Instead, he's putting his best foot forward in a letter addressed to the person in a position to make the hiring decision.

The woman returning to work after raising her family can skip the resumé too, because the usual elements that would be included are so outdated. The applicant's many achievements in the years since she was employed defy categorization in a conventional resumé and are better stated in letter form. Her prospective employer very likely will give high marks to extensive community involvement.

BEGINNER'S LETTER OF APPLICATION

Mr. Emil Goetz
Managing Editor
The Daily Beacon
street address
city, state ZIP

Dear Mr. Goetz:

Were there any days last summer when the Beacon found itself short-handed? With so many employees scheduling vacations at the same time, there were probably periods when an extra person would have come in handy.

I hope to be that person next summer. A versatile, energetic jack-of-all-trades, I will have by then completed my first year at Grove University where I am majoring in journalism.

I have no illusions about my journalistic skills at this point. I realize there is a big difference between the theories taught in school and the realities of getting out three editions each day of a large metropolitan newspaper. More than anything I want to be a part of it all. You'll find me eager to learn and willing to do any job.

Experience as editor of the high school year book enables me to bring to the Beacon a better than average knowledge of graphics, layout, production and printing along with the ability to write concisely and well.

The spring semester at Grove ends May 20, and I will be available to start on Monday, May 23. Fall classes resume August 28.

I'll soon be home for the Christmas vacation. May I call you during the first week of January and arrange an appointment to discuss how I may be of use to the Beacon for three months next summer?

Yours truly,

HOMEMAKER'S RE-ENTRY

Personnel Office
Evansville Village Hall
street address
city, state ZIP

Your ad in today's Gazette for a secretary to the Village Manager certainly looks interesting. With the youngest of our children now in high school, I am looking forward to returning to work after a 20-year "vacation."

Before starting a family, I was secretary for three years to the District Sales Manager of U.S. Gumball Corp. While my shorthand could use a bit of brushing up, my typing speed has actually improved.

In recent years I have been involved in many volunteer activities in Evansville, which, I believe, give me a unique insight into the workings of our community. They include:

1984	Fund raiser, United Charities of Evansville
1982–83	Volunteer consultant, Career Center, Evansville High School (experience in IBM 14 computer)
1980–81	Publicity chairman, First Presbyterian Church of Evansville
1979	Co-Chairman of Fourth of July parade, drum and bugle competition and fireworks display, village of Evansville
1978	President of the Parent-Teachers Association, Hilltop Elementary School
1977	Vice President, Hilltop PTA
1976	Secretary/Treasurer, Hilltop PTA
1973–75	Editor of the Hilltop News (monthly school paper)

In addition to having prepared countless thousands of meals and kept a home and its occupants looking spiffy, I have skills in managing a budget and coordinating busy schedules.

I offer to bring to the post of Secretary to the Village Manager a combination of secretarial skills, a long history of community involvement, maturity and the ability to work tirelessly.

Sincerely,

LETTER LEVERAGE

A follow-up letter sent a day or two after an interview is a final touch too many applicants ignore. After the individual who will do the hiring has spoken with a number of candidates, they often begin to blur, and such a letter gives you additional exposure.

The follow-up letter thanks the interviewer for taking the time to review your qualifications. It restates briefly the special skills you would bring to the job. Finally, it indicates your continuing interest and availability.

FOLLOW-UP LETTER AFTER INTERVIEW

Mr. Arthur Draper
Vice President, Sales
Liberty Lumber Company
street address
city, state ZIP

Dear Mr. Draper,

I appreciate your taking the time yesterday to discuss with me the possibility of my joining the sales staff of Liberty Lumber Company. It sounds like a wonderful opportunity, and Liberty seems to be a company in which one could build a rewarding career.

I was especially impressed with the fact that Liberty is a major supplier to the fast-growing market of rehabilitating older homes with such a variety of innovative products. As an amateur woodcrafter and do-it-yourselfer, I can appreciate the market that exists.

If there is anything further I could add to a review of my qualifications or goals, please don't hesitate to call. I hope to hear from you soon.

Yours truly,

FOLLOW-UP LETTER AFTER INTERVIEW

Ms. June Kerr, R.N.
Administrator, Nurse Recruitment
Memorial Hospital
street address
city, state ZIP

Dear Ms. Kerr,

I appreciate the time you spent with me yesterday. It is an honor to be considered for the position of head nurse for your 30-bed family-centered obstetrical unit.

I was impressed with the progressive, dynamic nursing service at Memorial Hospital, and with the steps you are taking to move toward providing the most modern techniques in patient care. I, too, am committed to using my professional skills to the fullest, and I couldn't imagine a more conducive atmosphere in which to do so.

I welcome the challenges, the opportunity to have my ideas heard and to participate in decision making. It would be a privilege to join you and the staff at Memorial Hospital.

Yours truly,

FOLLOW-UP LETTER AFTER INTERVIEW

Mr. Malcolm W. Hughes
Director, Data Processing Center
Gargantua Company
street address
city, state ZIP

Dear Mr. Hughes,

It was good to meet with you yesterday to discuss the opening you have at Gargantua Company for a senior systems analyst.

I was particularly impressed with the sophisticated and stimulating working environment which cannot help but bring out the best in everyone.

My diverse background includes meaningful hands-on experience as well as the analytical and communications skills necessary to direct projects from idea to implementation. I welcome increasing responsibilities in a quick-paced setting.

It would be an honor to join your team of computer professionals and share in the growth of your unique organization.

Sincerely,

LETTER LEVERAGE

While most jobs are obtained through conventional channels, there's certainly no harm in putting out lines to friends and business associates. Discretion by all concerned is imperative if you're looking for another job while still employed.

If you're between jobs, there's nothing to be lost by pulling out all stops. Old high school and college friends, former professors, professional acquaintances are all possible sources of leads. Even if you haven't been in touch for some time, it's worth the price of a stamp to tap into another potential source. Most associations have printed directories which list members by name and position.

This type of letter attracts more notice if it appears to be one of a kind. If you find it easier to have the letters printed, as did the recent grad contacting his fraternity brothers and the art director writing to members of the Art Directors Club, be sure to personalize each copy with a hand-written postscript.

TO FRATERNITY BROTHERS

Dear Alpha Delts,

It's hard to believe nearly six years have passed since we all went our separate ways after graduation. Those rip-roaring days in the Alpha Delt house are forever etched in my memory.

I've never been one to keep in touch as regularly as I should, but if you can overlook the mass-produced appearance of a printed letter, I'll explain the reason. I'm out of a job and hope some of you can provide a lead or two. As Professor Emerson in Economics 104 used to say, "Leave no stone unturned."

As you may recall, I signed on with General Switches Co. shortly after graduation. I'm enclosing a resumé which tracks my altogether-too-brief career in financial planning until that fateful day last month when I learned that our entire department was being phased out as a result of General Switches' acquisition by ConGlom Corp. I'm told this happens frequently to acquirees in the merger mania prevalent today.

I'm still single and flexible enough to consider relocating wherever the right opportunity may be. Please set aside a few minutes from the pursuit of your first million to look over my resumé and see if anything comes to mind.

Either way, I hope you drop me a line. And if, heaven forbid, you ever find yourself similarly sidetracked in the years to come, let me know what I can do to help. After all, that's what friends are for.

Best regards,

P.S. Charlie, it's been a long time. Can you still down two 6-packs a night?

Enclosure

TO PROFESSIONAL ASSOCIATES

Dear Fellow Art Directors:

Two years ago at one of our monthly club meetings, I chaired a panel discussion in which several guests advised the group on "how to get a new job after losing your old one."

Part of my introductory remarks have proved prophetic. I recall having said at the time that the sudden loss of a job is the sort of thing that could happen to anyone.

Three weeks ago, as many of you know, the ax fell at Creative Concepts when our largest account took its business elsewhere. The departure of Empire Motors from the agency decimated the group which had been servicing the account, and many good people found themselves on the street.

It would be wishful thinking to dream of the day we are all together once more to do award-winning advertising for another large automotive client.

Instead, I am sending my resumé to each one of you in the hope that you'll keep me in mind if anything comes up. You'll notice in addition to the Empire campaign, I have an extensive background in food and appliance accounts in all media, with a special emphasis on television.

Since most people in our field tend to rely more on the grapevine for referrals rather than want ads, I'd certainly appreciate a call at 000-0000 if you get wind of anything.

Hope to see you all at the May meeting.

Sincerely,

P.S. Bill, I'll call you next week and we can have lunch at the Fireside.

Enclosure

TO INDUSTRY COLLEAGUE

Dear Craig,

Quite a bit has happened in the four months since our paths last crossed at the Industrial Relations Conference in Houston. As you may recall, I mentioned at the time that there were rumors that as soon as our old chairman retired, the new CEO-designate was planning to thin the ranks.

Since Mallory took over as top banana, it has become apparent that he regards the entire Human Resources division as excess baggage. We have had to let go 15 of our 40 people so far and it looks as if this is just the start.

So I'm whispering rather than shouting, but nonetheless the message is MAYDAY. I'm ready to jump ship before it goes under. If this means relocating to another city, so be it.

How do things look at your place? Or, for that matter, anywhere out west? I'm putting out discreet feelers in places I hadn't even considered before.

If you're on to anything, please get in touch. Needless to say—at my home address shown above. Or call (000) 000-0000 evenings or weekends.

Many thanks,

P.S. I haven't put together a formal printed resumé yet, but will send one your way within a week or so.

TO FORMER CLASSMATE

Dear Amanda,

Four years ago when we were graduating from Compton's Commercial College we all had good jobs lined up and were looking forward to exciting careers. All my dreams seemed to be coming true at Commco—security, good salary, two promotions with promise of future advancement, great people to work with and a convenient location.

In fact, because Commco is such a dynamic and flourishing company, expansion is needed. Since the cost of land and buildings in this area is so high, the company will be relocating in South Carolina where it is erecting a complex of buildings.

After considerable deliberation I have decided to not accept the offer to be part of the South Carolina team. In eight weeks I will no longer be working for Commco.

In your position as president of the local chapter of The National Secretaries Association, I thought you might hear of an opening now and then. I would appreciate any leads you could give me.

You can reach me at the office during the day at 000-0000 or evenings and weekends at home at 000-0000.

My resumé is enclosed. Feel free to photocopy it if you know someone who is looking for a top-notch executive secretary with a high recommendation from her present employer.

With gratitude,

Enclosure

TO COLLEAGUE ON BEHALF OF . . .

Dear Max,

I am taking the liberty of sending you the resumé of a promising young draftsman, Frank Cleary.

As you've probably heard, our company is undergoing a major reorganization and quite a few departments, including mine, are being consolidated. In the process, there are the inevitable casualties. Frank Cleary, with less than two years service, is one of them.

In his short time with us Frank has shown remarkable aptitude in mechanical drafting. He is able to develop drawings working closely with design engineers. I'm sorry to be losing Frank, but recommend him enthusiastically and without reservation.

Max, if you could use this talented young man in your research and development department, or know of any openings elsewhere, please give him a call. Frank's office number (for the next two weeks) is 000-0000; his home phone is 000-0000.

Best regards,

Enclosure

LETTER LEVERAGE

After a hiring decision has been made, it is good business to write a brief letter to the other candidates who were interviewed.

In a small business this is often done by the owner. In a large corporation either the contact in the Personnel section or the department head who did the interviewing should notify the runners-up.

While there's no need to justify your decision, a word of encouragement following the gentle letdown can leave the unsuccessful applicants with a lasting favorable opinion of your company.

Unsolicited letters of application should also be acknowledged.

NOTICE OF DECISION AFTER INTERVIEW

Dear Miss Olsen:

It may be scant consolation, but you were one of the leading contenders for the position of staff photographer until the final decision was made Tuesday.

Thank you for taking the time to come in for an interview last week. I enjoyed talking with you and was impressed with your samples. They show a great deal of creativity and are an indication that you will go a long way in your field.

I will keep your resumé on file in the unlikely event that another such position opens up here. Meanwhile, the best of luck to you.

Sincerely,

NOTICE OF DECISION AFTER INTERVIEW

Dear Mr. Tyson,

At the conclusion of your interview two weeks ago, I promised to let you know our decision—one way or the other.

Had our requirements and your experience converged two or three years from now, the job very likely would have been yours. As it turned out, after lengthy consideration, we opted for a candidate with a broader background in international banking.

You have made remarkable strides in your career to date, and it was a genuine pleasure to meet with you. I wish you the best in the years to come.

Sincerely,

ACKNOWLEDGING LETTER OF APPLICATION

Dear Mr. Bell,

We appreciate your interest in Bixby International. Unfortunately we do not have any openings in our auditing department at this time.

Your credentials are impressive, and I have no doubt that your search for the right job will have a happy ending.

Thanks again for thinking of our organization and good luck.

Yours truly,

ACKNOWLEDGING LETTER OF APPLICATION

Dear Ms. Kelly,

One of the most difficult aspects of my job as personnel manager is letting well-qualified persons know that we don't have an opening.

I appreciate the interest you've shown in our organization. It's obvious you have great potential and your resumé is impressive.

Don't be discouraged—you're too talented to be without work for long.

Sincerely,

15

Make Radio and TV Listen to You

While most listeners and viewers have never bothered to call or write a radio or television station, the electronic media are very attuned to audience preferences.

An elaborate and accurate system of rating points measures audience size. These figures play a large role in determining how much to charge advertisers for airing their commercials.

With their fingers on the pulse of the public and so many dollars riding on programming decisions, it's no wonder that radio and television executives pay close attention to their mail. Don't hesitate to let them know your likes and dislikes.

Following are sample letters covering a variety of situations. For best results, call ahead to the switchboard of the radio or television station and ask for the name of the General Manager or Program Director. Address your letter directly to that person. You'll very likely receive a prompt response.

Even if your views don't prevail, there's one consolation. Unlike some of life's irritations, annoying radio or TV can be remedied easily—just turn it off or flip the dial.

RADIO MUSIC COMPLAINT

Mr. Harlan Pierce
Program Director
WXYZ-AM
street address
city, state ZIP

Dear Mr. Pierce:

For the past two years I have listened to WXYZ during my 40-minute ride to work each morning. Your civilized music selection, coupled with timely news, weather and traffic bulletins, helped get my day off to the right start.

One week ago all hell broke loose on the station I had come to trust. The raucous sounds of rock filled my car, but not for long. A flip of the "off" switch provided a temporary fix. Next morning, same thing.

I learned from a friend that WXYZ had decided to change its format to appeal to a younger audience. This herd-like instinct to bow to youth has recently been adopted by nearly every station on the AM band.

Overlooked altogether now, with your defection, is the affluent 40-plus market comprised of people who are earning more money and spending more money than they ever have in their lives.

Oh well, the choice is yours. This former listener is now in the market for a tape deck.

Formerly yours,

RADIO MUSIC COMPLIMENT

Mr. Sam Stowe
General Manager
WXYZ-AM
street address
city, state ZIP

Dear Mr. Stowe:

After a personal boycott lasting over 10 years, I have once again become an avid listener of AM radio . . . more specifically, a fan of station WXYZ.

The reason I'm back is your long-overdue change of musical format. The re-discovery of original versions of hit songs from the '40s and '50s is the most talked-about event in my circle in some time. At last one AM station has shown they haven't forgotten mature listeners.

As a small token of my appreciation I am sending under separate cover a number of vintage albums in tip-top condition. Consider them a gift. Included are old hit recordings by such stars as the Andrews Sisters, Nat King Cole, Frank Sinatra and others.

If you wish, you have my permission to reproduce and circulate this letter to your present and prospective advertisers. Be assured that I'll go out of my way to buy the products of companies that sponsor such fine programs.

Yours truly,

WHEN YOUR FAVORITE D.J. GETS THE AX

Mr. Lionel J. Harvey
General Manager
WXYZ-AM
street address
city, state ZIP

Dear Mr. Harvey:

With the dismissal of Floyd Lloyd by station WXYZ, I note with regret the passing of an era—not just the loss of a clever entertainer, but also the loss of the last local station that dared present a controversial personality.

While Lloyd's taste was questionable at times, I shrugged it off, knowing that before long he'd get a laugh from me—not a particularly easy thing to do on the freeway at 8:00 A.M.

From your own viewpoint, I suppose the safest thing to do is replace the unconventional Lloyd with someone who can just drone on with the routine weather, traffic reports and music. Other stations have offered this dull catalog for years and have a following of rather dull listeners.

For my own part, I'll leave the radio off in the morning and reflect on one's chances in this world for daring to be different.

Formerly yours,

CRITICISM OF LISTENER-SUPPORTED STATION

Ms. Nora Harrison
Program Director
WXYZ-FM
street address
city, state ZIP

Dear Ms. Harrison:

I have one weakness—fine chamber music. So I set aside more pressing matters last night to relax and enjoy your tape-delayed broadcast featuring the Classico String Quartet. They were, as usual, flawless.

But the interpretive commentary interspersed throughout the performance was unsettling at best. I have until now assumed that a classical music station billing itself as "listener-supported" would have a sophisticated audience that would not require or welcome these intrusive explanations.

Lately the cluttered program content of WXYZ-FM is beginning to resemble conventional radio's endless commercials. But, then again, the rest of the AM and FM band is still "free," whereas I help fund your station with contributions.

If these commentaries continue at this pace, I will probably not renew my annual pledge to WXYZ-FM. Diverting that sum to the purchase of records and tapes could provide the assurance of enjoyable listening without interruptions.

Yours truly,

A MUSICAL REQUEST

WXYZ-FM
street address
city, state ZIP

Dear WXYZ-FM,

Saturday, November 6 will be a very special day for my husband and me. We will be celebrating our fortieth wedding anniversary.

I'd like to ask a favor of you. That morning as we're driving to Indiana to spend the day with our son, we'll be tuned in as usual to WXYZ-FM. Could you arrange to play the Wedding March from Mendelssohn's Midsummer Night's Dream sometime between 10:00 and 11:00 A.M.?

I would very much appreciate it.

Sincerely yours,

SUGGESTION FOR TALK SHOW HOST

Mr. Flash Finkle
c/o Station WXYZ-AM
street address
city, state ZIP

Dear Flash,

I have for some time been a passive fan of your late night talk show. Until very recently I have been content to hear your views, the opinions of your guests and the input from call-in listeners.

Then one night last week I felt strongly enough about the right-to-life issue to call you with my two cents' worth. If you and your audience are still unaware of how I feel, it's because the switchboard operator put me on hold for 20 minutes, then came back and said I'd be on the air shortly. Twenty minutes more passed before I gave up.

The same thing happened last night—this time, 30 minutes of holding the phone and waiting in vain.

For most of your listeners, Flash, this would be merely wasted time. For me, it was money wasted on a toll call as well.

Your show carries to three, perhaps four states in addition to your primary area of reception. Perhaps you could use your influence to have WXYZ establish a toll-free "800" number for listeners in fringe areas. Now that I've come this close to being on your show, I can hardly wait!

Yours truly,

LETTER LEVERAGE

When writing to comment on a television show, some letters should be directed to the network in New York and others to the local affiliate. (Independent channels, of course, are solely responsible for their own programming.)

The three hours preceding the late news are considered prime time and generally programs being aired during this period come directly from the network. The programming choice is made locally for most programs aired in non-prime time with the exception of some of the "soaps," the coast-to-coast morning shows and late-night programs. Local station managers decide which syndicated material to use.

A brief call to the local television station will help you determine the name of the person to whom to address your letter, and also—if there's any doubt—whether the program was network-originated or not.

Names of individuals in this volatile business change frequently, but the headquarters of the three major television networks are likely to remain at the same location for a long time. Their addresses follow:

ABC
1330 Avenue of the Americas
New York, NY 10019

CBS
51 W. 52nd Street
New York, NY 10019

NBC
30 Rockefeller Plaza
New York, NY 10020

TV GAME SHOW COMPLAINT

Mr. Avery Randall
General Manager
XYZ Television Network
street address
city, state ZIP

Dear Mr. Randall:

I have enjoyed the game show "Win Bux" from its beginning. I especially enjoy the excitement of knowing I might be chosen as the at-home partner.

Richard Roden was an excellent host and did a great job. I was sorry he left for "greener pastures." It didn't occur to me that a change of hosts could make such a dramatic difference, but since Vince Wagner has taken over, the show is a drag. Where did you dig him up? His hugs and kisses for the women and his idiotic questions for the men ("How's the weather up there?" he asked a tall gentleman) are an insult not only to the contestants, but to the viewers as well.

I can't imagine how he got this job—he certainly didn't earn it with his talent. Please consider either replacing him or killing the show altogether. You'd be doing everyone a favor.

Yours truly,

TV SOAP OPERA COMPLAINT

Ms. Marlene Niles
General Manager
XYZ Television Network
street address
city, state ZIP

Dear Ms. Niles:

For the past 10 years I have faithfully followed "The Life of Lonesome Lulu." I worked my schedule around the program and did my best to make sure I didn't miss an episode. Over the years I've been through a lot with Lulu, and I must admit that, each time a new situation came up, I couldn't wait to see what happened.

The last few programs have upset me as I see a shift in the moral undertones (or lack of same). You may think I'm old-fashioned, but since when do we need to see people in bed together on mid-day television? These scenes add nothing to the plot. I imagine they're just to raise the ratings. All they have raised around here is my temper and my resolve to forget Lulu and the rest of the bunch.

Actually, I should be thanking you for curing me of my Lulu addiction. I flipped to channel 14 and discovered a wonderful exercise program that has gotten me up off the sofa and feeling alive again. Farewell Lulu, I won't miss you!

Yours truly,

TV CHILDREN'S PROGRAM COMPLAINT

Mr. Frank Curtis
Program Director
Channel 10/WXYZ-TV
street address
city, state ZIP

Dear Mr. Curtis:

My children and I looked forward to the much-advertised "Children's Special" that was aired Saturday morning at 11:00 A.M. It was a below-zero, blustery day, and we were cooped up and ready for a good TV show.

After 30 minutes of disappointment we turned it off in favor of a game of Monopoly. Either my children, ages 6, 8 and 10, have very sensitive minds or that show was pure trash. In my mind the latter is true. Your promos had enticed us with promises of laughter, adventure and surprises. Little did we know that the laughter was supposed to come from ridicule and ethnic slurs, and the adventure and surprises from people driving off cliffs and bopping each other with soda bottles.

Is this really what the children of today want to see? What are you trying to accomplish with programming like this? You must remember that any TV program children watch is an "educational program" in that they learn from and imitate what they see and hear.

I have no doubt that other parents felt a similar revulsion while viewing "Children's Special." Until I feel I can trust what you "promise" to show, we'll stick to video tapes that I know will be worthwhile for my children.

Yours truly,

COMPLIMENTING TV CHILDREN'S PROGRAM

Ms. Lucia Gayle
Program Director
Channel 10/WXYZ-TV
street address
city, state ZIP

Dear Ms. Gayle:

The new children's program, "Show Me" is a delight. I have three children under six, so I feel I'm an expert on what appeals to the pre-school set.

My children love the show because it is entertaining, and I love it because it is educational and fun at the same time. After each show, we play the games you taught us and have even tried a couple of the projects.

Thank you for stimulating a sometimes worn-out mom with fun and ideas, and for the creative ways you involve the children in each show.

Sincerely,

PROTESTING POOR TASTE IN TV SHOW

Mr. Simon Wellington
Program Director
XYZ Television Network
street address
city, state ZIP

Dear Mr. Wellington:

I have just switched off the TV after the first half-hour of "Sin City." It was offensive and in poor taste. I am writing while my emotions are fresh to implore you to return to your former standard of excellence.

Responsible programming is not an option, but a duty. The shows reach millions of homes, and you must consider the consequences of the impressions you're creating.

Sincerely,

PUBLIC TV COMPLAINT

Mr. J. Carleton Wallmond
General Manager
Channel 10/WXYZ-TV
street address
city, state ZIP

Dear Mr. Wallmond:

For years I have enthusiastically endorsed the concept of public television with both donations and countless hours of viewing.

When you recently began to air commercials, things seemed no longer the same. I understand that this change was caused in part by cutbacks in government funding, and that you have to take up the slack somewhere.

But obviously you can't have it both ways. To the extent that you have become commercialized, you will surely lose contributors. I suggest that you consider retaining your original commercial-free format and reduce the hours of programming.

To do otherwise will likely result in a botched attempt to split the difference, and in so doing, you'll blur the essential distinction which justified public television in the first place.

If these commercials continue and I perceive your need blending into greed, you will have one less listener/donor on your roster.

Yours truly,

REQUEST FOR REBUTTAL TIME

Mr. Grant Baxter
General Manager
WXYZ–Channel 10
street address
city, state ZIP

Dear Mr. Baxter:

I have just finished watching your editorial on gun control. At its conclusion, viewers with responsible differing opinions were invited to contact the station to arrange rebuttal time.

I believe I could make a convincing case for the other side of the issue of gun control, and would very much appreciate the opportunity to deliver a response to your audience.

I would, of course, be willing to submit my prepared text in advance for your review.

If you'd care to discuss this proposal further, I'd appreciate an indication of how much rebuttal time I'll be allowed, along with a printed transcript of your remarks.

My flexible schedule would permit a taping session at your convenience.

Yours truly,

LETTER LEVERAGE

Following a particularly objectionable television show, hundreds of calls and dozens of letters of protest—addressed to no one in particular—will descend on the network and local affiliates. They will be tallied and most of the letters will be discarded after a superficial glance.

It's far more effective to complain directly to the Chairman or President of the sponsoring advertiser(s). If the program really got under your skin and you have enough stamps, send a copy of your letter to each member of the sponsoring company's board of directors. Reference books in the business section of most libraries will furnish their names and addresses.

The defection of a once-loyal customer will invariably get their attention. While you shouldn't expect to change corporate policy with a single letter, at least you have reached the real decision makers.

On the other hand, a particularly well-done show will rate plaudits. By sending a complimentary letter you'll be encouraging similar presentations in the future.

It's always a good idea to keep copies of your letter for future reference.

PROTESTING OFFENSIVE TV SHOW TO SPONSOR

Mr. R. G. King
Chairman of the Board
Regal Foods, Inc.
street address
city, state ZIP

Dear Mr. King:

The only effective way I can protest your company's sponsorship of "Grass and Hash" on television last night is to stop patronizing your stores. And I shall suggest to my other "straight" friends that they do likewise.

When such deplorable behavior is depicted as normal, or even desirable, I feel it's time to begin doing business with another retailer more in touch with mainstream America.

Yours truly,

cc: (Directors of Regal Foods)

PROTESTING OFFENSIVE TV SHOW TO SPONSOR

Mr. O. C. Yates
President
Monolith Industries, Inc.
street address
city, state ZIP

Dear Mr. Yates:

I consider myself open minded, unbiased and liberal-leaning. I'm certainly not a prude or a "do-gooder." No matter how I try to justify in my mind any worthwhile impressions being made by "Hell is in Harlem" the effort is futile, and I find myself getting angrier and angrier.

The fact that you run a respected corporation in America and still sponsor this trash revolts me. I am only one person, but I have the freedom of choice. And from this day forward I choose to avoid the use of all Monolith products.

Sincerely,

THANK SPONSOR FOR GOOD TV SHOW

Mr. Benjamin Kaiser
President
Bingo Dairy Products
street address
city, state ZIP

Dear Mr. Kaiser:

Congratulations on your sponsorship of the superb television presentation of "The Saudis and Their Audis." Your company took a calculated risk in putting advertising dollars behind such a controversial subject.

I urge you take with a grain of salt the predictable backlash which will come from some offended viewers. Rest assured that there are millions of Americans who, while not moved to write and say so, applaud your courageous stand.

Yours truly,

TV COMMERCIAL COMPLAINT

Mr. Marshall Marsh
Chairman of the Board
Con-Glom Industries, Inc.
street address
city, state ZIP

Dear Mr. Marsh:

Over the years the advertising industry has made commendable progress in eliminating offensive ethnic and racial stereotypes. It's equally true, and regrettably so, that tasteless television commercials have contributed significantly to the disintegration of the American family.

Typifying this disgraceful trend is your latest campaign for SoakUp paper towels. To continually depict the father in such ludicrous situations, gaily mopping up spill after spill, while the youngsters make fun of him is irresponsible at best.

Is it any wonder that so many children are disrespectful of parents when multi-billion dollar corporations such as Con-Glom run such drivel? Perhaps the Dagwood-like creative types at your ad agency who think this stuff is cute don't really know any better. But the real fault lies with the company that approves these commercials and spends good money to run them.

For my part, I'll do without SoakUp towels until you clean up your act.

Yours truly,

cc: (Directors of Con-Glom)

TV COMMERCIAL COMPLIMENT

Ms. Vivian Beatty
Vice President, Marketing
Ever Sure Household Products Co.
street address
city, state ZIP

Dear Ms. Beatty:

Since I have been house-bound the past two years, I watch many hours of TV. It brings me much pleasure and helps pass the time.

During these two years I have seen many a commercial. I have come to dread some, hate others, hardly notice a few and can count on one hand the number I have actually enjoyed. As I sat here chuckling over the commercial I just watched I resolved to write to you and tell you how refreshing it is to know there are truly creative people out there in the advertising world with a sense of humor.

Your latest campaign for Sudsy-Soapy detergent is great. Turning something as mundane as washday into the event of the week was no easy task. I'm convinced from your commercials that Sudsy-Soapy and *only* Sudsy-Soapy will do. And yes, I asked my sister to buy some, and we are delighted with the results.

Keep up the good work and especially the humor that is plain old fashioned fun, not the kind that comes at someone else's expense. You are on the ball and I wish you much success.

Sincerely,

16

Getting a Fair Shake
From Insurance Companies

All insurance offices, large or small, share one thing in common—a mountain of paperwork including policies, claims and, yes, even letters. Paperwork is the very lifeblood of the industry . . . as vital a part of the insurance business as rubber is to a tire manufacturer.

So write, don't call, if you want to make a change on your policy or if you encounter problems of any kind. Your correspondence will become a part of your file with the company and will provide a reference point long after a conversation is forgotten. If you must call, follow up at once with a confirming letter.

If you're dealing directly with an agent who places your business and receives commissions it generates, all the better. He can cut through the red tape and get things done quickly. Develop a rapport with the agent and you'll be pleasantly surprised at how smoothly routine matters are handled. Chances are, he'll be in your corner if and when any problems arise.

When contacting your agent or the company that issued your policy, indicate the policy number(s) above the body of the letter.

CONTACTING AGENT WHEN YOU BUY A NEW CAR

Policy #000-00-000

Dear Mr. Kozak:

This letter is to confirm my phone call yesterday when I informed you of the purchase of my new car and asked that my policy be changed to insure it. I traded in my '78 station wagon and now own a new Penguin four-door sedan. The serial number on the new car is 4N35X71102334; it is not being financed.

I wish to continue with the same coverage on the Penguin as I had previously, with one exception. Please change the collision deductible to $200.

Yours truly,

INSTRUCTING AGENT TO MAKE A CHANGE IN YOUR POLICY

Policy #00-000-00

Dear Mr. Powell:

I would like to make a change on my auto insurance when the present policy expires on May 31.

Now that the car is nearly six years old, I wish to discontinue the collision coverage. All other provisions of the policy are to remain the same.

Yours truly,

ASKING AGENT TO ADD NEW DRIVER TO YOUR POLICY

Policy #00-000-00

Dear Mr. Walters:

My 16-year-old son, William, Jr., has successfully completed the Driver's Education course at Roosevelt High School and obtained his driver's license.

I would like to change my auto insurance policy to include William, Jr. as an occasional driver. All other provisions of the policy are to remain as they are. The car will continue to be used for non-business driving only, and I don't anticipate the annual mileage to change.

I am enclosing a copy of my son's most recent report card which, as you will notice, makes him eligible for the good-student discount.

Yours truly,

FURNISHING AGENT WITH CLAIM INFORMATION

Policy #00-000-00

Dear Mr. Peterson:

This morning at 3:00 A.M. the police called to inform me that my car which I had reported stolen on Wednesday had been recovered. A side window had been broken to gain entry and a number of items taken from the glove compartment.

Below is an itemized list of the stolen articles, including their approximate value and date of purchase in keeping with your telephone instructions to me. My homeowner's policy should cover it.

Item	Price	Date of Purchase
2 prs. sunglasses (man's and woman's)	$24.00	Spring '83, summer '83
1 flashlight	10.00	Summer '83
1 pr. leather gloves	32.00	Fall '82
1 portable AM/FM radio	40.00	Summer' 83

Again, my thanks for your help in settling this matter.

Yours truly,

SUBSTANTIATING CLAIM WITH PHOTOGRAPHIC EVIDENCE

Mr. Alfred A. Slocum
Claims Manager
Goober Insurance Co.
street address
city, state ZIP

Policy #00-000-00

Dear Mr. Slocum:

I've completed and signed the enclosed claim form itemizing the extent of the damage to my household contents in the fire of September 10. Also enclosed are 24 interior photographs taken in May of last year which show, from several angles, the furnishings and possessions in each room. You'll note that the back of each photograph is keyed to the attached list describing the item, year of purchase and approximate cost.

Your prompt attention in expediting the settlement of this claim will be much appreciated.

Yours truly,

Enclosures

INQUIRY TO COMPANY REQUESTING STATEMENT

Infinity Life Insurance Company
street address
city, state ZIP

Policy #00-000-00

Gentlemen:

Please furnish me with a current statement indicating the cash value of the above life insurance policy, along with accrued interest and dividends to date.

After evaluating this information, I will either continue the policy in effect, or cancel it and request payment of the accumulated amount. Should I decide to do the latter, please send, along with the statement, whatever forms are necessary to cancel the policy and request payment.   .

Sincerely,

NOTIFICATION TO COMPANY OF INTENT
TO CASH IN POLICY

Infinity Life Insurance Company
street address
city, state ZIP

Policy #000-00-000

Gentlemen:

Thank you for your prompt response to my inquiry of May 10. I have decided to cancel the above-numbered policy and hereby request payment for $420.65 plus any sums which may have accumulated in my account since your statement of May 17.

I am enclosing the policy and the appropriate signed form.

Yours truly,

Enclosures

REQUESTING PAYMENT ON LIFE INSURANCE POLICY

Infinity Life Insurance Company
street address
city, state ZIP

Policy #00-000-00

Gentlemen:

As you requested, I am enclosing the completed and signed claim form, along with a copy of the death certificate for my late husband, Rudolph Fletcher. His legal address at the time of his death was _____.

I would like the settlement in one lump sum, as soon as possible.

Yours truly,

Encl.

REQUESTING CHANGE OF AGENT

Mr. Armand H. Swanson
Administrator, Illinois Division
RevUp Insurance Company
street address
city, state ZIP

| 1980 Ford station wagon | Policy #000-00-00 |
| 1982 Chevrolet 4-door | Policy #000-00-00 |

Dear Mr. Swanson:

I have been a RevUp policyholder for about six years and would like to change from my present agent (Ken Douglas in Chicago) to an agent closer to my home (Russell Burke in Lake Forest).

Please send me the necessary forms to make this transfer for my two cars.

Yours truly,

WHEN MORE THAN ONE INSURER PAYS ON A CLAIM

Juvenile Sports Insurance Assoc.
street address
city, state ZIP

Gentlemen:

Several weeks ago I submitted the following bills for treatment for my son, Charlie, following a Little League accident, together with your form signed by both the manager of Charlie's team and the doctor:

June 6	Riverside Hospital emergency room	$132.50
June 9	Dr. Mason (orthopedist)	130.50
June 8	crutch rental	6.00
June 22	Dr. Mason	52.00

Since then I received the enclosed $18.00 bill from Dr. Kimball, the pediatrician who examined Charlie's foot on June 28.

My employer's insurance company sent me a check (explanation enclosed). This group insurance plan covers accident-related expenses at 100% *within 5 days*.

That leaves only the following items for which I now make claim:

June 22	Dr. Mason	$52.00
June 28	Dr. Kimball	18.00
		$70.00

Sincerely,

Encl.

LETTER LEVERAGE

Most advertising depicts insurance companies as large enough to provide financial stability but concerned about each policyholder and willing to provide individual attention. Many indeed will appear to be just that—until you make a claim. Just as a salesman gets commission from writing a policy, a claims adjuster is considered to be doing his job well when he minimizes the amount of the settlement.

The singular exception is life insurance. The insured is either alive or he isn't, and a death certificate still triggers an undisputed payment of the amount due. No other form of insurance, however, is as clearly defined in black and white. The various shades of gray soon become apparent as adjusters attempt to whittle down the size of your claim.

There are several avenues open to an individual policyholder who feels the settlement offer is too low or that he is being treated unfairly. The first is the state regulatory agency that licenses insurance companies. Your letter to the person in charge should state the name of the insurer, the policy number and the specifics of the complaint. The state will then contact the insurance company which must respond in detail. The complaint division will review both sides of the issue. If it concludes that the insurance company's actions or settlement offer were unfair they usually *recommend* action. The recommendation is just that, not a ruling in a court of law. But a finding by the state insurance commission carries quite a bit of weight with the companies it regulates, and claims managers usually comply with its recommendation.

Another avenue of appeal is the small claims court where the insured will get a fair hearing from an impartial judge.

Large claims resulting from deaths or serious injuries are best referred to an attorney. *Never* sign a release if you're dissatisfied with the initial settlement offer and plan an appeal.

Finally, it can be of some assurance to know that whatever the outcome you can have the last word. If dissatisfied, cancel the policy and take your business elsewhere.

APPEALING NON-RENEWAL NOTICE
TO STATE REGULATORY AGENCY

Mr. Basil Borden, Chairman
State Board of Insurance Commissioners
street address
city, state ZIP

Dear Mr. Borden:

I would like to request a hearing before the State Board of Insurance Commissioners to protest the arbitrary termination of my automobile insurance policy by Gargantuan Insurance Company (policy #000-000-000).

I noticed in the paper last week that the company's computers had pinpointed certain sections of the city in which a disproportionate number of claims are filed.

The article also stated that the company intended to discontinue coverage of policyholders living in what they now define as high-risk areas. Today I received notice that my policy would not be renewed when it expires in two months.

My appeal to the state board is based on the belief that fairness would dictate a review of individual policyholders rather than discriminatory action affecting everyone living within a specific area. At the hearing I would expect Gargantuan to show cause why my policy should be terminated.

In return, I am prepared to present evidence of many years of careful driving. It's a matter of record that over the past 15 years I have never received a ticket for a moving traffic violation nor been involved in an accident. In addition, my car is kept in a locked garage each night.

During my years of coverage with Gargantuan, I have always paid my premiums promptly and never filed a claim. To be cast out at this point and forced to secure coverage with another company in what is now designated a high-risk section of the city would cause undue hardship and expense. I am confident that once the facts are brought to light you will require Gargantuan to maintain my policy on the present terms.

Yours truly,

APPEALING NON-RENEWAL NOTICE TO COMPANY PRESIDENT

Mr. Dwight Davidson
President
Colossal Insurance Co.
street address
city, state ZIP

Auto Policy #000-000-000

Dear Mr. Davidson:

I have just been informed that Colossal intends to cancel my automobile insurance policy effective July 20. The cryptically-worded notice cited a "high incidence of claims" as the reason.

To set the record straight, I have filed two claims in the ten years I have had my cars insured by Colossal. The first involved a minor fender-bender one year ago. The only other claim was for a set of wheel covers that was stolen last month. Two such incidents in a ten-year period are hardly reason to categorize me as a bad risk.

I am confident, Mr. Davidson, that after reviewing the underwriter's arbitrary decision, you will reinstate my coverage. Should you decide the cancellation was warranted, I will immediately take the following steps:

—Cancel the homeowner's policy #000-000-000 in effect with Colossal since 1974;

—Cancel my whole-life policy #000-000-000 written by Colossal in 1971;

—File a complaint with the State Department of Insurance and ask it to review the decision to cancel.

I hope that once you have all the facts in hand this misunderstanding can be cleared up, and that I will remain on your list of satisfied policyholders.

Yours truly,

REQUESTING ARBITRATION FROM STATE

Mr. Arturo Gomez
Administrator
State Department of Insurance
street address
city, state ZIP

Dear Mr. Gomez:

On September 4, my three-year-old Pontiac sedan was totally destroyed by fire. I filed a claim with the Armadillo Insurance Company (policy #000-000-000).

The company offered to settle for $3,000. I consider this amount unacceptable and furnished Armadillo with a separate appraisal placing the car's worth at $3,600. In addition, several reference books used widely in the industry show a range of $3,400 to $3,800 as the value of a comparably equipped auto of its age.

Armadillo refused to budge from its position. I am so convinced that their settlement offer is unreasonable that I am asking you to initiate procedures for a hearing in which an arbitrator from the State Department of Insurance will issue a ruling that would be binding on both parties.

In the event of a finding notably in excess of the original $3,000 offer, I would recommend that the State Department of Insurance undertake an investigation of the practices of Armadillo Insurance Co. If such disparities are found to be commonplace, I would hope that the Department would consider suspending the license permitting them to sell insurance in this state.

Yours truly,

SEEKING INTERVENTION FROM INSURANCE COMMISSION IN ANOTHER STATE

Mr. Kurt Barlow
Manager, Complaint Division
State Board of Insurance Commissioners
street address
city, state ZIP

Dear Mr. Barlow:

While vacationing in your state in June, my car was struck from behind while stopped at a red light. The police determined at once that the other party, Glenn McAble of Montpelier, was responsible. Mr. McAble is insured by the Hawkeye Insurance Company, and his policy number is 000-000-000.

My insurance company is Eversure, Inc., and my policy number is 000-000-000. Eversure eventually collected the money from Hawkeye for the necessary repairs, but was unable to collect the cost of my rental car. I made several long-distance phone calls to Hawkeye and wrote them once.

There's no indication that they ever intend to reimburse me. I would appreciate it if you would contact Hawkeye and try to determine why they continue to ignore a valid claim. Please send me a copy of the correspondence.

Thanks in advance for your cooperation.

Yours truly,

ASKING INSURANCE COMMISSION TO HELP SPEED UP SETTLEMENT

Ms. Jane Gunderson
Director
State Insurance Commission
street address
city, state ZIP

Dear Ms. Gunderson:

I am writing to ask your help in expediting payment of a long-overdue claim. I am insured by the Monastic Health & Accident Company (policy #000-000-000). Their delay in settling what should have been a routine matter is unconscionable.

I broke my wrist last summer and was treated in the Ogden Hospital emergency room and subsequently became a patient of one of the orthopedists on their staff, Dr. Marvin Geller. I promptly paid the hospital, the doctor and the X-ray laboratory with personal checks, amounting to a considerable sum of money.

Mr. Clarence Bird of Monastic's claim department said I was to wait until I had the final bills together and turn them all in at the same time. Three months have passed since I submitted these bills along with the claim form, physician's statement and supporting records.

Still no check. "These things take time, don't get impatient," says Mr. Bird. His supervisor, Mr. Gallo, has alluded to unfortunate computer breakdowns and misplaced documents.

Having complied with Monastic's instructions to the letter, I don't think it unreasonable to expect prompt reimbursement. Yet all I hear are excuses. Can you help?

Yours truly,

THREATENING TO SUE WHEN CLAIM SETTLEMENT IS INADEQUATE

Mr. H. D. Burgess
Claims Manager
Calico Insurance, Inc.
street address
city, state ZIP

Dear Mr. Burgess:

I am returning the check you issued for the repair of damages caused on May 6th when your insured, Frank Forrest, sideswiped my car.

Your adjuster's determination that $360 was sufficient compensation was far off the mark. I'm enclosing three written estimates which I obtained on my own—two from authorized Ford dealers and one from an independent auto repair shop. Any attempt at a settlement for less than $582, the lowest of the three estimates, will prompt me to file suit in Small Claims Court to recover the actual cost of the repairs.

If I don't have your check in hand by June 10th, I will initiate court action.

Yours truly,

Encl.

THREATENING SUIT IF LIABILITY DENIED

Mr. Horace Harris
CARE-LESS Parking, Inc.
street address
city, state ZIP

Dear Mr. Harris:

At 7:30 last night I pulled into the CARE-LESS parking lot, was given a ticket stub, and handed my keys to one of your attendants. Moments later he screeched away and roared up the ramp in my car. Four hours later when I returned to pick up the car, a much more subdued attendant (with the name Max lettered on his shirt) brought it back down.

As is my custom on the rare occasions in which I entrust my car to such individuals, I walked slowly around to inspect it. The moment I saw the dented left front fender I pointed out to "Max" that the damage had occurred here. This brought forth loud denials and a confrontation before your night manager. He predictably sided with "Max" and said it was his word against mine.

I called the police and an accident form was filled out on the spot. If it's the policy of CARE-LESS to deny liability automatically in such matters, rest assured it won't work this time.

Either you arrange to have an adjuster from your insurance company contact me before the end of the week, or I will initiate court action next Monday morning to recover damages.

Yours truly,

IF NOT TREATED FAIRLY, CANCEL

Mr. T. W. Sanders
Vice President, Claims
Indigo Insurance Company
street address
city, state, ZIP

Dear Mr. Sanders:

A decision has been made regarding my claim on the loss of my $500 diamond ring. Apparently there is no "court of appeal."

The two adjusters who came to interview me were patronizingly polite, but it was clear they had made up their minds in advance. They attempted to put me on the defensive from the start by strongly inferring that the ring may just have been "lost" and that, if and when I found it, I might be too embarrassed to say so and return the amount of the settlement check. I very much resent their implication that I had filed a false claim.

Was it foolish of me to have expected a fair hearing on my first claim after 12 years of on-time premium payments for my homeowner's policy?

I certainly didn't need this aggravation following the loss of my ring. I have decided to cancel my policy and place the coverage with another firm.

You can be assured of my eagerness to tell and re-tell the story to all my friends, relatives and neighbors about your company's high-handed, tight-fisted manner of handling claims.

Yours truly,

17

Vacation Plans and Pitfalls

When planning a vacation well in advance, a letter expressing your interest to a Chamber of Commerce or Visitors' Bureau can bring forth an avalanche of information about the area.

Subsequent letters can deal with specific questions and arrange accommodations—at a fraction of the cost of long-distance phone calls.

The pace of running a busy resort often doesn't allow for much time providing information over the phone. The proprietor usually is in a better position to give your written inquiry more attention during the off-peak hours when he's not as pressed for time.

Free road maps of each state are yours for the asking, but no longer at gas stations. Write the state tourist information office in the state capital and ask them to send you a map.

REQUESTING GENERAL INFORMATION

Chamber of Commerce
street address
city, state ZIP

Dear Sir:

My wife and I and our three children, ages 8 through 12, plan to visit Cape Conch for the first time next June. I'd appreciate your sending me a map of the area along with a description of the attractions and events scheduled for that month.

Would it also be possible to furnish me with a list of moderately priced beachfront motels?

Thanks in advance,

REQUESTING BROCHURE AND RATES FROM RESORT

Sea-Isle Motel
street address
city, state ZIP

Dear Sea-Isle:

My family and I are planning a week's vacation in Cape Conch in late June. Please send us a brochure on the Sea-Isle Motel and a schedule of rates.

We're a party of five, including three children, ages 8 through 12. Hopefully, one good-sized room can accommodate us all. A rollaway cot for our youngest will suffice.

Hope to hear from you soon.

Yours truly,

SENDING RESERVATION AND DEPOSIT

Sea-Isle Motel
street address
city, state ZIP

Dear Sea-Isle:

Thank you for your prompt response to my inquiry for a brochure and rate schedule. We'd like to reserve an ocean-view room for one week beginning Saturday, June 20.

As I had mentioned, we're a party of five, including three children, ages 8 through 12. I understand that the weekly rate for an ocean-view room plus one rollaway bed is $400. I'm enclosing, as requested, a $100 check as a deposit.

We'll be looking forward to seeing you around mid-afternoon on Saturday, June 20.

Yours truly,

Enclosure

COMPLIMENTARY FOLLOW-UP LETTER TO HOST

Mr. & Mrs. Gerald Miller
Sea-Isle Motel
street address
city, state ZIP

Dear Mary and Gerry:

Our vacation in Cape Conch was even better than we expected. And the Sea-Isle was a fine place to stay . . . great location, spic-and-span surroundings and a friendly, helpful staff.

You run a first-rate establishment and we look forward to coming back again soon. What's more, we will recommend the Sea-Isle to our friends.

All our best,

REQUESTING INFORMATION ON NATIONAL PARKS

United States Department of the Interior
National Parks Service
Washington, D.C. 20240

Gentlemen:

Our family is planning a camping trip this summer. Please send me a free copy of "Guide and Map of the National Park System."

Thank you,

REQUESTING STATE ROAD MAP

Department of Tourism
126 Van Buren Street
Tallahassee, Florida 32301

Gentlemen:

Please send me a free road map of Florida.

Thank you,

WHEN TRAVELERS LEAVE THINGS BEHIND

Dear Mr. Sanders:

We were relieved to learn a few minutes ago that the items we left behind when we checked out of your motel early this morning have turned up.

You can't imagine the shock of traveling 500 miles and unpacking at the end of the day only to find so many things missing. As I mentioned on the phone, I'm enclosing a check to cover the cost of mailing the package to our home. Please address it to:

_____

(name)

_____

(street address)

_____

(city, state ZIP)

Thanks again for your thoughtfulness.

Yours truly,

Encl.

LETTER LEVERAGE

Most travelers who settle for something less than a suite on the QE2 would agree that getting there is no longer half the fun.

It's not uncommon for an airline to overbook and have to bump ticketed passengers from a flight. And checked baggage still disappears. There are established procedures and endless forms for dealing with such occurrences, but they're designed primarily to limit the carrier's liability. The right letter on the right desk can help tilt the scales in your favor.

Bargain-priced charter tours are not always what they appear to be. If you ever take one that promises more than it delivers, don't seek an adjustment from the travel agent. Write instead to the tour operator. By now he has all the money you paid, less the agent's commission.

Better yet, make some inquiries before signing up. If you have any doubts about the promoter of a charter package, check his reputation in the destination city. Verification of the operator's agreement with the hotel and car rental firm he purports to use can put your mind at ease, too.

Despite his often imperious mannerisms, the desk clerk at a hotel is *not* the final arbiter on disputes—the manager or owner is running the show. Trouble is, he's often not around at the time of the contested charge or complaint. A letter, however, will bring the problem to his attention. Be sure to include a copy of your bill, mention the specific nature of your complaint and suggest a compromise or prorated refund that seems fair.

If your vacation is marred by a disappointing experience and chances of an adjustment are nil, you can still have the last word. Drop a line to your favorite travel editor and suggest that some future column warn readers to avoid that particular place.

WHEN AIRLINE LOSES YOUR BAGGAGE

Ms. Victoria Wallace, Manager
Consumer Affairs Department
Air Lines International
street address
city, state ZIP

Dear Ms. Wallace:

On May 2, I arrived on ALI flight 603 from Baltimore to St. Louis. However, the suitcase I checked at your counter prior to the flight never arrived in St. Louis and hasn't been found in the six weeks since. Nor have I been reimbursed for the value of the suitcase and its contents.

When it became apparent that my luggage was missing I reported it to your Miss Reynolds at the baggage claim area in St. Louis. Before leaving the airport I filled out a report. I am enclosing a copy of that report with this registered letter. Also enclosed is a copy of the claim check I was issued in Baltimore, along with an itemized list of the contents of the suitcase and the approximate value.

I realize that your liability covers only the depreciated value of the missing items and not the cost of replacing them. Since the total amount of the claim is well under the $750 per passenger liability limit for baggage-loss claims on domestic flights, I see no point in further delay in processing the claim.

Yours truly,

Encl.

WHEN LOST BAGGAGE SETTLEMENT OFFER IS INADEQUATE

Mr. Cecil Lane
Vice-President, Marketing Services
Air Lines International
street address
city, state ZIP

Dear Mr. Lane:

I'm willing to concede that luggage is occasionally lost, even on a well-run airline like ALI. On January 20, it happened to be my three-suiter which disappeared somewhere on flight 603 between the check-in counter in St. Thomas and the baggage claim rack in New York. I filled out the appropriate forms at the airport and went home, assured that the suitcase would be delivered as soon as it turned up. Wishful thinking, as it turned out.

Now, two months later, I am consoled only by the fact that the loss occurred on my return trip rather than on departure leaving me stranded in a far-away city with nothing to wear but the clothes on my back. Offsetting this is the loss of a significant part of my wardrobe and a number of gift items I was bringing home.

I complied to the letter with your requirement that I list the contents and their estimated value. Doubtless it's been your experience that, at times like this, passengers sometimes exaggerate the worth of lost items, and I can understand your initial skepticism. But there can really be no question of the amount of my loss since three of the items on the attached list were purchased in St. Thomas the day before my return flight and I have receipts to prove it, copies of which are enclosed.

The combined value of the clothing and gifts, as you can see, exceeds by far the $750 per ticketed passenger which I understand to be the maximum payment any airline will make on such claims.

I am again willing to concede that your liability has to end somewhere, and agree that $750 would be a fair settlement for *substantiated* claims.

ALI's offer to settle for $420 is totally inadequate. As a frequent business and pleasure traveler I fly upwards of 50,000 miles each year, approximately one-third of it on your line. And while it's not likely my luggage would be lost another time, I'll certainly never again board one of your planes unless this claim is settled fairly.

                                             Sincerely,

Enclosures

DEMANDING FAIR COMPENSATION
WHEN YOU'RE BUMPED FROM FLIGHT

Ms. Victoria Wallace, Manager
Consumer Affairs Department
Air Lines International
street address
city, state ZIP

Dear Ms. Wallace:

On December 14, I prepared to board ALI flight 143 from St. Louis to New York. I had a confirmed reservation for a coach seat and was at first unconcerned when I heard the announcement that there were more passengers at the gate than there were seats on the plane. Your agent then asked if anyone would like to volunteer to stay behind and briefly outlined the procedure for compensating those volunteers.

One or two passengers offered to give up their seats, but that wasn't enough. By whatever standards your people arbitrarily employ, it was determined that I was a low-priority flyer, and I was told that other arrangements would have to be made. I was handed a check for $170, the price of my ticket, and put on another flight two hours later.

By this time, a severe storm had closed most of the runways at LaGuardia, and we had to land in Cleveland. After a three-hour layover there we finally got back on board and prepared to leave. But mechanical difficulties delayed the takeoff for another hour. We finally landed in New York at 3:15 A.M.

The check for $170, which seemed adequate at the time, looks pitifully small in hindsight, considering the aggravation and time wasted, the out-of-pocket expenses incurred at the Cleveland terminal, and the additional delay in trying to get home from LaGuardia in the early morning.

I'm sure you'll agree that this extraordinary chain of events is more than most of your "bumped" passengers face. I see that my endorsement of the compensation check within 30 days concludes the matter. This simply won't do. What would seem more appropriate is an apology accompanying a check for twice that amount, in compensation for a never-to-be-forgotten night.

I'll waive the apology, but am enclosing the original check—unsigned—with this letter. I'll expect another check for twice that amount before considering the matter closed.

Yours truly,

Encl.

SEEKING REFUND FROM HOTEL MANAGER

Dear Mr. Keyes:

On the weekend of June 3–5, three friends and I attended the Political Women's Seminar held in your hotel. We had a room reserved for the two nights, but on one of those nights were able to get very little sleep.

On the night of the third there was a high school prom in the hotel. From midnight till 3:00 A.M., the teens were roaming the halls shouting, banging on doors and being as rowdy as they could. Our calls to the desk brought promises, but no action.

The next morning we went to the registration desk and asked for a refund for that night and were told that was impossible. Since we had paid for the two nights in advance, we were stuck.

We understand these were unusual circumstances, Mr. Keyes, but if you wish to continue to draw seminar groups to your hotel, some changes in policy must be made. If we do not receive a refund for that night we will make sure the Political Women no longer have their annual seminar in your hotel.

Yours truly,

SEEKING REFUND FROM HOTEL MANAGER

Dear Mr. Pane:

My family and I planned and looked forward to our overnight stay in your hotel before our arrival on July 14. We arrived at 5:00 P.M. and were told our room wasn't ready.

We left our luggage with the clerk at the reservations desk and went to dinner. Our room still wasn't ready after dinner. In fact, it wasn't ready till 9:30 P.M. which made the evening a total loss and was very hard on our two small children who are usually in bed by 8:00 P.M.

The people at the desk were quite harried that evening, and I had the impression the hotel was understaffed. They all remained courteous, but could do nothing for us.

Well, you can do something for us, Mr. Pane. You can see that compensation is made to us in the form of a check for $62.32, the cost of our room for that miserable night.

Yours truly,

SEEKING REFUND FROM HOTEL MANAGER

Dear Ms. Moss:

I made a reservation at the Palace Hotel for the night of September 22. I know you hold reserved rooms only until 6:00 P.M. Since there was a good chance I would be arriving after that hour, I guaranteed my reservation by giving my credit card number.

When my flight was grounded in Florida because of hurricane conditions we were told we wouldn't be able to take off till morning. It was 5:00 P.M. your time when I called to cancel my reservation. I spoke to Miss Hover who assured me she would take care of it.

She didn't "take care of it" very well. When I received my monthly statement today there was my charge for the room I never occupied and which I cancelled an hour before the 6:00 P.M. deadline.

Please confirm the time of my cancellation with your Miss Hover and issue me a credit for $48.00 without delay on my credit card account number 000 000 00.

Sincerely,

WHEN ILLNESS FORCES A CANCELLATION

Mr. Elmer Holmes, President
Holmes Travel Agency
street address
city, state ZIP

Dear Mr. Holmes:

This letter is to confirm my phone call this afternoon in which I requested that my wife's reservation and mine for the tour to Hawaii scheduled to depart December 20 be cancelled.

I am enclosing a letter from Dr. Robinson which explains the nature of my wife's sudden illness and the need for prompt surgery.

We had looked forward to this vacation, and are disappointed that we won't be able to go at this time. We hope to re-schedule the trip as soon as possible after her convalescence.

Meanwhile, with the prospect of sizeable medical bills looming, I would appreciate a prompt refund of the amount we prepaid to your agency.

I regret the inconvenience this unavoidable cancellation has caused you.

Yours truly,

Encl.

COMPLAINT ABOUT TOUR PACKAGE

Mr. Julius Jones, President
Jones Tours, Inc.
street address
city, state ZIP

Dear Mr. Jones:

I have just returned from a week's vacation which your ads bill as, "Island Living at Its Best." In reality, it was a disaster.

The round-trip plane transportation was the only part of the package deal that wasn't misrepresented. On arrival, I expected to be met by a bus and taken to the Briny Breeze Hotel. There was, of course, no bus so I took a cab to the hotel. The desk clerk could find no reservations in my name and simply shrugged as he stated their policy of "no reservation, no room."

None of the nearby hotels had accommodations for unannounced arrivals either. I took a lengthy cab ride before finally finding a fleabag motel two miles away from the beach.

First day of the seven: totally wasted.

Day two was little better. Since the price of the prepaid vacation included the use of a car with unlimited mileage for one day, I presented my certificate at the Rollaround Rental facility and encountered the same blank stare I'd seen the day before on the desk clerk. No amount of explanation could pry loose the car I'd been promised. "You should have known better than to have given your money to those people," said the manager.

I could enumerate additional indignities, but suffice it to say, your organization has a justifiably dreadful reputation on the island.

Rather than just chalk it up to experience, I have decided to extract some measure of compensation in return for the miserable week caused by your misrepresentations and negligence. I have attempted to determine an equitable amount to be refunded me from the $800 I paid in advance.

Enclosed are copies of my bill for lodging, receipts for one day's car rental, as well as cab trips to and from the airport and in search of a hotel. In addition, a prorated $1/7$ of the total for the wasted first day I spent seeking alternate accommodations.

The total, Mr. Jones, comes to $330. Lest you regard this letter with the same indifference your organization has displayed so far, be clear on two points—the amount of $330 is non-negotiable; and if I don't have your check for that amount in hand one week from today, I will initiate legal action to recover damages.

I assure you that I will pursue the matter with documentation and diligence.

Sincerely,

cc: American Society of Travel Agents, Inc.
Encl.

INQUIRY ABOUT TOUR OPERATOR

Dear Chamber of Commerce of San Banana:

The Gravel Travel Agency advertises a vacation package that sounds almost too good to be true. It includes—for the price of $179.95—round trip air fare from Chicago to San Banana on a scheduled flight, plus accommodations for four days and three nights at the Melvin Hotel, and one day's use of a rental car with unlimited mileage.

I have been unable to learn anything about the tour promoter, Budgetours of San Banana, other than that they claim to have been in business for ten years. Before laying out money for this package deal I would appreciate any information you may have about Budgetours of San Banana.

I'd be particularly interested to know if their tours are indeed as represented. Also, while at this price I wouldn't expect the Melvin Hotel to be in the deluxe category, I'd like very much to know if it's in a safe neighborhood and reasonably well run.

Thanks for your help.

Cordially,

VERIFYING TOUR OPERATOR'S RELATIONSHIP WITH HOTEL

Manager, Melvin Hotel
street address
city, state ZIP

Dear Sir:

I have talked to the Gravel Travel Agency about their vacation package, which includes for $179.95 round trip air fare to San Banana, plus accommodations for four days and three nights at the Melvin Hotel, and one day's use of a rental car with unlimited mileage.

Please let me know whether you do indeed have such an arrangement with Budgetours of San Banana, the tour promoter. Are there any surcharges or time restrictions? We are tentatively planning to take our vacation in early July.

Yours truly,

INSURANCE PROTECTS AWAY FROM HOME, TOO

Policy #000-000-000

Dear Mr. Phillips:

While vacationing in Mexico last month I was the victim of a pickpocket who stole my wallet.

I reported the theft on December 27, the day it occurred, to the police in Guadalajara. In addition to several pieces of identification and a number of credit cards, I lost approximately $120 in U.S. dollars and $70 in Mexican pesos.

It is my understanding that up to $100 of this loss is covered under my homeowner's policy numbered above. Please send me the necessary claim form and contact the Guadalajara police for a copy of their report.

Sincerely yours,

TO TRAVEL EDITOR—WARN YOUR READERS!

Dear Mrs. Franklin:

I have for years been a faithful reader of your weekly travel columns in the Gazette. To the extent that my limited budget and time permit, I have on numerous occasions followed the itinerary you suggested. And always with very satisfactory results—until my recent vacation in San Banana.

The portion of the trip which fell short of expectations was the day-long bus excursion down the coast to Periwinkle Beach and back. While the scenery was as breathtaking as you described it, the bus ride was dreadful. The driver was surly, and the air conditioning and rest room were out of order.

The charming little cafe, of which you wrote three years ago, is now off the schedule. Instead we stopped for lunch at a run-of-the-mill sandwich shop which was obviously not prepared to serve an entire busload at one sitting.

I hope you'll warn your readers to avoid the side trip by bus the next time they visit San Banana.

Cordially,

TO CONSUMER ACTION COLUMN

Gentlemen:

I'm in a pickle, and I hope you can help. While my wife and I were on vacation in San Banana we were invited to attend a dinner meeting hosted by Travel Clubs, Inc.

At the session we were informed that members of Travel Clubs, Inc. are eligible for special discounts on airline fares and hotel rates all over the world. The savings quoted were fantastic. We were impressed, signed a contract and paid the membership fee.

It wasn't till we returned home that I took a closer look at the contract and price lists, and I became suspicious. I made a few phone calls to airlines and discovered that my "special discount rates" were the same as the regular airline rates.

I immediately wrote to Travel Clubs, Inc. requesting cancellation of my membership and a refund of my dues. They refused to refund my money. Travel Clubs insists that since I signed the contract, I am legally bound to it. If that is true in spite of their misrepresentations, what recourse is there for me to take?

Believe me, this costly lesson has taught me to read everything I sign thoroughly. I hope the appearance of this letter in your column will convince others to do the same.

Sincerely,

COMPLAINT ABOUT UNSANITARY RESTROOM

Mr. Zachary Royce
Vice President, Marketing
Glopp Oil Company
street address
city, state ZIP

Dear Mr. Royce:

Enclosed are the shredded remains of what was once my Glopp credit card. Over the years it has been used to purchase rivers of gasoline plus occasional fan belts, batteries, tires and the like.

The reason I will never again set foot in one of your facilities can be traced to the Glopp "service" station in southern Nebraska along Interstate 00 at Route 000.

I have always felt that travelers had every right to clean restroom facilities, especially in gas stations located along vast stretches of highway. The nightmarish conditions that greeted me and my family at this location defy description. Suffice it to say that one look was enough to make us hurry back to the car and go down the road to one of your competitors.

A fleeting glance at the doorway indicated that one Oliver Owens is the proprietor. If this station hasn't already been closed by some state agency charged with maintaining minimal sanitation conditions in public facilities, it should be soon.

Meanwhile I suggest that you tell Mr. Owens to clean up his act. It's an absolute disgrace.

Yours truly,

18

When Your Castle Becomes a Hassle

The closer you read the standard apartment lease, the more heavily it seems stacked against the renter. Most key points are clearly spelled out to the advantage of the landlord.

The time to object to and request modification of any of these provisions, of course, is before you sign the form. Once the lease is approved by both parties, it becomes the final word for the term of the agreement.

That doesn't mean the tenant need be the doormat for an unreasonable landlord. There are safeguards in the system to prevent such abuses. If you feel you're being treated unfairly, write the owner or building manager and list your grievances. If it seems appropriate to mention that his failure to resolve these matters will be brought to the attention of the proper authorities, be sure you're on solid ground. Your credibility will vanish, for instance, if you threaten to take up the problem of safety code violations with the local real estate board rather than with the proper enforcement authorities.

One of the most frequently disputed items is the return of the tenant's security deposit. The last word here doesn't belong to the landlord, despite what he may tell you. The threat to take the matter of a delayed return of all or part of your security deposit to court will usually bring the landlord around. If not, be prepared to follow through.

GETTING BACK YOUR SECURITY DEPOSIT

Dear Mr. Goldberg:

Several calls to your office have failed to pry loose a check for the $650 of mine which you still retain. That sum represents the security deposit equal to two month's rent on the apartment at 1400 Elm Street, which I vacated at the expiration of my lease on April 30th.

The building supervisor verified that he found no damage during his inspection of the apartment in mid-April, and he assured me that a check for the amount of the security deposit would be issued to me within a week after my departure. It is now two months.

I have sent this certified letter to your home so there will be no mistaking my intentions. If I don't have the check for $650 in hand by next Monday, June 11th, I will file a claim in court. I am prepared to present my copy of the lease agreement, furnish cancelled checks, and, if necessary, ask for a subpoena requiring the presence in court of both you and the building supervisor.

In a nutshell, Mr. Goldberg, I have you cold. It remains to be seen whether you're a smart enough businessman to get off that check at once.

Yours truly,

GETTING BACK YOUR SECURITY DEPOSIT

Dear Mr. Quinn:

This certified letter is my third—and last—reminder that you are required by law to refund my $350 security deposit with interest within 45 days of the expiration of my lease.

Five weeks have passed since I vacated the premises. Before leaving I took photos to support the fact, should it prove necessary, that I left apartment 4-B in the same condition it was in when I moved there two years ago.

My new address is (street address), (city), (state, zip). If I do not have the entire amount due me in hand by June 15, I will take the matter to court.

As you are doubtless aware, the court's decision in my favor would make you liable for double the amount of the security deposit, plus accumulated interest, attorney's fees and court costs.

Yours truly,

NOISY TENANTS UPSTAIRS . . . ONE OF US HAS TO GO

Dear Mr. Hamilton,

Enclosed with my check for the February rent is this brief note which will explain why I may not renew my lease when it expires in two months. The apartment is lovely; the building is well maintained; the rent is reasonable, but one problem overshadows all. The Russos in apartment 2D directly above ours fight constantly. The sounds of their domestic discord intrude into our lives day and night. My wife and I have spoken to them about it, but the chaos continues unabated.

I realize how busy you are running your business and a 24-unit apartment building from the other side of town, and didn't want to bother you about a matter which I had hoped could be resolved between us. I was wrong, and we have arrived at an impasse. Either the Russos go or we do . . . and the problem will fall into the laps of your next tenants in 1D.

Out of respect for your time, I'll not mention this matter again. The first four of the five years we've spent here have been most enjoyable, but the past year has been intolerable. We realize the decision will ultimately be yours, and we are prepared to move if nothing is done.

Yours truly,

A THREAT MAY BRING THE EXTERMINATOR

Dear Mr. Fultz:

Apparently you've chosen to disregard my two phone calls suggesting that you hire an exterminator to eliminate the bug problem in this building. I wish I could ignore the bugs the way you ignore me, but unfortunately they just don't go away.

Don't assume I will go away if you continue to pretend I don't exist or you'll find that I can be just as pesty as the bugs.

If the premises aren't completely free of bugs one week from today, I will file a complaint with the Board of Health and the City Building Department.

Yours truly,

APPLYING PRESSURE TO GET THINGS FIXED

Mr. Pulaski:

According to the terms of my lease, I am required to pay you $300 per month, and you are to maintain the building in livable condition. If I had been as lax in meeting my obligations as you have been in meeting yours, you very likely would have initiated eviction proceedings by now.

I am referring specifically—and for the final time—to the following points:

(1) Oven thermostat off by at least 50 degrees.
(2) Rain continues to seep in through bedroom window and drip down wall.
(3) Front door so warped that it takes all my strength to open it.
(4) Defective toilet flush mechanism.

Items (1) and (2) are annoying, but I will probably have to rely on your sense of fairness to effect repairs. Items (3) and (4), on the other hand, are serious enough to be brought to the attention of the City Department of Building Inspection for possible violations—non-compliance with the fire code requiring easy-opening exterior doors; and infraction of the sanitary code.

If these conditions haven't been corrected by next Thursday, I will have no choice but to file a report with the proper authorities.

(sign)

ONE DOG IS ONE TOO MANY

Dear Mr. Flynn:

Three years ago when we moved into Fairview Gardens it was made quite clear that no pets would be permitted. We have complied with the terms of the lease as have the other tenants in the building—with one exception.

The Olsons in Apartment 2-F have recently acquired a small-to-medium-size dog whose 'round the clock noise is quite annoying. The animal is left alone most of the day. Something as trivial as the sounding of the downstairs door buzzer has been known to set off a lengthy barking session.

I've already spoken to the Olsons and was told, in effect, to mind my own business. Well, since I live next door to these people, it becomes my business.

Have the rules been changed or has one family been granted an exception? Please let me know what will be done about this.

Sincerely,

EMERGENCY IN RENTED HOUSE

Dear Mr. Arnold,

Enclosed is a check for the September rent. In the six months since you were transferred to Connecticut and our family has been leasing your house, absolutely nothing has gone wrong that I couldn't fix in a matter of minutes with simple tools. Until now.

We asked the gas company to come out before the start of the heating season to clean and inspect the furnace. They found a cracked heat exchanger, and shut off the gas to the furnace as a precaution. We were told that continued operation of the furnace in this condition would cause carbon monoxide poisoning.

My wife told the serviceman that it is our understanding that the furnace has been in operation since the house was built—about 18 years ago. The serviceman indicated that if this were his house, he'd replace the entire unit.

Please advise as to who you'd like to furnish written estimates. I'll be glad to send them along for your consideration. I've enclosed a list of local heating contractors that I've copied from the classified directory.

One final thought—the gas company serviceman said that heating contractors are quite busy in the fall, and suggested that we contact someone as soon as possible.

Best regards,

Enclosures

A WAY OUT OF A LEASE

Dear Mr. Rozanski:

I have just been notified by my employer that I am being transferred to our firm's San Francisco office on November 1. This allows me only three weeks to tie up all the loose ends here.

First and foremost among my concerns is my apartment lease which runs until April 30 of next year. Since there is no provision in the lease for subletting, I have a proposal which I hope you will consider.

Would you agree to accept $400 for the November rent and consider it my last month if I vacate the premises by the end of October? In addition, I would be willing to give you an extra $50 to offset the cost of advertising for a new tenant.

If this arrangement is satisfactory, you would then cancel the existing lease and return my security deposit after having inspected the apartment to determine that there was no damage.

The apartment, the building and the neighborhood have more than met my expectations. Were it not for this unexpected transfer, I would very likely have stayed for quite some time.

I'd appreciate your giving my proposal some thought, Mr. Rozanski, and letting me know your decision as soon as possible.

Sincerely,

LETTER LEVERAGE

Certainly not all landlords are mean-spirited ogres. The majority are hard-working people whose savings have enabled them to buy a building on which they have every right to expect a reasonable return.

Too often, renters will try to take advantage of such a landlord. And they'll frequently get away with it for longer than they could in a large, professionally-managed apartment building.

If you own a small-to-medium-sized rental building, you'll have to cope with these things as they occur. The ultimate trump card you hold is the threat of eviction. Use it if all else fails, but not frivolously. It's the final step in the escalation from personal or phone conversations to letters to court action.

PLEASE PAY YOUR RENT ON TIME

Dear Mr. and Mrs. Benton:

I am writing to remind you that, according to the terms of the lease, the rent for your apartment is due on the first day of each month.

Perhaps the delay was an oversight. Perhaps I have bent the rule too often in the past by saying nothing when your check was a week or so late. But in both September and October it was necessary for me to call you in the middle of the month when the check still hadn't arrived.

As you know, there are many details and expenses involved in owning and managing an 18-unit apartment building. That's why it is absolutely necessary that rents be paid on time.

Could you imagine me telling the janitor that I don't have the money to pay him? Or that I ask the gas company to wait beyond the due date for their payment until all rent checks have been received?

I couldn't operate that way, and I'm sure you wouldn't want to live in a building where essential maintenance is deferred for lack of the money to pay for it.

I feel certain, Mr. and Mrs. Benton, that you would not willingly endanger your credit rating. To ensure that this does not happen, please make it a point to pay your rent by the first day of each month.

Thanks in advance for your cooperation.

Yours truly,

PAY OVERDUE RENT NOW OR FACE EVICTION

Mr. Barnes:

This certified letter is your final notification. Unless your back rent for March and April—a total of $600— is paid within seven days from this date, I will file suit to have you evicted.

I have on several previous occasions had to initiate similar eviction actions with tenants for the same reason, and the process is always pretty much the same.

You will receive a summons to appear in court on a certain date. After a court judgment is issued, sheriff's deputies will be empowered to remove you and all your belongings from the premises.

If you wish to avoid the eviction proceeding, please make certain I have received payment for the entire $600 within seven days.

(sign)

EITHER THE DOG GOES OR YOU GO

Dear Mr. and Mrs. Crown:

I have mentioned to you several times that the lease agreement you signed prohibits keeping an animal in your apartment. And yet your dog remains here and continues to annoy other tenants.

This will no longer be tolerated. If you wish to stay in this building, you must make arrangements at once to find another home for the dog.

Unless the dog is gone within seven days, I will initiate court proceedings to have you evicted from the premises.

(sign)

LETTER LEVERAGE

It may be that some day the meek will inherit the land, but if they plan to build on it, a more assertive approach can save them a lot of aggravation.

Builders and remodelers are often long on promises and short on delivery. Just as airlines and hotels have been known to overbook, builders frequently commit themselves to more than they can possibly deliver.

Who gets the short end of the stick? Almost without exception, it's the customer who accepts it uncomplainingly. Call the builder and let him know you're dissatisfied. Stop in to see him. Or, if nothing else works, write him a letter. Make clear in the letter that you won't settle for unacceptable delays or second-best materials or shoddy workmanship.

You have the upper hand when you threaten to withhold payment until the terms of the contract are met to your satisfaction.

If he already has your money, but everything is coming unglued, there may still be a way to apply some leverage. Resourceful condominium owners, for example, could move along with the builder to the site of his next project and get his attention there with picketing.

NO MORE MONEY UNTIL IT'S DONE RIGHT

Dear Mr. Kincaid:

The reputation of Kincaid Construction Company for quality workmanship was a major factor in my selecting your firm to build my house on Pelican Lake. Now, three months later, I feel I may have made the wrong choice.

If you and I can't discuss the matters summarized on the attached list before construction proceeds much further, it may soon be too late to make necessary corrections. Your foreman on the job site is totally uncommunicative, and has made it clear that he takes his orders from you alone. To make matters worse, you haven't returned my phone calls of the past week.

The difference between your accessibility and willingness to accommodate *before* I signed the contract and the apparent uncaring attitude *since* makes a startling contrast. I'm left with the impression you don't take a woman seriously. But be clear on one matter, Mr. Kincaid—my money is as good as anyone else's. And you won't see any more of it until you take steps to ensure that the problems cited on the attached list have been corrected.

Yours truly,

Enclosure

PRODDING A SLOW CONTRACTOR INTO ACTION

Dear Mr. Hurse:

Progress has moved at a snail's pace on our family room addition since I signed the contract and made the initial payment. When your sign went up, along with the Village Permit seven weeks ago, people I didn't even know would ask what we were doing and how we came to select Hurse Remodeling Company.

Many had seen your commercials on late-night television and wondered whether any remodeling contractor could be as good as you claimed. Lately I have replied that I am disappointed. I feel that there is no excuse for the project remaining less than half done even though the contract stipulates completion by June 30.

An entire week will pass without any sign of a workman. Expensive construction material sits along the side of the house inviting theft. My calls are not returned.

More than once I've wondered, Mr. Hurse, just how you can afford the ripple effect of negative publicity from a dissatisfied customer. Especially in a town this size.

Exactly what steps will be taken if the addition isn't completed by the agreed-upon date will be determined then, with the advice of counsel. Needless to say, no more money will be coming your way until progress is made.

Sincerely,

PICKETS WILL GET A BUILDER'S ATTENTION

Dear Mr. Gordon:

If you had followed through on the many promises you've made over the past months, there would have been no need for us to write this certified letter. But with the warranty on our new condo units due to expire in two weeks and numerous construction flaws still uncorrected, we wanted to go on record and let you know that continued stalling won't work.

The attached list specifies, once again, the repairs that should be made. Your failure to do so within the warranty period will result in our taking what we feel will be an unusual but effective retaliatory measure.

As dissatisfied owners of units in the 1220 Building, we will take turns on a picket line two blocks away to dissuade would-be purchasers of your new condo development, the 1440 Building, from making the same mistake we did. Leaflets will invite prospective buyers to come over and see first-hand the shoddy workmanship in your earlier condo.

Picketing your new building is not our idea of an enjoyable way to spend future weekends, Mr. Gordon, but make no mistake about it—the owners of 1220 are prepared to exert whatever pressure it takes to ensure fair treatment.

Your prompt attention to correcting *all* the repairs itemized on the enclosed list would, of course, eliminate the need for such action.

(all sign)

Enclosure

LETTER LEVERAGE

In the relatively short time since condominiums have become so popular, many people have found themselves in positions of considerable responsibility and authority after election to their governing boards or associations. When you hold such a position, it will be necessary from time to time to contact fellow property owners . . . and a letter is the best way to do it.

The surest way to obtain the cooperation of residents is to remind them that this is their association and that participation and suggestions of members are welcomed. A tactful rather than a heavy-handed approach will work best. This is, after all, quite unlike the typical landlord/tenant relationship.

Of course, not all matters are of a routine nature so it may be necessary occasionally to impart a firm tone to a letter when earlier, gentler contacts have failed. Again, a touch of diplomacy is a requisite.

If you, as owner of a condominium unit, ever find yourself temporarily unable to pay your monthly maintenance fee, inform the board members at once. Early notification can make their budgeting easier and lessen the likelihood of group action against you.

GET INVOLVED—BECOME A BOARD MEMBER

SUNNY SHORES CONDOMINIUM ASSOCIATION

Dear Member,

An election will be held on December 8 to determine the make-up of the Association's Board of Directors for the coming year.

Members of the nominating committee are seeking the most qualified candidates for the offices of President, Vice President, Secretary and Treasurer. If you are interested in running for office, but hesitate because you're not sure what is involved, feel free to call on any of the current board members. The term is for one year; the compensation comes entirely from the realization that you are helping make Sunny Shores a pleasant community in which to live (as well as enhancing your investment here).

If you decide that this is the year to become involved in the decision-making for your Association, please contact one of the following members of the nominating committee:

Bernice Perez	000–0000
Duane Abbott	000–0000
Steve Tyson	000–0000

You are needed!

Sincerely yours,

President

YOUR BOARD NEEDS YOUR INPUT

SUNNY SHORES CONDOMINIUM ASSOCIATION

Dear Neighbor:

Your Board of Directors is committed to do the best job possible in the coming year as we make decisions regarding the schedule of operations and maintenance.

We have prepared the enclosed survey in order to obtain your thoughts and views as to what services you expect—and are willing to pay for—before we proceed. The budget for the year ahead will be based to a large extent upon your response to the survey.

Your signature is not necessary on the form. The information you provide will be confidential and a vital guide in our decision-making process. Please return it to us in the enclosed postage-paid envelope.

Sincerely,

Secretary

Enclosures

WHY HIGHER MONTHLY ASSESSMENTS ARE NEEDED

SUNNY SHORES CONDOMINIUM ASSOCIATION

Dear Member,

Sunny Shores is one of the loveliest places in the Midwest to live and we, as a board, are determined to keep it that way. At this point we feel we must face the facts and make some hard choices to ensure that our operating budget will be sufficient to maintain our combined properties at their present level.

It has been three years since we have had an increase in our monthly maintenance assessment. Careful management by past boards has even allowed us to accumulate a reserve, but increased operating expenses have chipped away at it relentlessly. Today, we are barely solvent.

Sunny Shores has reached the age where extensive renovations are needed for the first time. We all know the roads and parking areas need resurfacing. The east border has suffered severe erosion after our wet spring and needs rebuilding with tons of new dirt and probably a few more trees. The pool has been patched in the past, but will need considerable work before opening in June. The docks on the lake need painting and minor repairs.

On Saturday, April 10th at 10:00 a.m. there will be a special meeting for all association members in the recreation center. Please read carefully the enclosed proposal which summarizes the repairs and maintenance required and an estimate of the cost. Plan to attend the meeting . . . we'll appreciate your input.

Sincerely,

Your Board of Directors

Enclosures

CLARIFICATION OF RULES AND REGULATIONS

SUNNY SHORES CONDOMINIUM ASSOCIATION

Dear Owner:

The enclosed booklet has been prepared as a summary of the rules and regulations governing the Sunny Shores Condominium Association. It is not intended to replace the formal Declaration of Condominium, but rather to provide owners with a capsule version of the legal document.

In recent months the Board has received numerous requests from owners involving modifications or alterations that we have had to deny because they were clearly in violation of the Declaration of Condominium. Among the more frequently heard were requests to:

—install a CB antenna on the roof

—expand the patio area

—put up awnings

—hang beach towels out to dry

—post garage sales

The answer in every case was "no" because to do so would have broken the agreement which all owners signed at the time they purchased their units. Unauthorized modifications or alterations of the exterior of the building are not permitted. Nor are any intrusions into the common elements.

We hope that owners will familiarize themselves with the rules and regulations pertaining to these matters. Board members are not arbitrarily making these decisions; instead we are upholding the integrity of the rules which have been set up for the benefit of all.

Please retain the booklet for future reference.

Yours truly,

Board of Directors

Enclosure

MONTHLY MAINTENANCE FEES MUST BE PAID

SUNNY SHORES CONDOMINIUM ASSOCIATION

Dear Mr. Kirby,

As Treasurer of the Sunny Shores Condominium Association, it is my duty to notify you that you are $600 in arrears on your monthly maintenance assessment.

When I brought this matter to your attention in March, you indicated that the withholding of your payment was an attempt to get the attention of Luther Leghorn, the builder, and pressure him to make some long-overdue repairs. Much as I sympathize with your situation, the fact is that the builder has turned over the accounts to the association board and is no longer legally liable to make good on such claims. Similar action a year ago might have brought the results you seek, but now it's a futile gesture—and one that's hurting innocent parties.

Your obligation to pay $150 per month is completely unrelated to your dispute with Mr. Leghorn. In a small condo such as ours, each of the 22 unit owners is responsible for his share of the assessment. You are doubtless aware that the by-laws in the Declaration of Condominium contain provisions to recover delinquent payments, and I really hope it doesn't come to initiating action to place a lien on your title.

Many of us share your disappointment that everything doesn't measure up to expectations, but on balance, Sunny Shores is a nice place to live and probably will continue to appreciate in value over the years.

I hope you'll make arrangements to settle this matter as soon as possible.

Yours truly,

Treasurer

PAYMENT WILL BE DELAYED

To the Board of Directors,
Sunny Shores Condominium Association:

As some of you may know, I lost my job six months ago and have not yet been able to find another.

Our failure to pay the current monthly maintenance assessment was not an oversight . . . we simply don't have the money right now. Sandy and I are sorry this has happened, and ask your patience and understanding.

She's already gone back to work and I'm still hopeful of finding another job. As soon as we're back on our feet, we intend to make good on any and all back payments. That's a promise.

Meanwhile, if any of you hear of an opening for an accountant, please let me know.

Yours truly,

19

Mending Medical Misunderstandings

Years ago when the Norman Rockwell-type doctor was the rule rather than the exception, the patient handed the doctor three or four one-dollar bills after each visit. The doctor added them to an impressive wad in his pocket and the transaction was concluded.

Today, it's a bit more complicated. With the increase of third-party payments, the avalanche of paperwork can swamp a busy physician or dentist. He's retreated behind layers of receptionists, book-keepers and assistants who take care of billing, insurance forms, and the like.

Medical insurance companies require substantiation of treatment before paying a claim. This usually involves a copy of the invoice plus signed statements by the insured and the attending physician or dentist. The sooner you can get these to the company, the sooner you'll be paid.

The best way to secure the prompt cooperation of the person who prepares these forms for the doctor's signature is to state clearly and briefly what you require. If you also include a self-addressed, stamped envelope, chances are your request will be easier to handle than most, and go to the top of the pile. If you still can't pry loose the signed form, it's time to alter the tone of your letter.

With the passing of the old pay-as-you-leave era, doctors encountered rising postage costs and cash-flow problems as well as a certain number of people who simply wouldn't or couldn't pay their bills. As a result, doctors have come full-circle to a modern-day version of cash-and-carry. Only this time around, a sign posted at the receptionist's desk reminds patients that "Payment Is Expected at Time of Treatment."

This is directed primarily at new patients and those inclined to pay slowly or not at all. It's a procedure often waived at the request of established patients.

There are also times when a letter can best explain why you're unable to make full payment.

ROUTINE REQUEST FOR INSURANCE INFORMATION

Dear Dr. McGuire:

Please fill out the "Attending Physician's Statement" section of the enclosed insurance form and return it to me in the self-addressed, stamped envelope I've provided.

Thank you,

REQUEST FOR ELABORATION ON INSURANCE FORM

Dear Dr. Dixon:

I'm sorry to have to bother you again on this matter, but my employer's group insurance company returned the enclosed form as incomplete.

Would you be good enough to itemize on the reverse side the dates, specific nature of treatment, and cost per visit? Then please return it to me in the enclosed self-addressed, stamped envelope.

Thank you,

REMINDER THAT INSURANCE FORM IS LONG OVERDUE

Dear Dr. Von Schacht:

It's nearly two months since I sent you an insurance form and asked that you complete the "Attending Physician's Statement" and return it to me.

When it never came, I called your office and was assured it would be mailed to me in a few days. Two weeks ago I called again and once again was promised that it would be taken care of shortly. And still no form.

I paid your bill promptly, Doctor. Now I'd like to be reimbursed by my insurance company. But as it is, absolutely nothing can happen until I file the claim, and I can't do that without your signed statement.

If the form has been misplaced, please notify me and I will obtain another. I'm enclosing a self-addressed, stamped envelope for your convenience.

Yours truly,

TO DOCTOR AT HOME WHEN ALL ELSE FAILS

Dear Dr. Weber:

In desperation I am sending this letter and the enclosed insurance form to your home. Nearly three months have passed since I sent a similar form to your office, requesting that you complete the "Attending Physician's Statement" and return it to me.

When it never came I made the first of many calls to your bookkeeper asking that she prepare the form for your signature and send it to me. In subsequent calls I pointed out that I had paid your bill promptly and did not think it unreasonable to expect to be furnished with the evidence of medical treatment required by my insurance company. In order to obtain reimbursement, I must first file a claim, and that is impossible without your signed statement.

Yesterday your bookkeeper became quite agitated with me and managed to convey the message that I could wait until hell freezes over before she'd lift a finger to help.

I'm certain this is the first you have heard of this matter, and, as I indicated, contacting you at home is an absolute last resort. But I thought you'd be interested to know of one patient's exasperation with the snags in your back-office operation.

I would greatly appreciate it if you'd take a few minutes to fill out, sign the form and return it to me in the enclosed self-addressed, stamped envelope.

Yours truly,

A WAY AROUND THAT "PAY NOW" SIGN

Dear Dr. Johnson:

As I was leaving your office after my appointment this afternoon, your receptionist called me back and pointed to a sign which indicated that patients are expected to pay immediately. At first I was embarrassed, because I didn't have my checkbook or enough money. My next reaction was one of hurt at the implication that I might not be trusted to pay my bill promptly, or at all.

Grudgingly, your receptionist gave me an envelope and a copy of the bill and urged that I write a check and mail it as soon as I got home.

In the more than ten years that you have been my physician, I have never failed to send my check shortly after receiving your bill. I realize that the "pay now" sign was not intended as an affront to patients, but rather as a means of saving you postage and eliminating the slow-pay problem as well as improving your cash flow.

The problem is . . . *my* cash flow. With the Social Security check (my prime source of income) arriving around the first of each month, it is more convenient to schedule my own bill payments accordingly. If that's okay with you—or if it isn't—please fill out and detach the bottom portion of this letter and return it to me in the enclosed stamped, self-addressed envelope.

Yours truly,

— —

Dear Mrs. Brown:

_____We'll make an exception in your case, and I'll so notify my receptionist.

_____Sorry, but there can be no deviations from the new policy.

_____

— —

WHY I'M CHANGING DOCTORS

Dear Dr. Everett,

Perhaps you'd be interested to know why, after 10 years as your patient, I have changed doctors.

It had nothing to do with your professional competence—I'll consider myself fortunate if my next physician is as capable. Nor were your fees unreasonable.

What I found intolerable were the countless hours wasted in your waiting room. I've concluded that your receptionist was instructed to "overbook." This callous disregard for the value of patients' time was, in the end, more than I could tolerate.

It's unfortunate that, in the vast reservoir of knowledge accumulated by a doctor these days, basic consideration for others is so notably lacking.

Yours truly,

EXPLANATION OF PARTIAL PAYMENT TO DENTIST

Dear Dr. Kramer:

It is with no small measure of embarrassment that I write you this letter. Your November 21 statement for $300 for my bridgework restoration has been sitting in an ever-growing pile of unpaid bills.

Since losing my job early last month, I have been juggling bills and trying to keep expenses for necessities at a minimum while I continue to look for work.

I am enclosing a check for $100 which is all I can afford at this time. Rest assured that the balance will be paid promptly as soon as I obtain a new job. Till then, I'll pay a small amount each month.

Thank you in advance for your understanding and patience.

Sincerely,

LETTER LEVERAGE

Frequent complaints have been heard about the condescending attitude of the supportive staff in many doctors' offices. It's usually difficult to find an appropriate time to mention this to the doctor in person, but a letter will certainly make him aware of the situation.

When you feel you have been well cared for remember that, busy as they are, health care professionals still deserve words of appreciation for an exceptional job.

On the rare occasion when you encounter a complete lack of professional competence, it's important to keep in mind that each state regulates and licenses its medical practitioners. Don't hesitate to let them know if you've been victimized.

A COMEUPPANCE FOR PATRONIZING OFFICE HELP

Dear Dr. Brock:

I am sending this letter to your home instead of discussing the matter with you in the office because I didn't want to interrupt your busy schedule or be overheard by one of your associates. And, frankly, I'm afraid it would be sidetracked if sent to your office.

It concerns the condescending manner of your nurse, and, to a lesser extent, of your receptionist. While it's been a minor annoyance for some time, I decided, after the rudeness displayed by these two yesterday, to bring the matter to your attention.

I find it inexcusable that, while taking my temperature and drawing blood, Mrs. Gargoyle persists in berating me with such insults as "You've obviously put on a few pounds since last time and Doctor won't like that one bit" and "Doctor and I feel that you could push yourself away from the table a little sooner."

While I'm at least three times Nancy's age she summons me in from the waiting room by my first name. Before scheduling my next appointment she has the audacity to ask, "When will we be seeing you again, dearie?"

Curiously, such incidents never occur when you're within earshot. I have never expected the red carpet treatment, but I am always on time for appointments, pay bills promptly and follow your advice as best I can. It would seem not an unreasonable expectation to be treated with common courtesy in return.

Yours truly,

"I'LL PAY NOW IF YOU'LL BE CIVIL"

Dear Dr. Larson:

Being aware of financial matters myself, I understand and sympathize with the need to require patients to pay for services rendered before they leave the office. What you are doing makes good business sense, and I appreciate that.

What I don't appreciate is your receptionist's way of handling this new policy. I overheard her badgering a few patients before me, and when it was my turn I was well prepared for her tactless manner.

I think you'll find that your patients will cooperate willingly if you make clear to your receptionist how to explain your policy kindly and sympathetically rather than to brusquely state, "Doctor says you *must* pay before you leave."

Yours truly,

SOME THINGS MUST REMAIN CONFIDENTIAL

Dear Dr. Levin,

We have been pleased to have you as our dentist since the days when you had a small office over the hardware store and we were a family of three. Now there are six of us and you have your own building, two associates and a large staff.

I'm writing with a complaint that may sound trivial at first, but after you've given it consideration I think you'll agree to take some action. After a child has had a checkup, instead of calling in the parent, the hygienist stands at the door of the reception room and gives the parent the child's report loud and clear before all. I've seen many a mother cringe as these prim young things state, "Mrs. Jones, Susie has two cavities. She does a terrible job of brushing, you know."

Over the years I knew my day would come, and it did today. That's what prompted me to write and suggest that you have the hygienists call each parent in to give her report—whether good or bad—in private.

I've been meaning to mention this to you, but put it off until I was directly affected. I wouldn't be a bit surprised if many of your other patients are offended by this practice, too.

Sincerely,

COMPLAINT ABOUT RUDE NURSE

Director of Nursing
Memorial Hospital
street address
city, state ZIP

Dear Director:

A long hospital stay is always a difficult experience, and one of the nurses on your staff made it even more so.

Now that I'm convalescing at home and beyond her reach, I am in a position to report Nurse Emma Hammer without fear of retribution. Two weeks ago when I mentioned her insolence to Dr. Condon, word apparently got back to Nurse Hammer and her rudeness intensified.

I haven't chronicled every day's abuse, but the following incidents, which occurred on Thursday, December 10, were typical:

— My son and daughter-in-law traveled quite a distance to visit me. They had been at my bedside for just a short time when at 7:45 p.m. Nurse Hammer barged into the room and loudly announced, 'All visitors are to get off the floor NOW." My son pointed out that 15 minutes remained until visiting hours ended and she called him a fool.

— That afternoon I had buzzed intermittently for 20 minutes. When Nurse Hammer finally arrived, I asked for a glass of water. A half-full glass of lukewarm water came 15 minutes later. I asked her to raise my bed, but she left in a huff.

— A short time later I was disturbed by the loud and strident sounds of an argument in the hall outside my room. I buzzed and in seconds Nurse Hammer and an orderly appeared in the doorway. "Mind your own business, you old pest," she hissed.

I suppose by most standards my stay at the hospital was a success. The operation went well, and Dr. Condon has assured me that I will recover completely.

But I will be forever skeptical of any institution that could employ so uncaring an individual as Nurse Hammer.

Yours truly,

cc: Hospital Administrator

COMPLIMENTS TO HOSPITAL STAFF

Dear Dr. Jasper,

In this age of impersonal, uncaring attitudes by so many, I was delighted to discover that the staff at Tall Oaks Hospital was exceptionally cordial and helpful during my stay two weeks ago.

It was my first hospital stay and my first experience with surgery, and I must admit I was scared to death. If I had to put up with impatient people around me I think I would have fallen apart. Since complaints usually go to the top, I thought a note of appreciation should, too. There's a possibility that I will be back for more surgery in the months ahead, and thanks to the staff on 2 West, I will be calm and unafraid as I enter those doors.

Cordially,

THANKS TO ORTHODONTIST

Dear Dr. Perry,

You are indeed an expert rearranger of teeth! When Tom came home last night with his braces finally removed, he displayed the broadest smile I've seen in years.

Frankly, there were times—as when complications required oral surgery—that we doubted the outcome. But all's well that ends well.

Many thanks.

Yours truly,

cc: Dr. M. Roberts (family dentist)

GRATITUDE TO STAFF OF REHABILITATION CENTER

Dear Staff,

Now that I am home and on my own again I am happy as a lark. During the time I lived at the Rehabilitation Center and was under your tender care, I promised myself I would write a letter of gratitude as soon as I was able.

Abundant thanks to each one of you for your patience, expertise and genuine concern. You helped me believe in myself and gave me the assurance that I could walk again. Forgive me for the times I lashed out at you in frustration, and thank you for understanding and remaining firm with me.

Never stop your beautiful way of working with people. If any of you ever feel the least bit discouraged give me a call and let me remind you of the miracle you brought about in my life.

Affectionately,

THANKS TO NURSING HOME

Dear Staff,

While my mother was still well enough, she mentioned many times how pampered she was at Melody Hill Extended Care Facility. Now that she is gone, my family and I wish to express our appreciation to all of you for making her last few months as comfortable as possible.

It was a difficult step, turning her frail life over to someone else, but once she was at Melody Hill and I came to know so many of you, my apprehensions ceased as did hers.

Thank you and many blessings to you as you continue your vital work with terminally ill patients and their families.

Fondly,

COMPLAINT ABOUT BAD DOCTOR
TO STATE LICENSING AGENCY

Mr. Oliver Clinton, Director
State Board of Medical Regulation and Registration
street address
city, state ZIP

Dear Mr. Clinton:

I am writing to report a documented case of gross medical incompetence and unprofessional conduct. On February 6 Dr. Alvin Bohn, an orthopedic surgeon, performed surgery in Memorial Hospital for the removal of a bunion from my right foot. What should have been a routine procedure has turned into a nightmare.

Complications resulting from the initial surgery and a subsequent operation to undo the mistakes of the first have left me in constant pain and unable to work. I am now under the care of another specialist and am told the road to recovery will be a long one.

My attorney, Paul Glickson of 1200 Main Street, has filed a malpractice suit against Dr. Bohn. This is the eleventh time that Dr. Bohn has been sued in this state. In five of the suits he either lost or settled out of court. He was exonerated in one case, and four other cases are pending. In addition, I've learned that a hospital revoked his staff privileges and his license was suspended in California before he moved to this state five years ago.

I find it incredible that an agency formed to set standards and monitor medical care in this state permits Dr. Bohn to continue with his butchery. How many more patients will be maimed before this man is finally called in for a hearing before the Medical Disciplinary Board?

While the damage has already been done in my case, I am more than willing to cooperate in an investigation by substantiating all charges. Please let me know what I can do to help put a stop to this carnage.

Yours truly,

cc: Governor

"I WON'T PAY THESE BILLS"

Dear Dr. Abbott:

While on vacation two weeks ago I came to the Lake du Lac Hospital emergency room with an injured finger. After viewing the X-ray and examining the finger, you concluded it was not broken.

I complied to the letter with your follow-up advice to the patient on the green form that was issued. It said to "ice and elevate, after 24 hours heat," and I kept the splint on for several days. Then I removed the splint and tried to restore movement to the injured finger despite increasing pain.

To my astonishment on August 20 I received a note from you dated August 18 which informed me that the radiologist who looked at the X-ray several days later determined that there was indeed a fracture and that I might want to put a splint back for a few weeks and/or contact a doctor back home.

I would have willingly accepted reverse charges by telephone at home rather than wait the two days between the date of your letter on August 18 to its delivery on August 20. During that period, as I indicated, I was no longer wearing the splint.

After receiving your note, I went to an orthopedist in my home town. He saw the fracture on the X-ray immediately, and I'm under his care now.

It seems each day's mail brings a new and startling insight into the wonders of medicine as practiced in rural Lake du Lac. Because yesterday along came a $60 invoice from the hospital, together with a $30 statement from Radiology Specialists, Inc. for the belated diagnosis. Adding insult to injury, I received today a bill for $35 from Abbott Clinic Associates for your "treatment."

I have kept these bills, but will not pay them. They will remain in my file, along with the original copy of the form detailing follow-up instructions to the patient from the hospital emergency room and your incredible note of August 18, a copy of which is enclosed.

You can consider the matter closed. Unless, of course, the finger doesn't heal promptly in which case Abbott Clinic et al will be hearing from me.

Sincerely,

Encl.

20

Letters to the Clergy

Priests, ministers and rabbis are eager to help you and listen to you. However, many of us are hesitant to approach them when we're displeased or when we feel we need help in our personal lives and are too embarassed to ask. A letter is a perfect way to communicate your thoughts with the assurance that you will receive a reply.

A letter of appreciation or encouragement is especially important because so much of their work involves serving others. We all know that the chronic grumblers in any group, however small a minority, feel free to make their thoughts known.

Most of the model letters are self-explanatory, with a few notable exceptions at the end of this chapter.

The forms of address for clergymen of various denominations rate some attention here.

Protestant clergy

Methodist Bishop	The Very Reverend Arthur Park Methodist Bishop street address city, state ZIP (Reverend Sir: or My dear Bishop:)
Episcopal Bishop	The Right Reverend Stewart Darby, D.D., LL.D. Bishop of Baltimore street address city, state ZIP (Right Reverend Sir: or Dear Bishop Darby:)
Minister with advanced degree	The Reverend Warren Brae, D.D., Litt.D. or The Reverend Dr. Warren Brae (Dear Dr. Brae:)

Minister without advanced degree	The Reverend Warren Brae (Dear Mr. Brae: or Dear Reverend Brae:)
Episcopal priest with advanced degree	The Reverend Henry D. Swift, D.D., Litt.D. or The Reverend Henry D. Swift (Dear Dr. Swift:)
Episcopal priest without advanced degree	The Reverend Henry D. Swift (Dear Mr. Swift: or Dear Father Swift:)

When addressing the minister of your own church with whom you are familiar, it is also proper to address him as Paster Brae, which has a more personal, affectionate tone.

Women in any of the above positions would be addressed in the same manner, substituting Ms., Miss or Mrs. for Mr.

Jewish clergy

Rabbi with advanced degree	Rabbi Micah J. Strauss, Ph.D. (Dear Rabbi Strauss: or Dear Dr. Strauss:)
Rabbi without advanced degree	Rabbi Micah J. Strauss (Dear Rabbi Strauss:)

Roman Catholic clergy

The Pope	His Holiness, The Pope or His Holiness Pope Luke II Vatican City, Italy (Your Holiness: or Most Holy Father:)
Cardinal	His Eminence, Chester Cardinal Farner Archbishop of New York street address city, state ZIP (Your Eminence: or Dear Cardinal Farner:)
Bishop/Archbishop	The Most Reverend Walter Novak, D.D. Bishop of Newark street address city, state ZIP (Your Excellency: or Dear Bishop/Archbishop Novak:)
Monsignor	The Right Reverend Msgr. Patrick A. O'Reilly (Right Reverend and Dear Monsignor O'Reilly: or Dear Monsignor O'Reilly:)
Priest with advanced degree	The Reverend Kenneth C. Murphy, Ph.D. (Dear Dr. Murphy:)

Priest without advanced degree	The Reverend Kenneth C. Murphy (Dear Father Murphy:)
Brother	Brother Hugh West (Dear Brother: or Dear Brother West:)
Sister	Sister Mary Martha (Dear Sister: or Dear Sister Martha:)

WELCOME TO OUR CONGREGATION

Dear Reverend Olander:

On behalf of my entire family, I would like to welcome you as our new pastor. We are excited to have you as our new shepherd and look forward to getting to know you and your charming wife in the weeks ahead.

We will also be praying daily that the Lord will help you adjust to your new environment quickly and that lasting friendships will be made.

Feel free to call on Irene or me if we can help in any way.

Yours truly,

THANKS FOR SPECIAL ASSISTANCE

Dear Rabbi Cohen,

My family and I want to thank you for the many hours you spent with my dad during his long illness and with us during the days immediately following his death.

Thank you also for following through on his wishes and conducting the funeral just as he wanted it.

Your constant prayers and compassion were a source of great strength for all of us.

Sincerely,

PERSONAL PROBLEM, ASK FOR CONSULTATION

Dear Pastor Nelson,

Over the past few years Faith Community Church has been a haven for me. Your sermons have always been inspirational and the people of the church have become my best friends.

Lately I have been fighting a losing battle with bouts of depression which are affecting my relationship with my family and my ability to cope with everyday situations.

Rationalizations and tears have gotten me nowhere. I would appreciate the opportunity to talk with you. I will call you next week for an appointment for consultation.

Yours truly,

A COMPLIMENTARY LETTER

Dear Father Ryan,

I have thoroughly enjoyed your latest series of sermons on Sunday mornings. You have stimulated me into thinking through what I've been doing with my life.

Keep up the good work.

Yours sincerely,

A LETTER OF CRITICISM

Dear Reverend Marshall,

As you know, I've been a member of the church for the past 20 years. It's been a second home to me and means very much to me and my family.

There's been much concern lately over the loss of members and much conjecture as to the reason why. In my opinion, the main problem is that the services are dull. New people do visit occasionally, but they never return.

Surely there is something you can think of to bring more joy into the service with less droning on about money problems. You won't get more money by badgering people for it; you will by ministering to their needs. Then they will give from the heart.

Forgive me for sounding harsh. It's not my intent to discourage you, but to prod you into considering turning your focus back to the people and away from the balance sheet.

Yours truly,

GREAT JOB WITH YOUTH

Dear Pastor Dell:

It is so exciting to see teenagers "turned on" about church! Thank you for doing a wonderful job with the youngsters.

From what the kids tell me, the Bible study and discussion times are what keep them coming back. They enjoy the socials, but it's getting down to the nitty gritty that touches them and changes their lives.

Keep up the good work. God bless you.

Warmly,

WHAT ABOUT OUR YOUTH?

Dear Reverend Babcock,

Our family has enjoyed the fellowship of the Woodlands Church for the past five years. Now that our oldest child, Heather, is in high school we have our first complaint.

Heather was looking forward to being a part of the Youth Group at the church, but after four months she has become discouraged because she feels she isn't wanted. Her best friend from church moved away last summer, and it seems the rest of the girls have their own cliques.

We hate to see her drop out, Reverend Babcock. Can anything be done to make her feel a part of the group? She is basically shy, so I'm sure she isn't trying her best to make friends, but I know she'd respond eagerly if someone would be friendly toward her.

We would appreciate anything you could do to have someone reach out to her before she becomes unreachable. Thank you.

Cordially,

SUGGESTIONS FOR YOUTH PASTOR

Dear Mr. Lindon,

As you know, with two youngsters in high school we are kept up to date on what's happening in the Youth Group at Village Church. Our son and daughter so looked forward to having a new youth pastor and they, along with the rest of the kids, gave you a royal welcome last spring.

Now it is a year later and we have seen the number of young people involved in the group steadily decline. The social events are fewer and fewer, and it seems the Sunday School classes are terribly boring.

We realize teenagers can be harsh critics, but we feel their complaints are justified. We have been praying for you and feel that now is the time to put our prayers into action.

We are eager to see the youth group work. Let's give the teens of our church a place where they can be themselves and have a haven to come to . . . to be exposed to dynamic Christian leadership and teaching that will establish them in their faith and prepare them for adulthood . . . to see that prayer works, not only for adults or "holy rollers," but for ordinary teens like them. We are willing and ready to help.

Perhaps we could form a committee made up of concerned parents and teenagers and headed by you. We could meet together and try to come up with some new ideas. We *are* available and we *are* eager to help in any way we can. Let's get started!

Sincerely yours,

MUSIC APPRECIATION

Dear Mr. King,

The selections of contemporary music during recent services have been both inspirational and a refreshing change. I like the way you always maintain a balance, never neglecting the old familiar hymns yet interspersing just enough contemporary sound to make each service stimulating.

Your expertise is greatly appreciated. I dream of singing beautifully in heaven some day, but for now I'll enjoy the voices of others while I sing in my heart.

Thank you for your hard work and up-beat personality. Your enthusiasm is contagious.

Sincerely yours,

MUSIC COMPLAINT

Dear Mrs. Blodgett,

You have served our church faithfully for many years as choir director, and I appreciate your diligence and patience with all of us.

For the past three months I have been conducting my own personal survey, asking people their opinions about what kind of church music they prefer. It was very interesting to hear the majority say that they love the old hymns, but they also appreciate some of the new, contemporary songs they have been hearing on Christian radio and television. I was happy to hear that, because I've been trying to get up the nerve to suggest that we broaden the format.

I believe this change of pace would be a blessing to the people of our church and put a spark into the choir as well. After singing the same hymns for 20 years, a new song would perk us all up.

Let me know what you think. If you would like me to take an official survey of the congregation, I'll be happy to do so. I'll be glad to help in any way I can.

Yours truly,

MUSIC COMPLAINT

Dear Mrs. Bluestone:

On Sunday mornings in church I expect a respite from the rollicking sounds heard all week long on AM and FM radio.

Instead, we have of late been given an overdose of so-called contemporary music. These new sounds are fine in their place, but I'm convinced they don't belong in our worship services.

The traditional hymns that have inspired generations of Christians over the years should not be put to pasture.

Yours truly,

LET'S NOT FORGET THE OLDER FOLKS

Dear Pastor Winters,

I enjoyed your sermon on being our brother's keeper this morning, but as I sat there agreeing with what you were saying I wondered to what extent our church lives up to that teaching. I was thinking particularly of the elderly and shut-ins of our congregation.

There is so much we could be doing. Volunteers could maintain frequent telephone contact . . . a list could be compiled of people who would be available to drive seniors to and from church . . . and to doctor appointments . . . Sunday services could be taped and brought to those senior citizens and shut-ins who can't get out . . . a visitation schedule could be established . . . anything to let them know we care.

My husband, Tom, and I have talked it over and wanted to let you know that we would be happy to help organize caring ministries to our brothers and sisters who aren't as independent as they used to be.

Let us know what we can do.

Sincerely yours,

REQUESTING PARTICIPATION AT BANQUET

Dear Father Richards,

On behalf of Boy Scout Troop 420 I would like to request your participation in our annual awards banquet. We would appreciate having you give a blessing before the meal and a benediction at the end of the evening.

The banquet will be held at Fritz's Steak 'N Bake, Tuesday evening, May 27th at 6:30 p.m. We usually finish between 8:00 and 8:30 p.m.

You can give me your answer by phone. During the day I can be reached at 000–0000; in the evening at 000–0000.

We're hoping you are available. We would appreciate your presence.

Sincerely,

REQUESTING PARTICIPATION AT CEREMONIAL EVENT

Dear Rabbi Schiller:

I have been named Grand Marshal for the annual Memorial Day parade in Peaksville this year, and would like to ask a favor of you. The Parade Committee and I are hoping you'll be available to make some appropriate remarks at the memorial ceremony in the Village Square.

The parade route begins, as usual, at 11:00 a.m. on Memorial Day starting at Beacon Road and Dudley Avenue, proceeding west on Beacon to Main Street, then north on Main to the Village Square. This year we're expecting over a dozen Veteran's groups and high school marching bands. We'd like you to ride along with Mayor Parker in an open car right behind the first flag bearers.

Please let me know, at your convenience, if you'll be available.

Cordially,

LETTER LEVERAGE

Many denominations have a Church Board or a Board of Elders, comprised of church members elected for specified terms. The board has the responsibility of making key personnel decisions after securing the approval of the congregation. Among them are the selection of the pastor and his staff, determining the terms of the position to be offered, and occasionally the difficult matter of asking for a minister's resignation.

Countless hours of preparation, traveling and interviewing are in store for any church member who serves on a Search Committee. After identifying a candidate, the Chairman of the Search Committee often makes the initial contact by letter. Such a letter would request the candidate's consideration of the position available. In addition, it would give a brief history of the church as well as its size, rate of growth, composition of present staff, and a brief description of what's expected in the position to be filled.

In what's commonly referred to as the "letter of call," the Chairman of the Church Board—after selection of the candidate has been made and voted upon by the congregation—contacts him with a formal offer of the position. The letter spells out in detail the salary, housing allowances or use of the manse, vacation time and benefits. Accompanying this letter is a separate printed job description.

Not all stories have happy endings, even in the ecclesiastical world. Occasionally it becomes necessary to write a letter of termination, requesting the resignation of a pastor or a staff member. Tact and discretion in such a letter are required.

Churches of the mainline denominations have personnel decisions made for them by the administrative hierarchy. However, if many members desire to have a particular clergyman removed, they can appeal by letter to the person in authority to have him replaced. In such a case the letter must include details—facts and dates, not merely complaints about a personality conflict—and the letter must be signed by those who are willing to verify what has been stated. *Never* send an anonymous letter. It will accomplish nothing.

LETTER FROM SEARCH COMMITTEE

Dear Dr. Young:

I'm writing on behalf of the Search Committee commissioned by Grace Church of Pleasant Hills, Pennsylvania. We would like to invite you to candidate for the position of Senior Pastor.

Reverend Robert C. Noble will be retiring at the end of December after 15 years of faithful service to our congregation. They have been 15 years of exciting growth and expansion, and we're looking forward to continued growth under new leadership.

A complete history of our church is enclosed, beginning with our founding 26 years ago. As you will see, we now have a staff of three pastors—Senior Pastor, Assistant Pastor and the Christian Education Pastor as well as two full-time secretaries.

We have received three separate recommendations that we extend an invitation to you to be one of the first men we ask to meet with us. After reviewing the recommendations, the Committee voted unanimously to contact you.

Please give our invitation prayerful consideration. Please contact me when you reach a decision. If you are available, we will send you round-trip plane tickets and arrange a meeting at your convenience.

Very truly yours,

Encl.

LETTER OF CALL

Dear Dr. Young,

Thank you for the time you spent with us last week. We feel we had a good opportunity to get acquainted with you and your wife, Julia.

As chairman of the Church Board at Grace Church, I have the privilege of notifying you that we would be honored to have you serve as our Senior Pastor.

At the congregational meeting last night, the Search Committee recommended that we consider a 75% majority a deciding vote. The final count gave a 90% majority in favor of calling you to our church.

The congregation voted to accept the terms you had proposed along with those that had been determined by the Search Committee. The details are listed on the enclosed sheet, including salary, housing, insurance, vacation and travel time and a suggested job description.

If you have any questions, feel free to call me. Upon notification of your acceptance, we will arrange to have the parsonage ready by January 15 and expect you to begin your full duties on February 1.

Yours sincerely,

Enclosure

LETTER OF TERMINATION

Dear Reverend Bennett,

I am writing on behalf of the Church Board, which, at a special congregational meeting last night received a two-thirds majority vote to ask you to submit your resignation.

This is a very difficult decision, but we feel we have been fair after having you address the congregation two months ago in response to our complaints. At that time you promised changes; those changes never materialized. We, as a church, feel we cannot afford to continue in this manner. We believe the center of our attention should be the Lord and His teachings, not the political theories of our pastor.

Many good things were accomplished in your three years at Central Christian Church. However, the repetitious airing of your political views fom the pulpit has had a divisive effect upon the congregation. As much as we respect your opinions, we feel the Sunday sermons are an inappropriate forum for their delivery.

The congregation voted to continue your salary and benefits through the end of April, during which time you may continue to live in the manse. At that time a final payment equal to six weeks' pay will be made to you, representing compensation for unused vacation time during this calendar year and a termination allowance of one week's pay for each year's service.

Reverend Donald Erickson has agreed to serve Central Christian Church as interim pastor until your successor is named. He will be conducting all services beginning next Sunday.

We very much regret having had to take this action, but extend our best wishes to you for success in the years to come wherever the Lord leads you.

Sincerely,

REQUEST FOR REPLACEMENT

Dear Bishop Novak:

After months of prayerful consideration, we, the undersigned, have decided to initiate action to have Father Kenneth C. Murphy relieved of his duties at St. Gregory's Church in Fairview.

Father Murphy's three years at St. Gregory's have been marked with controversy because of his persistent use of the pulpit to air his political views. The enclosed list of the dates and topics of his sermons will give you an idea why most people in the parish feel it's time for a change.

On numerous occasions many of us have asked Father Murphy to confine his preachings to religious matters. He has ignored these appeals, and has become increasingly one-dimensional in recent months.

Each of the 54 parishoners whose signatures appear below is prepared to verify and, if need be, expand upon these complaints.

We very much regret having had to take this action, and hope your consideration of a replacement for Father Murphy will restore normal conditions at St. Gregory's.

Respectfully yours,

Enclosure

21

Little League
and Scouting

Never before have so many parents been so involved with virtually every aspect of their children's play hours.

Scouting, of course, goes back generations, but Little League is strictly a post World War II phenomenon. Neither could exist without legions of adult volunteers. Many mothers and fathers enjoy these activities; others feel coerced into participating and do so reluctantly.

As might be expected, there is as wide a range of competence and temperament among the adults involved as among the children they oversee. Keep in mind in your occasional letter of praise or protest that these are usually unpaid volunteers. If you're dissatisfied, try to come up with a positive suggestion for a better way of doing things rather than with just a complaint. When you have a beef, take up the matter in person with the individual concerned. Most such problems can be solved long before the letter-writing phase.

The court of last resort in Little League is usually a Board of Directors headed by a commissioner or president. These unpaid volunteers are responsible for the local baseball association. The scouting hierarchy moves, in ascending order, from the patrol or troop level to the troop committee, followed by the charter organization.

If the charter organization is a school or place of worship, the letter can be directed to the principal or clergyman. Higher up the administrative ladder, with paid staff and broader responsibilities, are the field director, the Scouting council, the regional office and national headquarters.

THANKS FOR GREAT COACHING JOB

Dear Mr. Dawson,

Just a note to tell you what a great job you did as coach of the Cardinals this past summer. Mark has definitely become a better ball player and has gained a greater insight and appreciation for the finer points of the game.

More importantly, the example you set stressing good sportmanship and fair play have made what I hope will be a lasting impact on our son and the other players.

Thanks for taking the time to be a Little League coach. Hope Mark winds up on your team again some day.

Yours truly,

THANKS FOR GREAT COACHING JOB

Dear Mr. Gable,

Another year of Little League is over and thanks to you our son, Randy, will have happy memories of his year on the Tigers. My husband and I want you to know how much we appreciate your combination of fairness and firmness with the boys through all the games and practices.

Randy will never be a professional baseball player, but he loves the game. Thank you for encouraging him and letting him know he was important to the team.

Yours truly,

A MANAGER'S THANKS TO LEAGUE COMMISSIONER

Dear Hal,

It was quite a kick to manage the Dodgers this season. And while we didn't win any more than we lost, a good time was had by all.

In the aftermath of an exciting season I reflected on what makes the whole thing happen. The Fairview Youth Baseball Association is more than kids playing ball. Its success is due in large part to the hundreds of adult volunteers in our community. Not just the highly visible coaches, managers and umpires, but the entire behind-the-scenes staff as well.

Without field maintenance crews, salespeople at concession stands, bookkeepers, scheduling coordinators and everyone else involved, the program would soon collapse under its own weight.

That brings me to one final thought. As commissioner of FYBA you pull the whole thing together in a remarkable fashion. I'm sure it takes countless hours, but the results are worth it. Our Little League players and participants at every level will be enriched by many years of happy memories.

Thanks again.

Sincerely yours,

ASKING LEAGUE PRESIDENT TO REMOVE
INCOMPETENT COACH

Dear Mr. Anderson:

This is the sixth consecutive season in which at least one of my sons has participated in Little League baseball in our town. I've been impressed with the dedication and enthusiasm of the adult coaches—until this year.

My son, Timmy, is on the Braves' team in the Intermediate League coached by Hank Hunk. Unlike other coaches, Mr. Hunk is so consumed by the desire to win at any cost that such considerations as good sportmanship and fair play are ignored entirely.

For example, in last night's game, Brave base runners were repeatedly told that "if the catcher blocks the plate, kill him." And I learned after the game that when one of our players was hit by a pitched ball (which was obviously accidental) the Brave pitcher was told to "biff" one of their hitters in return. Continual loud and crude harangues protesting at least a half-dozen of the umpire's calls made this a disgraceful contest, but, unfortunately, a typical one.

As League President I'm sure you have more on your mind than individual coaching performances. But I feel certain that if you were to ask any of the parents of other Brave players or, for that matter, any other coaches in the League they'll agree that Mr. Hunk has no business coaching youngsters.

I urge you to remove this man from Little League coaching for the good of the game and the children.

Yours truly,

ANGRY PARENTS PROTEST TO COMMISSIONER

Dear Mr. Hagerstrom:

Below you will find a list of names of parents whose sons played on the Orioles' Little League team this season. The manager was George Grunch, and we would like to file a formal complaint against him and strongly request that he not be allowed to manage a team again.

Repeated instances of poor judgment, bad temper and overall boorish behavior toward umpires and players alike have ruined the season for the youngsters and spectators. Beside each name is a phone number so you can reach any of us for elaboration, if necessary.

We're sorry it had to end this way, but several of us tried to advise Mr. Grunch to calm down and also volunteered to help but were rejected.

We trust that as League Commissioner you will take appropriate action.

(all sign)

cc: George Grunch

ONE PARENT'S REASON FOR NOT PARTICIPATING

Dear Harry,

I'm feeling guilty after telling you again this year that I'm too busy to coach a Little League team. While it's true that my job calls for occasional travel, the real reason I declined is that I don't agree with the basic concept of Little League.

It may sound old-fashioned, but I believe that while boys and baseball go together, the supervision and involvement of adults at every level of the sport is unnatural. We will probably never again go back to the dawn-to-dusk sandlot baseball games I played as a youngster, but the highly structured Little League of today has gone too far in the opposite direction.

The only time young ball players ever saw an adult in the old days was when we were called home for dinner. Today nothing happens without fathers calling the shots. True, there are fewer arguments when a full-grown, uniformed umpire makes a call. And nowhere else can the kids compete in an environment simulating Big League play.

But when the season ends in early July, that's it. Our Park District continues to keep the diamonds in top shape well into the fall, but the players are gone. It seems that without regularly scheduled games, today's youngsters lack the initiative to get together with a half-dozen or so friends and just play ball.

My own boys were amazed when I told them that an improvised version of baseball can be played with less than nine on a team. They're totally unfamiliar with such things as left field hitting only, pitcher's hands out or choosing sides by hand-over-hand on a bat.

As a result, lacking the push from grownups, too many kids in the second half of the summer prefer to watch a ball game on TV rather than get up one of their own. Nobody loves baseball more than I do, Harry. But I believe kids can have more fun being themselves once again rather than what we parents expect them to be.

Best regards,

BOY SCOUTS ARE NOT MINIATURE SOLDIERS
(to chairman of troop committee)

Dear Mr. Magnuson:

As a former den mother, I realize the Cub Scouts and Boy Scouts rely to a large extent on adult volunteers. And I thoroughly enjoyed the two years I worked with the boys in my son's Den.

My involvement was timely because at the point when Joey reached the age to enter Boy Scouts, his father and I were divorced. His father moved across the country, and the fact that Joey would have a Scoutmaster as an honorable role model was a comfort to me.

To say I was disappointed with Mr. Hawk, Scoutmaster of Troop 205, would be an understatement. Now that Joey is a *former* Boy Scout, I feel free to report that Mr. Hawk's militaristic, indeed fascist, methods are counterproductive at best.

As I mentioned earlier, I realize Mr. Hawk is a volunteer and as such cannot be fired or penalized for his dogmatic approach to what should be an enjoyable experience. But I believe he could be reminded of the true purpose of Boy Scouting and asked to leave if he fails to change.

If you check the records, you will find that Troop 205 has an unusually high drop-out rate. That alone should warrant an investigation.

Yours truly,

SOMETHING MISSING IN GIRL SCOUTS (to field director)

Dear Ms. Grant:

A number of years have passed since I was a Girl Scout, and I have many fond memories of the troop I was in. I have shared my remembrances with my daughter as she grew old enough to join the Scouts. We were both looking forward to her involvement.

Apparently I was naive to think that the Girl Scouts could have maintained the format that worked so well for so many years. My daughter discovered right off that the only thing that matters is a "competitive spirit."

We used to strive for unity and team cooperation, but now the girls are pitted against each other as they strive for advancement through higher rank and more badges. Fun has taken a distant second place. Instead of encouraging one another, the more aggressive girls ridicule the slower ones.

I'm sure this trend is considered very "now." It seems the emphasis is placed on preparing the girls early on for the corporate life so they won't be devoured when they get out in the real world. Well, even women in business have to know how to work as a team.

The Girl Scouts organization has the opportunity to continue the tradition of teaching young girls the value of the Golden Rule combined with self-reliance. Half that formula is as good as none.

Sincerely,

cc: National Headquarters

SCOUTMASTER EXTRAORDINAIRE

Dear Mr. Benton,

Many thanks for the excellent job you did this year as Scoutmaster for Troop 122. My husband and I are especially grateful for the way you were able to relate to our son, Ty.

Ty had been through a rough year; he had become rebellious and was having difficulty at school. My husband tended to blame himself because his job requires that he be away from home much of the time.

You've helped Ty regain his self-confidence by giving him projects that he enjoyed doing and did well. You were free with praise and encouragement. Ty's attitude began to improve considerably after the spring camp-out.

If you ever had doubts or were frustrated with your work with the Scouts, let me assure you that you are doing a fine job. We feel this year has been a criticial one for Ty—he could have taken a turn for the better or continued to be depressed and unruly. Thanks to your guidance and the fine Boy Scout program, he has become his old self again.

Sincerely,

BROWNIE MAYHEM (to Field Director)

Dear Mrs. Harding,

Since she was a tot, my daughter, Linda, has been waiting for the day she would be old enough to be a Brownie like her big sister. This is the year she has been waiting for, but it has been a nightmare rather than a dream come true.

I realize that Mrs. Novak is a volunteer and probably is doing her best, but I think you should talk to a few more mothers (as I have done) and be aware of what goes on at the Brownie meetings in her home. Linda has come home in tears more than once because her Brownie time turned out to be total confusion again and again.

I've called Mrs. Novak and offered to help her with the crafts or anything else and she turned me down, stating, "They sure are a lively bunch!" According to Linda, "lively" includes throwing food, making fun of Mrs. Novak and just plain being brats.

Linda will not be going to another Brownie meeting this year. Be sure to put me down as a willing mother, eager to learn how to be a Brownie leader for the year ahead.

Yours truly,

GIRL SCOUT COOKIE PRESSURE CAUSES SLOW BURN
(to Girl Scout Council)

Dear Council Members:

I'm sure the annual sale of Girl Scout cookies is a very effective fund-raising activity. And I agree that each of the children should participate. But even what's generally recognized as a good thing can be overdone.

My daughter, May, is a member of Troop 332. An inherently reserved child, May nonetheless enjoyed the camp-outs, games, crafts and other Scouting activities.

Things took a turn for the worse when Bertha McGirth, Leader of Troop 332, told the girls what was expected of them in the upcoming cookie sale drive . . . and hinted at unpleasant consequences awaiting any girl who fell short of her quota.

Try as she would, May lacked the requisite forcefulness to sell many boxes of cookies either door to door or at shopping centers. As a result, she has been ridiculed severely in front of the other girls by Mrs. McGirth, who evidently places a higher priority on fund raising than on any other aspect of Scouting.

I spoke to Mrs. McGirth and she affirmed how essential it was that quotas be met. She strongly suggested that one means of compensating for "May's laziness" would be for me and my husband to sell cookies to co-workers and relatives. And that is where we draw the line.

I'd like to know one thing before deciding whether to give up Scouting altogether. Is the relentless pressure to "sell, sell, sell" coming from above at the Council, regional or national level? Or is one overzealous troop leader the exception?

I'll await your response with great interest.

Yours truly,

BOY SCOUT TROOP THAT DOESN'T LIVE UP TO THE PLEDGE
(to Boy Scout Council executive)

Dear Mr. Case:

My 12-year-old son, Phil, is a Boy Scout in Cobra Patrol in Riverdale. But he won't be much longer.

Phil is the object of ridicule in his Patrol. The older Scouts are on him constantly—perhaps because of his tendency to stutter, or because he is not as well coordinated as some boys his age.

On the camp-out last weekend, for example, Phil was thrown in the lake, had his tent knocked over and had food spilled on him. I'm told the Scoutmaster, Mr. Bush, looked on amused.

In spite of this abuse Phil wants to continue with Scouting. Not, understandably in Cobra Patrol, but perhaps with a fresh start elsewhere.

Is there room in the Boy Scouts for a cheerful, energetic lad who wants nothing more than to be accepted as a teamplayer? If so, please advise on the steps to be taken to get my son relocated in another group.

Yours truly,

22

Corresponding With Police and Fire Departments

While we've been trained since childhood to call the police or fire departments in an emergency, it might stretch the imagination to come up with occasions for *writing* them.

Certainly there is no substitute for the phone when help is needed fast. But for all other matters, a letter is more effective. It stands a much higher chance of coming to the attention of a high ranking official than would a call.

If you're making a request or suggestion, be specific and furnish ample supporting evidence to make your point. When you're criticizing departmental procedure or performance, state your grievance concisely.

If a response is warranted, make it clear at the conclusion of the letter that you'll be expecting a reply.

REQUESTING A STOP SIGN

Dear Chief Randall:

For the past 10 years I have lived on the corner of Plain and Fifth, and have observed with dismay the incidence of traffic accidents increase over the years.

I had applauded the decision to change the zoning for the area west of town so office buildings could be erected and therefore ease the tax burden of the home owner. At the time I realized there would be increased traffic, but the hazards of this particular corner weren't yet apparent.

If you check the records, you will see that in the past year there has been an average of three accidents a month. Would four-way stop signs be possible? I would appreciate your looking into this matter before someone is killed or seriously injured.

Yours truly,

REQUEST TO BE A CROSSING GUARD

Dear Chief Hanson:

I have a proposal which, I believe, could save our town money and, at the same time, contribute to public safety. It would involve putting crossing guards at busy street corners during the periods children walk to and from school.

At the present, children are assisted across some of these intersections by regular police officers and at others by volunteer patrol boys. This is a classic example of the protector being either over-qualified or under-qualified.

Why not split the difference and hire senior citizens—at or near the minimum wage—to do it instead? This would free the higher-paid officers for other duties, and save money in the process. At the same time it would improve safety, because many patrol boys, despite their best intentions, aren't taken seriously by other children or by motorists.

I, for one, would gladly serve as a crossing guard for periods in the morning and afternoon as well as during the lunch hour. I'm 68 years old and in excellent health. I enjoy being with children and can earn their respect and confidence in a short time. I know of many other well-qualified retired persons who would also be happy to be part of such a project.

Other communities have established senior citizen crossing guard programs with good results. I would be happy to stop in at your convenience to discuss this matter further. Please give me a call.

Cordially,

REQUESTING CROSSING GUARD FOR BUSY CORNER

Dear Chief Sullivan,

On behalf of the Wilson Elementary School PTA Board, I would like to request that you assign a crossing guard to the corner of Oak and Apple Tree. As you know, that is an intersection with four-way stop signs and is very difficult and often hazardous for the children to cross.

The morning motorists are especially impatient and most of them barely stop, let alone wait for a group of children to pass in front of them. We would appreciate your help and anxiously await your decision.

Sincerely,

name
Chairman, Health & Safety

WHEN HELP DOESN'T COME IN TIME

Dear Chief Parker:

Fifteen minutes to respond to an emergency call with the nearest police station just six blocks away is inexcusable in a city this size! Yet that's how long it took two nights ago when I placed a call for help as an intruder tried to get into my apartment through the front door.

The police dispatcher needn't have known any more than my name, address, apartment number and that there was a breaking-and-entering crime in progress. But he insisted in asking me whether I was alone, if I knew the individual trying to get in, has this ever happened before and numerous other irrelevant questions. Were it not for my second dead bolt lock and the timely appearance of the building superintendent, the intruder would have been in, done whatever he wanted to do and left before the police arrived.

Before another incident of this kind occurs—with much more serious consequences—I am asking you to review the tape of my call at about 11:00 p.m. on the night of February 10th. If you agree that the dispatcher took too long with his interminable questions, I think the department should reprimand him and state clearly that time is of the essence in such emergencies.

Chief Parker, you yourself have stressed the need for every citizen to be vigilant and take steps to prevent crime. Could I or should I have acted any differently? I'll await your response.

Yours truly,

COMPLAINT ABOUT ABUSIVE OFFICER

Dear Captain Hoover:

Yesterday, for the first time in 14 years, I received a speeding ticket. Officer Malloy issued me a citation for going 42 in a 35 mph zone. He also was verbally abusive. My wife and children were shocked to hear a police officer raise his voice and curse without provocation.

It would be no more than speculation to suggest that Officer Malloy was hinting at a curbside payoff, but the drift of his conversation was unmistakable. When I refused to take the bait, the belligerence erupted.

I'll pay my fine if found guilty in court. And I'll go out of my way to avoid any future confrontations with this disturbed patrolman. I hope he seeks professional help before really going berserk.

Yours truly,

cc: Police Commissioner Grady

DIRECTING TRAFFIC AT SPECIAL EVENT

Dear Chief Erickson:

I am heading a committee which is in the early stages of organizing a novel fund-raising event for St. Timothy's church at 1400 N. Riverside Drive.

We are planning to set up a huge tent in the church parking lot and conduct a 24-hour rummage sale beginning at 6:00 p.m. Friday, June 5. This sale will be widely publicized, and we expect people from all over the city to attend.

To keep things running smoothly, we'd like to arrange to have an off-duty uniformed patrolman on hand to direct traffic at peak hours. There will be a band and refreshments will be served, so the guests probably won't begin thinning out until about midnight. While items will be specially priced during the early morning hours, we don't anticipate a full house until 9:00 or 10:00 a.m. Saturday. If all goes as expected, the traffic flow will be considerable from then until the 6:00 p.m. closing time.

I'd very much appreciate your advice on such matters as how to contact the officer(s) who would be willing to assist, what is the customary hourly rate for such duties, and any other suggestions you might have. I can be reached evenings and weekends at 000–0000.

Thanks in advance for your cooperation.

Sincerely yours,

OFFICER FRIENDLY IS A BORE

Dear Chief Clancy:

At the present time we have three children in the Bates Elementary School between the ages of 8 and 11. As a mother, I would like to appeal to you to make some revisions in the Officer Friendly presentations, especially in grades 4, 5 and 6.

I realize the importance of emphasizing bicycle safety each year, but when the children see the same film over and over, it becomes boring and they tune it out.

Before becoming a full-time homemaker I taught graphic arts at Career College for four years. I would be happy to volunteer to help prepare an up-to-date version of the Officer Friendly presentation.

Yours truly,

OFFICER FRIENDLY IS GREAT

Dear Chief Clancy:

I am a fifth grade teacher at the Bates Elementary School. Yesterday our class was visited by "Officer Friendly" (patrolman Len Fleming).

His message to the boys and girls was particularly appropriate. At this age youngsters frequently tend to think it's "dumb" to follow all the rules.

Knowing this class as well as I do, it was apparent that more than a few young minds were changed by Patrolman Fleming's presentation. The question-and-answer session which followed showed him to be exceptionally able to relate to youngsters.

My compliments for continuing this worthwhile program. "Officer Friendly" has made a lasting impression on our class.

Cordially yours,

THANKS TO PARAMEDICS

Dear Captain Carter:

My father is alive today only because of the skill and promptness of two of your paramedics.

They were at the door within two minutes of my frantic call last week after my father's sudden collapse from a heart attack. Immediate on-the-spot care followed by a speedy trip to the hospital saved his life. He's now out of the intensive care unit and is expected to come home in a day or two.

I don't know the names of these two men, but it should be a matter of record. I'd appreciate it if you'd convey to them our family's deep appreciation and thanks for what they did.

Yours truly,

HERE'S WHAT REALLY HAPPENED THE NIGHT
MY HOUSE BURNED DOWN

TO: Board of Trustees
     Fire Protection District #156
     street address
     city, state ZIP

FROM: Name
       street address
       city, state ZIP

One week ago our home was destroyed by fire. In my estimation, our loss would not have been as great if the fire chief had been on hand to supervise.

Apparently a spark from our fireplace ignited the shag carpeting in the family room, and by the time we were aware of it and called in the alarm, half the room was in flames. Our family escaped unharmed, but we were dismayed at the performance of the fire fighters. Our neighbors as well will testify to their ineptitude.

The first truck to arrive found the nearest fire hydrant, but couldn't get the hose attached, and called for the pumper while they worked on it. The pumper arrived and the fire fighters spent at least five minutes untangling hoses. Another five precious minutes were wasted while they argued what to do next as it seemed the hoses didn't reach far enough. During the next half hour as they fought the blaze, there was confusion as more than one person tried to take charge. Finally, 45 minutes after our initial call, Chief Canning arrived. It wasn't long before things were under control and the fire was out, but by then the entire house had been destroyed.

When I confronted Chief Canning, demanding to know what took him so long, he reluctantly admitted that it was the evening of the Community Theater's annual play and since he had a lead part, he had left his beeper at home.

I am requesting a full investigation into the performance of these men. We chose this community because of its reputation for good schools, and excellent police and fire protection. We were willing to pay high real estate taxes, because we felt we were paying for the best in this state.

It's too late for me and my family, but I hope other families in this town will benefit from whatever discipline or re-training is necessary to get our fire department into shape.

(sign)

FIRE PREVENTION NEEDS PROMOTION

Dear Chief Robbins,

My husband and I want you to know how pleased we were with the home inspection by your two fire fighters, Bob Winton and Jeff Stroud. They were very thorough and helpful, and we appreciate the advice they gave us.

We learned of this service while visiting the fire house with our small son. We feel many more home owners would take advantage of the home inspection service if they were aware of it. Please consider publicizing it during Fire Prevention Week.

Thank you.

Sincerely,

LETTER LEVERAGE

The job of the police is made harder when witnesses to a crime clam up because they "don't want to get involved."

Many citizens realize they should step forward to provide information or make an identification, but are reluctant to appear in court to testify. Worse yet, they fear retribution from the accused who is usually out on bond within a day or so. Instead, they pretend they saw nothing.

A third alternative—an anonymous letter to the police—can be justified only by reasoning that some information is better than none at all. Some people may prefer to send a letter rather than phone in the information because it is widely known that most law enforcement agencies routinely tape incoming calls.

If a letter is to be useful to the authorities, it must be mailed promptly before the trail grows cold. It should include all specifics: time, place, names/descriptions of people involved.

IDENTIFYING SUSPECT BY NAME

Police Department:

I believe I know who started the fire last night in the apartment building at 4260 Orion Drive.

I live in one of the buildings across the street and happened to be looking out of the window shortly after 11:30. A man emerged from the gangway, looked to the right and to the left, and hurried away on foot. Moments later I saw the flames and called the fire department.

That man is Harry Smith, and he lives about three blocks north of here. I know Smith to be a dangerous individual and fear what he might do if I came forward and publicly accused him.

There's no use trying to find out who I am because I'd deny seeing anything. But I'm sure that if you question Smith as to his whereabouts last night, or even obtain a warrant to search his apartment, you'll be on the road to solving this crime.

WITNESSED HIT-AND-RUN ACCIDENT

Police Department:

I was a witness to a hit-and-run accident this morning. I was passing through town and wish to report it anonymously because I won't be able to return to testify.

At 9:30 a.m. I was traveling on the 1500 block of Broadway. About five car lengths in front of me a 4- or 5-year-old blue Pontiac, Colorado license 0000, sideswiped the left side of a late-model red Buick, Colorado license 0000, which was parked at the curb. The Pontiac made no attempt to stop.

23

Miscellaneous Missives

The letters in this chapter are so varied they defy categorizing. But each is designed to deal with a specific situation not unlike those which crop up so frequently.

There can be any number of reasons for writing such a letter. It may be something as routine as asking a bank to correct an error in your monthly statement, or an occasion calling for special tact and persuasive power.

In any case the same guidelines apply. State the facts concisely, build a case for your viewpoint, and indicate unmistakably the hoped-for result.

WHEN UTILITY COMPANY DIGS UP YOUR LAWN

Mr. Everett H. James, President
Community Gas Company
street address
city, state ZIP

Dear Mr. James:

Three weeks have passed since the gas company crew completed repairs on the underground mains and service pipes in front of my home.

Before completing the work and moving on, the foreman assured me that landscapers would be out within a week to restore our once-lovely lawn. So far, no sign of them. Phone inquiries have brought one excuse after another, but no results.

I understand the reason why the company must occasionally dig up lawns. And I accept the inconvenience as a reasonable price to pay to keep the gas flowing safely. But I don't understand why it should take three weeks to put down new sod.

One phone call from you, Mr. James, could make it happen tomorrow. Will you help?

Yours truly,

LOST ITEM AT COAT CHECK COUNTER

Mr. R. W. Crane, Director
Metropolitan Art Museum
street address
city, state ZIP

Dear Mr. Crane:

Last Tuesday afternoon I paid a visit to the Museum. Earlier in the day I had been shopping and had purchased a dress and a raincoat and had them wrapped in a box.

Your coat check attendant indicated that Museum policy required that parcels of this size be checked, and she gave me a claim check number 260 which corresponded to the number of the hook on which she hung my coat. The package was placed on the rack above.

Several hours later when I returned to pick up the checked items, only the coat was there. The attendant searched for the package, but couldn't find it. She took my name, address, phone number, along with a description of the package and its contents. I was told I'd be hearing from her supervisor in a day or two.

Six days have passed and no one at the Museum has attempted to contact me. I have obtained from the store another copy of the receipt I was given at the time of the purchase of the dress and raincoat—for a total of $180.20— and I am enclosing it. The name of the attendant on duty last Tuesday was Marcia.

I would like to have my parcel or a check for $180.20 which will enable me to replace the items lost in your checkroom.

Sincerely,

Encl.

WHY AREN'T THINGS BUILT TO LAST?

Mr. Charles Jacobs
Vice President, Sales
XYZ Sound Co.
street address
city, state ZIP

Dear Mr. Jacobs:

Two weeks after the expiration of the 90-day warranty on my new Model 260 FM/AM radio cassette recorder, the 260 itself expired. Or so it seemed, as the tuning dial no longer moved and the tape speed jumped erratically.

I brought the recorder to your company-owned service center in Fairview. There I was told emphatically that there would be no exceptions to the terms of the warranty, and that it would take two to three weeks to fix the recorder.

Six weeks later came the notification that the recorder was ready to be picked up. I was astonished to be confronted with a bill for $42.20, nearly half of its $100 purchase price.

I asked the clerk whether it was common to have to make such expensive repairs on so new an item and the response was a shrug.

Before purchasing your Model 260 recorder I looked at the competition and decided to follow the advice of the slogan, "Buy American." In hindsight, this appears to have been a mistake.

Is it any wonder that imported goods continue to increase their market share when their domestic counterparts are so carelessly manufactured and so expensive to repair?

Sincerely,

SEEKING FINANCIAL COUNSELING

Family Service Assoc. of America
44 East 23rd Street
New York, New York 10010

Gentlemen:

I was recently widowed and have four small children. I'm overwhelmed and confused by the money matters my husband handled so well.

A friend suggested I seek financial counseling through one of your agencies. Please advise me where I can find such counseling in my area.

Thank you.

Sincerely yours,

AN APPEAL FOR HELP FROM SOCIAL SERVICE AGENCY

Ms. Barbara Benchmark, Director
Dell County Community Service Agency
street address
city, state ZIP

Dear Ms. Benchmark:

I'm hoping you will be able to help my elderly aunt who lives in Summit. She lives alone in a small apartment at 123 Fourth Street and is barely able to take care of herself because of severe arthritis in her legs.

I'm her only relative, and it's an hour's drive to her place. Since I have two children in elementary school and one in nursery school, it's hard for me to be much help to her. She values her independence, but desperately needs someone to look in on her, get her groceries, help her with housework.

Would your agency have any volunteer programs or local home health services that would be available to her?

Sincerely yours,

LETTER ACCOMPANYING DONATION

Dear Heart Association:

The enclosed donation is given in memory of Wesley Grant. Please notify his widow:

> Mrs. Wesley Grant
> street address
> city, state ZIP

The gift is given by:

> John and Jean Moore
> street address
> city, state ZIP

Please forward a receipt to me for tax purposes.

Yours sincerely,

Encl.

ASKING NEWSPAPER CONSUMER COLUMN TO STRAIGHTEN OUT BILLING ERROR

Dear Consumer Action Column:

Four months ago I had a PAY TV unit disconnected from my television. Each month since then I have received a bill. As time goes by the amounts get larger, and the wording becomes more threatening.

I've spoken numerous times to Laura Lyon, the PAY TV representative. She keeps assuring me the matter will be straightened out, but it hasn't been yet. My A-1 credit rating is very important to me, and I fear it is threatened by this error on PAY TV's part.

Enclosed is a photocopy of my dismantling receipt dated June 10. I would appreciate your intervention.

Sincerely,

Encl.

LETTER LEVERAGE

Their very size is one good reason for written communication with banks and governmental agencies. While phone calls are often forgotten, or even denied, a letter provides a reference point for future contacts.

No attempt need be made to direct this type of letter to any specific individual. It will, in time, find its way to the right person.

The more facts you can furnish, the better the chance your inquiry or complaint can be handled without delay. Retain all copies of both your correspondence and any replies.

CORRECT MONTHLY BANK STATEMENT

Gentlemen:

I am writing to call your attention to an error in my latest monthly statement for checking account #000–0000.

The statement does not include the $500 deposit I made on October 14. I am enclosing a photocopy of the deposit ticket I was issued on that date. As you can see it indicates that I cashed a check for $920, deposited $500 in my account, and received the balance in cash.

Please make the change and issue a corrected statement.

Yours truly,

Enclosure

CERTIFIED LETTER CONFIRMING LOSS OF BANK CHARGE CARD

Dear Ms. Emory:

This letter is to confirm our phone conversation today, during which I reported the theft of my charge card.

It is my understanding that prompt notification to you of the loss or theft of my card absolves me from any responsibility for subsequent charges made by someone else under that card.

The number of the card is 000–000–000, and it is listed in my full name.

Yours truly,

NOTIFYING BANK OF TAX REPORTING NUMBERS

Gentlemen:

Social Security cards have been applied for and issued to each of my three children. Please change your records for tax reporting purposes so that interest on their savings accounts and certificates of deposit (on which my wife and I will remain trustees) is reported under each child's number rather than mine. Following is all the pertinent information:

Name	Soc. Security Number	Savings Book	Certificate
Linda L. Daniels	000–00–0000	00000–0	00–00000–0
Nancy A. Daniels	000–00–0000	00000–0	00–00000–0
Polly S. Daniels	000–00–0000	00000–0	00–00000–0

Yours truly,

NOTICE OF RETIREMENT TO NEAREST
SOCIAL SECURITY OFFICE

Gentlemen:

Three months from now, on February 1 of next year, I plan to retire. It will also be my 65th birthday and the close of a 30-year career with ConGlom Corp. During that entire period my FICA payroll deductions were always at a maximum.

My Social Security number is 000–00–0000. My wife, Doris, is 63 years old. Her Social Security number is 000–00–0000, but she hasn't been employed for many years.

Please let me know the amount of my/our monthly benefits and the date on which I may expect to begin receiving them.

Yours truly,

NOTICE OF NAME CHANGE TO NEAREST
SOCIAL SECURITY OFFICE

Re: Social Security #000–00–0000

Gentlemen:

I am writing to notify you that three weeks ago I was married. On June 14 my name changed from Ellen Peterson to Ellen Robinson.

I am enclosing a copy of my marriage certificate. Please change your records accordingly and issue me a new Social Security card.

I will continue to work at MegaMotors, Inc., and have notified my employer of the change.

Sincerely,

Encl.

REQUESTING EDUCATIONAL AID FROM NEAREST VA OFFICE

Dear Veterans Administration:

One year ago I received an honorable discharge from the U.S. Army after five years of service. My employer has suggested I continue my education at night school, pursuing a degree in accounting.

I will be applying to Metropolitan College and will need financial assistance to pay my tuition and fees. Please send the appropriate forms for me to apply for aid under the GI Bill.

Thank you.

Sincerely yours,

CONTACTING MAIN VA OFFICE FOR EDUCATION ASSISTANCE

Veterans Administration
Washington, D.C. 20420

Gentlemen:

My attempts to reconcile an error with my local VA facility by phone have failed, so I am writing the main office in an attempt to resolve this matter.

My husband, Gerald Lock, served with the U.S. Marines during the Vietnam Era. He was killed in action when his helicopter was shot down. His serial number was 00000000; his period of service from _____(date)_____ to _____(date)_____ .

My son received financial assistance from the VA for his first year of college and will begin his sophomore year this fall. The VA office, however, apparently has lost the records. One person told me my son must reapply; another said there will be no aid because there is no record of my son's college attendance.

I am enclosing a copy of his grade transcript from last year along with a copy of his attendance record. We would appreciate prompt action as the beginning of the school year is approaching.

Yours sincerely,

Encl.

REQUESTING MORTGAGE LOAN FROM REGIONAL VA OFFICE

Dear Veterans Administration:

Please forward VA Form 26–1880, "Request for Determination of Eligibility and Available Loan Guaranty Entitlement."

Yours truly,

LETTER LEVERAGE

Every so often the mail will bring a reminder urging you to act now to renew a magazine subscription. It may hardly seem possible that a year (or two) has passed since you sent off a check.

You're probably right. Chances are, it hasn't been that long. Magazine circulation departments frequently jump the gun and send out renewal notices four or five months before subscriptions expire. And rarely is your expiration date noted on the form.

Your response should refer to the record you've kept of what you sent and when. If there's no name on the renewal notice, you'll find the circulation manager's name at the front of the magazine. Always retain a copy of the stub detailing the terms of the offer and indicate on your check the length of the subscription.

If the editorial content of your once-favorite magazine begins to slip or it takes a position on an issue which infuriates you, don't just go out with a whimper by not renewing. Instead, fire off a "cancel my subscription" letter and let them know the reason. For good measure, insist on a pro-rated refund for the unused portion.

PREMATURE MAGAZINE SUBSCRIPTION RENEWAL NOTICE

Dear Mr. Stiple:

This morning's mail brought the rather frantic plea to "renew your subscription now so you won't miss a single issue." Well, I have no intention of missing an issue of your fine magazine and certainly no intention of renewing five months before my present subscription expires.

Fortunately I keep a record of all such transactions. Across the back of my cancelled check dated April 2 of last year is the notation "FOR TWO-YEAR SUBSCRIPTION." As you must surely know, I've prepaid for my copies of the magazine until well into *next* year. Come mid-February I'll be in a more receptive mood to consider renewing.

Yours truly,

WHEN YOU DON'T REMEMBER EXPIRATION DATE OF SUBSCRIPTION

Dear Mr. Hollister:

I received your notification to renew my subscription now to avoid missing a single issue.

As it happens, I don't intend to let my subscription expire. But when does it? Nowhere on the card you sent is the date indicated. And while I have declined your frequent offers of two free issues if I renew immediately, I can't imagine that the basic subscription has lapsed.

Perhaps it has, and my memory with it. I'll have to take your word for it because I recently discarded all cancelled checks over a year old.

Please advise.

Yours truly,

MAGAZINE SUBSCRIPTION BILLING ERROR

Dear Mr. Connor:

You recently made me an offer I couldn't refuse—12 months of "Fishing Foibles" for just $6.99. The clincher was the two free issues I'd receive if I sent a check with the order rather than wait to be billed.

As promised, my first issue arrived today. With it, however, came an invoice for $6.99. I am returning it in the envelope you provided. You'll also notice a copy of the front and back side of my check for $6.99, dated October 6. Obviously it has been cashed, but my account has not been credited.

I trust you'll take care of this matter at once, and see to it that I'm not asked for any more money till my fourteenth issue is in the mail.

Yours truly,

Encl.

CANCEL MY SUBSCRIPTION (to editor in chief)

Dear Ms. Gardner:

The quality of your magazine has deteriorated noticeably with recent issues. Objectivity was totally lacking in last month's one-sided treatment of the Palestinian question.

So . . . *cancel my subscription*. And please send a pro-rated refund check for the issues still remaining. To expedite matters, I enclose my address label.

Cordially,

Encl.

LETTER LEVERAGE

Despite its formidable decorum, there is a certain amount of flexibility in the judicial system.

A jury summons, for example, can, under certain circumstances, be postponed if you have a valid reason. Your letter requesting deferral of service . . . either for yourself or for an essential employee—should be written as soon as possible after the notification is received. It should be respectful in tone and explain why it would cause hardship to serve at that time.

A court order determining child custody or the amount of support payments following a divorce must be obeyed. Circumstances, however, may change in subsequent years. If the former mates are still on speaking terms and can communicate rationally with each other, a letter can initiate discussions which could change the terms to their mutual satisfaction.

If you've grown farther apart from your ex-spouse, it may still pay to initiate communications. Hard feelings aside, it is usually preferable to come to terms without incurring costly legal fees.

REQUESTING DEFERRAL OF JURY DUTY

Dear Jury Supervisor:

I am honored to have been chosen to serve once again on the Criminal Court jury. A similar experience six years ago gave me an invaluable insight into the workings of the Court system.

Regrettably, the notice came after I had confirmed reservations to attend the annual convention of the National Computer Conference in Houston the week of January 8.

I would be most appreciative if you could arrange to defer my serving on the jury until a later date. My summons is enclosed.

Respectfully yours,

Enclosure

REQUESTING DEFERRAL OF JURY DUTY FOR YOUR EMPLOYEE

Dear Judge Mason:

I am the owner of a small business employing six persons. One of my employees, Susan Connelly of 1400 Baxter Drive, told me that she had just received a summons for jury duty for the two-week period beginning May 9.

As it happens, that is the busiest time of the year for us. Ms. Connelly, recently promoted to supervisor, was expected to play a key role in processing our orders.

Would it be possible to postpone Ms. Connelly's jury service until at least mid-June? She has indicated her availability and willingness to serve any time after that. We'd both be most appreciative.

Respectfully yours,

TO EX-SPOUSE ON CHILD CUSTODY

Dear Susan:

I understand from George Jr. that you are planning to remarry and move to California. When he and Becky stayed with me last weekend, I was brought up to date on a number of recent developments.

My initial concern, of course, was that I'd be a continent apart from the children and unlikely to see much of them again. It appears they, too, have some apprehension about the move, though both spoke highly of your fiancé.

An idea has occurred to me, Susan, and I'd like you to give it some serious thought. While we've had our differences, I believe both of us have one overriding concern—doing what's best for George Jr. and Becky. And the more I think of it the more I'm convinced that both would be happier staying here in Boston with me, their family and friends, and familiar surroundings.

I'm told your husband-to-be is a widower with children of his own. Also, that you speak frequently of making a "fresh start." It goes without saying that if you'll even consider my proposal I would agree to pay round-trip air fare for the children from here to your new home during the summer months and for occasional holidays.

The custodial agreement as spelled out in the divorce decree could be altered by mutual consent, on a trial basis if you'd like. If this idea seems reasonable, why don't you discuss it with your fiancé and the kids. I haven't, by the way, even hinted at any of this with either of them. Then, if you have any questions or suggestions, give me a call.

In any event, I wish you all the best.

Sincerely,

ASKING EX-SPOUSE TO INCREASE SUPPORT PAYMENTS

Dear Larry,

Congratulations! I read in the paper yesterday that you were named vice president of Clip-Corp. Nobody deserves it more.

In the time since our divorce, the years of hard work have certainly paid off handsomely for you. In retrospect, the $850 monthly child support payments must seem rather small. But I've appreciated your promptness with the checks each month, and it's more than some families are getting.

Now that you're on the "fast track," would you consider upping the payments to $1,200 a month? I'll not bore you with a recitation of the ravages of inflation. And, as you know, I'd never beg.

But if you think I've done an adequate job raising the children under difficult conditions, you just might find it in your heart to help out a bit more. Fair enough?

Cordially,

WHEN EX-SPOUSE IS BEHIND ON SUPPORT PAYMENTS

Dear Les,

You are now three months in arrears on your court-ordered child support payments. And I am unwilling to hear any more excuses or believe that "the check is in the mail."

To even begin to describe how difficult your obstinacy has made life for Les Jr., Lisa and me would create an intolerable indignity, and I simply won't do it.

Instead, let me remind you that the $550 per month figure isn't just a number plucked out of the air. It is the amount you agreed to in the divorce decree approved by Judge Whitney.

You know, Les, how distasteful the original proceedings were for me. And you may have assumed that I would hesitate to re-open old wounds. Well, you're wrong! If that check for $1,650 isn't in my hands by next Tuesday, it's back to court again . . . for both of us.

(signature)

LETTER LEVERAGE

There are times in a woman's life when her name as well as her address will change. When she gets married she must remember to notify all the banks and stores where she does business. In the event of a divorce, once again, the same people may have to be notified.

Weddings involve so many details, and nothing can be overlooked. To ensure confirmation of all arrangements made in advance and to avoid any confusion as to who is supposed to do what, put it all in writing.

A bridal registry service is designed to be the answer to the age-old problem of a bride receiving ten toasters. The bride provides the registry with a list of items she would like to receive. Friends and relatives can call and place their order so the registry will have a record of what she has received. The gift is then delivered to the bride, gift-wrapped, with a card inside. That is how it works when all goes well. When problems arise, a letter is in order.

BRIDE'S CHANGE OF NAME AND ADDRESS

account #0000–0–0000

Gentlemen:

I will be getting married on June 10. Please change my name and address on my account as follows:

from: Joy E. Willow
         street address
         city, state ZIP

to: Joy W. Kinsey
         street address
         city, state ZIP

Thank you,

CONFIRMING CATERER'S LIST

Chef Pierre Catering Service
street address
city, state ZIP

Dear Chef Pierre:

This letter is to confirm the arrangements we made for my daughter's wedding reception on June 14 at the Lovely Acres Country Club. An itemized list of the banquet you will be providing is enclosed.

Please verify the list and the total cost of $1,025. We understand that you will need 30 days' notice of any change in plans.

Cordially yours,

Encl.

BRIDAL REGISTRY COMPLAINT

Mr. T. H. Malcolm, Manager
Jones & Owens Department Store
street address
city, state ZIP

Dear Mr. Malcolm:

Something has gone haywire at the once highly regarded Jones & Owens Bridal Registry Service since it performed flawlessly for my own wedding 20 years ago. It's hard to believe that your computers are always down, and that inquiries made three months after an item has been back-ordered reveal it to be currently in stock.

A series of inexcusable complications has arisen from an attempt three months ago to order a place setting of flatware for Kathleen Malone (bridal registration number 00000).

I have tried repeatedly to reach someone in the silverware department, but the phone often rings 15 to 20 times before some clerk brusquely answers and puts me on hold.

Enough is enough. Please cancel the order and remove the $62.50 charge from my monthly statement. For future weddings I will be giving monetary gifts or something I select from one of the shops in my neighborhood.

Yours truly,

LETTER LEVERAGE

This year Americans will buy over $40 billion worth of goods through the mail. The problems encountered with such transactions consistently put mail order purchases at the top of the list of consumer complaints. They range from simple misunderstandings to cases of outright fraud.

Frequently a letter can bring results. A simple reminder that you have fulfilled your obligation and wish to discontinue participation should suffice to firms offering monthly selections to club members.

If someone mails you a package you didn't order, you have no obligation to return it or pay for it. A breezy note of thanks for the unexpected gift will usually send such schemers elsewhere. Report any attempt to bill you for unordered merchandise to the authorities and mail a copy of your letter to the sender.

If you never received an item by mail for which you've paid in advance, and routine letters of inquiry go unanswered, a carefully-worded ultimatum will usually bring a prompt resolution. Send the company a certified letter stating that you intend to bring the question of possible fraud before the U.S. Postal Inspection Service. If even that fails, follow through on your threat and report the incident to the postal authorities in the city where the company is headquartered.

Your local Better Business Bureau closely monitors ethical practices in regional mail order operations. The Council of Better Business Bureaus is concerned with such businesses which advertise nationally. Both are responsive to any reports of irregularities.

One way to avoid unwelcome solicitations is to contact the Direct Mail Marketing Association, a trade group which sells mailing lists to member companies. The DMMA will honor your written request that your name be removed from their mailing lists which are published quarterly.

WITHDRAWING FROM MAIL ORDER CLUB

Dear Membership Director:

Under the terms of my membership in the Revolving Record Club, I was required to purchase three selections within a 12-month period.

With the enclosed order, this obligation has been met. Please remove my name from your mailing list.

Yours truly,

STOP SENDING MERCHANDISE

Dear Membership Director:

My letter of April 16 evidently was ignored, so I am sending this one certified.

As I had indicated, I have fulfilled my obligation as a club member by purchasing three albums within a 12-month period. After clearly stating that I wished to withdraw and would not welcome further solicitations, I was dismayed to find yet another offering in today's mail.

Don't send that record! I will neither pay for it, nor return it, nor for that matter listen to it. In fact, any further albums, invoices and solicitations sent to me will be discarded at once.

Yours truly,

DON'T PAY FOR UNSOLICITED MERCHANDISE

Dear House of Treasures:

Thank you for the figurine I received unexpectedly in today's mail. I was particularly surprised to see an invoice enclosed in the package since I've never placed an order with your establishment and never will.

I have thrown away the invoice and intend to keep the figurine. It would be presumptuous of you to think I would do otherwise.

Sincerely,

THREATENING TO EXPOSE
MAIL FRAUD/UNORDERED MERCHANDISE

Gentlemen:

On August 8 I received a parcel from you containing a pair of pantyhose. I never ordered them; I can't wear them, and by law, I am under no obligation to pay for them.

Six weeks ago I wrote you a letter to this effect. Today I received another bill. This is my last communication with you. If I receive one more invoice I will forward the pantyhose, invoices and letters to the U.S. Postal authorities as evidence of an obvious case of mail fraud.

Sincerely,

THREATENING TO EXPOSE
MAIL FRAUD/UNDELIVERED MERCHANDISE

Dear Cassie's:

On June 19 I placed an order with you for an all-leather monogrammed purse (catalog #000). I enclosed a check for $43.26 to cover the cost of the purse, postage and handling.

Now, five months later, I am still waiting for the purse. I am also waiting for a response to the two letters I wrote inquiring about the delayed shipment. In fact, all I have to show as evidence is my cancelled check.

I am enclosing photocopies of my order, the two letters of inquiry and both sides of my cancelled check.

Ten days from now, unless I have in hand either the purse or a complete refund, I will furnish similar copies to the U.S. Postal Inspection Service. I will ask that they initiate an investigation into what appears to be a clear-cut case of fraud.

Sincerely,

REPORTING FRAUDULENT PRACTICE TO POSTAL AUTHORITIES

U.S. Postal Inspection Service
city, state ZIP

Gentlemen:

I have been victimized by a fraudulent mail order scam, and am writing to inform you of the details.

On June 19 I placed an order with Cassie's Catalog House for an all-leather monogrammed purse. I enclosed a check for $43.26 to cover the cost of the purse, postage and handling.

Now, six months later, I am still waiting for the purse. I am also waiting for a response to the three letters I wrote inquiring about the delayed shipment. In fact, all I have to show to date is my cancelled check.

I am enclosing copies of my order, the three unanswered letters of inquiry and both sides of my cancelled check.

There is no telling how many others have been similarly exploited by Cassie's. In any event, I would hope that this information is sufficient evidence for you to initiate an investigation.

Sincerely yours,

Encl.

REPORTING DECEPTIVE ADVERTISING

National Advertising Division
Council of Better Business Bureaus
845 Third Avenue
New York, NY 10022

Gentlemen:

Enclosed is an ad which appeared in Famous Magazine for a device which purports to cure back problems.

Four months ago I mailed in my $25 and soon after received the device and instructions for its use. I followed these instructions to the letter. Not only did my back pain persist, but it soon began to worsen.

After a month I stopped using the device and made an appointment with my doctor. "These gimmicks are worthless," he said. "In fact, they often are quite harmful."

I wrote the company, told them of my experience, and asked for a refund. They didn't even respond.

It cost me $25 plus the doctor's bill and a great deal of pain to learn my lesson. I would hope that you could do something to put a stop to these deceptive ads and the continuing exploitation of other backache sufferers.

Sincerely,

Encl.

REMOVE MY NAME FROM LIST

Direct Mail Marketing Assoc.
Mail Preference Service
6 East 43rd Street
New York, NY 10017

Gentlemen:

I do not wish to receive any more unsolicited mail.

Please delete my name from all such lists and notify all prospective senders.

Yours truly,

Part III

Letter Writing Is Easy Once You Know How

24

How to Write the Letter That Isn't Included in This Book

FOR STARTERS

If you haven't found among the preceding model letters exactly the one you need for a certain situation, don't be discouraged. Many people find the biggest hurdle to be overcome is the opening sentence.

Following is a wide range of openers on various subjects. Use whichever seems most appropriate. Once you've broken the ice, the rest comes easily.

TO FRIENDS AND LOVED ONES

For Old Time's Sake

I'm sorry to have taken so long to answer your last letter.

We were all so pleased to hear you will be coming to visit us.

We've been friends for too long to let a misunderstanding come between us.

When it gets to the point where I can't get you out of my mind, I know it's time to write you a letter.

The time has come for me to sit down and write to tell you how much I miss you.

As usual, your letter was like an envelope full of sunshine.

I hope you haven't given up on me, but . . .

In Appreciation

Just a note to tell you how much we appreciate the great job you did.

The excellent job you did this year as director of activities was greatly appreciated.

You have been doing a good job for so long I'm afraid I've taken you for granted, so . . .

In a few words I'm going to try to tell you how much you are appreciated.

Fran and I will be forever grateful for . . .

You'll never know how much we appreciated the delicious dinner that you brought over last night.

Your kindness in our time of need will never be forgotten.

Jim and I really appreciate your generous wedding gift.

We just love the beautiful cut-glass pitcher you gave us.

Hand-made gifts are the most creative and by far the most loving kind there can be!

The party you gave in my honor was quite a surprise and loads of fun.

Sympathy and Condolence

My heartfelt sympathy to you.

The news of Meredith's death brought a great sense of loss and flooded my mind with beautiful memories.

The time of grief is always difficult, but it will be greatly eased by the loving support of your dear family.

I pray that love, joy and peace will gently heal your wounds of grief, pain and separation.

All of us here at the office extend our deepest sympathy to you.

I wish I could express in words the fact that I am aching with you during your time of pain.

I heard of your accident today. I will come to see you as soon as you're able to have visitors.

Your friendship has always been special, but during Mom's illness and after her death, you were an angel of mercy.

Your timely visit gave me hope and encouragement.

During our time of grief your expression of love and concern brought us great comfort.

Announcements

I wanted you to be among the first to know the good news.

I have an announcement to make which is guaranteed to surprise you.

It gives me great pleasure to announce . . .

What's more fun than sharing good news!

TO BUSINESS ESTABLISHMENTS

Complaints

I would like to call your attention to an error on my latest monthly statement.

We have been doing business with your firm for the past 12 years and have always been satisfied until now.

After numerous futile attempts to solve this problem by telephone, I am now writing . . .

If my credit rating is affected by your persistent billing errors, you will have some explaining to do in court.

It seems to me that six weeks should be more than enough time to wait for delivery that was promised in ten days.

I refuse to pay for merchandise that was never delivered.

To say I am disappointed with my new _____ would be an understatement.

I have had one problem after another with my new car since you sold it to me three months ago.

My new car has given me nothing but trouble, and I think it's time you began taking my complaints more seriously.

If you were as concerned about consumer satisfaction as your advertising claims you are, this letter would be unnecessary.

I am becoming increasingly impatient with your snail-paced processing of my rebate check.

I would like to request a hearing to protest the huge increase in the assessed valuation of my house.

I am writing to request a State Board of Commissioners hearing in order to protest the _____ .

Routine Correspondence

Enclosed is check for . . .

I am enclosing a check in the amount of . . .

Enclosed you will find a check in the amount of _____ for_____ .

At your request, I am enclosing . . .

On January 21 I mailed an order to you for item #000.

Thank you for your prompt response to my inquiry of March 20.

Your prompt response to my inquiry of Nov. 20 is appreciated.

This is to notify you that . . .

As a responsible citizen of Fairview, I feel it is my duty to inform you that . . .

I have a question regarding the third item listed on my last statement (copy enclosed).

Please note the discrepancy between my latest monthly statement and the receipt issued by your clerk at the time of the transaction.

The enclosed copy of both sides of my cancelled check should be sufficient proof that I paid your April invoice.

Due to circumstances beyond my control I will be unable to pay my entire bill at one time.

Please send me any free information available on . . .

Job Hunting

Your ad in Sunday's Herald for an accountant looks as if it had been written with my background in mind.

I would like very much to be considered for the position of bank teller, as described in Sunday's Clarion.

I am writing in response to your ad for a payroll clerk.

You need a crackerjack secretary; I need an opportunity to utilize my skills to the fullest.

You need a salesman who doesn't mind working long hours; I need a chance to show you that quotas were meant to be broken.

Our mutual friend, Sam Shotwell, suggested that I contact you about a sales position with your firm.

I appreciate your taking the time to meet with me yesterday to discuss the opening you have in your department for an auditor.

I enjoyed meeting with you and Mrs. Prewitt yesterday and learning about the opportunities in the purchasing department of ConGlom Corp.

THE "MEAT AND POTATOES" PART OF A LETTER

The rest of the letter will come more easily if you remember to write what you'd say if you were to come face to face with the reader. Do it in words and phrases you feel comfortable using. Keep in mind the purpose of the letter and what you're trying to accomplish. Put yourself in the position of the person who will be reading it.

If you're like many people, you may find it hard to begin typing a letter from scratch on a sheet of bond paper or putting the pen to fancy stationery on an impulse. Start instead with an eraser-tipped pencil and a ruled pad. Then either outline the points you want to make or just begin writing and let it all spill out.

If you favor the outline approach, go back later and flesh out the points you want to make and arrange them in the proper sequence. If you've written a long, rambling draft, go over it carefully and strike out the irrelevant and repetitious parts. Note in the margin those parts which you feel are particularly important.

Tactful Diplomacy Goes a Long Way

If this is your first piece of correspondence on a contentious issue, take special care to state the facts in a straightforward, courteous way. Avoid threats. It's not to your advantage to strain the relationship in the first letter.

As you rework the letter into final form, make it clear from the beginning just what it is you're writing about. Give complete details in the middle portion. Finally, ask for action at the end.

If you're dissatisfied with a product or a service, don't assume that the reader will know what it will take to set things straight. Leave no doubt as to what response you expect and feel would be fair. Keep in mind that the reader's primary allegiance is to his employer, not to you. It will take a certain amount of persuasion to make him shed his initial defensive reaction and see things your way. Everything considered, however, he'd rather make a customer happy than not.

Don't burn your bridges. If you say flatly that you'll never do business with that establishment again, you leave little incentive for the reader to win you back with a concession. Instead, appeal to his sense of fair play. Suggest that with his intercession you can be retained as a customer.

Sometimes It Pays to Sleep on It

If you're really outraged about something and compose a scorcher of a letter, set it aside until the following day before heading for a mailbox. After sleeping on it, the letter may still express your sentiments exactly. On the other hand, you have a second chance to tone it down if in hindsight it appears too harsh.

YOU WERE ABOUT TO ASK . . .

Interspersed throughout this book under Letter Leverage captions are letter-writing tips of all kinds. Some are self-explanatory; others are not. Following are the answers to some questions which may have arisen.

Q.　Why should I bother to write a letter when I can just pick up the phone and call?

A.　The question answers itself—"just pick up the phone" describes the casual attitude with which we've come to regard a call—it's easier and quicker. Because a letter involves more time and thought, it has a greater impact on the recipient.

Friends will be touched to know that you were thoughtful enough to take the time to write. A letter can be saved and re-read long after the recollections of a phone call have faded.

In business situations there is no substitute for written correspondence. Instead of being put on hold, you'll have the undivided attention of the right person and will be able to make your point without interruptions. What's more, a letter can't be ignored, or later denied.

Finally, as even the most compulsive letter writer will tell you . . . a supply of stamps costs a lot less than your average monthly phone bill.

Q. How long should a letter be?

A. A newsy letter to an old friend can go on and on and still hold the reader's interest. A business letter, on the other hand, should be no longer than is absolutely necessary. Not just out of respect for the time of the person who will receive it, but also because the effectiveness of the letter is diminished by overembellishment.

For most business letters, one side of a standard $8\frac{1}{2} \times 11''$ sheet of paper, typed single-spaced, or its hand-written equivalent, should suffice. That's usually all that is needed to make your point concisely and convincingly.

Q. Does it matter if a business letter is addressed to any specific individual or not?

A. Regular matters such as a change-of-address notice or a routine inquiry can usually be handled adequately by anyone. A letter covering anything out of the ordinary, however, should be sent to the attention of the particular person who is a decision-maker in the organization.

Q. How can I obtain the name of the person I should contact?

A. Usually a phone call to the company's switchboard operator is all it takes to obtain the full name and exact title of whomever you wish to contact as well as the address of the firm. The business section of most libraries contains reference books which are a helpful source of such information for out-of-town firms. Professional and trade directories enable the job-hunter to target his cover letter and resumé to a key individual. This is an absolute must when you're sending an unsolicited letter of application.

Q. When should I send a copy of a letter to a third party?

A. If you're writing a follow-up letter of complaint, or seeking a refund or adjustment for the second time, send a copy to the president or chairman of the company. Be sure to indicate "cc:" at the bottom left margin. The person to whom you're addressing the letter—even if at the middle-management level or a divisional vice president—will invariably give it faster attention if he knows that his boss has also received a copy and is aware of the matter.

If it looks as if you're getting the run-around, a copy to the Better Business Bureau may prod your adversary into action.

Q. Why is record keeping important when it comes to writing letters?

A. Well-documented facts are an essential ingredient in any business letter, especially when you're trying to resolve a problem Whatever the nature of the dispute, your case is strengthened immeasurably if you have kept careful records.

Even when you don't anticipate a problem, it's a good idea to save receipts, repair orders, and cancelled checks for future reference. Then all the information is at hand should the need for a letter arise. Also retain copies of correspondence and a brief summary of who said or promised what and when on the phone or in person.

Q. Is it advisable to keep a copy of every letter I write?

A. There's no need to save a copy of routine correspondence such as a letter to a friend or a sick note for your child. It's generally a good idea, however, to retain a copy of other letters. You'll very likely want to refer to your original if a follow-up letter or any other type of action becomes necessary.

Q. Is it ever okay to send a form letter?

A. On occasions when the identical letter will be going to many people, printing it makes sense. This is done from time to time by professionals when they wish to make an announcement.

At other times if you send a printed letter, try to personalize it in some way—in either the salutation or with a postscript, or both. While job resumés are usually printed, never take that shortcut with the accompanying cover letter. It should be customized to fit each particular situation.

Q. Should I write or call for a job interview?

A. Unless the ad to which you are responding specifically indicates otherwise, mail a cover letter along with your resumé. When you're seeking an interview at a firm which has not advertised for help, always write to a specific individual.

Q. Is it ever worth the extra cost to send a certified letter?

A. It's well worth it if you anticipate having to prove that the letter was received. A certified letter travels through the regular mail and must be signed for at the time of delivery. When you request a return receipt, that signature is proof that the letter was received.

Q. Just what is the Small Claims Court that is referred to in some of the model letters, and how can it help me?

A. Until recent years the threat to sue unprincipled landlords or merchants was often a hollow one which was shrugged off because it was generally known that hiring a lawyer would probably cost more in legal fees than the claim was worth.

    Not any longer. More and more ordinary citizens are becoming aware of how to act as their own lawyers and sue an adversary in Small Claims Court in cases involving relatively small sums of money.

    Each of the 50 states sets limits on the amounts that can be recovered in Small Claims Court—most range between $500 and $2,000. A nominal fee to cover filing and the serving of a summons is all it takes. The trial follows in a matter of weeks, not months or years later as in conventional courts. Evidence is usually presented informally by the people involved in the dispute. The judge's ruling is binding on both parties.

    As a last resort, a letter threatening to seek redress of a grievance in Small Claims Court is often enough to bring your antagonist to terms. If not, be prepared to follow through. Call the Clerk of the Court in your district for details on the exact procedure for initiating a suit.

    Be sure to bring along and introduce as evidence at the trial all substantiating items such as your apartment lease, receipts, cancelled checks and copies of all correspondence.

25

The Basic Elements of a Letter

GUIDELINES FOR BUSINESS LETTERS

When sending a letter to a business establishment of any kind use one of the Sample Letter Layout forms that follow. Always include the date, your full name and address, and your signature. A typed letter is preferred, but if that's not possible, use your best penmanship, making sure all vital information is legible. A neat letter, whether typed or written, will be taken seriously.

It's usually best to address your letter to a particular person, but when that isn't possible, use one of the following salutations:

Gentlemen:

Dear Sir:

Dear Sir or Madam:

To Whom It May Concern:

Always follow the salutation in a business letter with a colon (:).

GUIDELINES FOR LETTERS TO FRIENDS AND LOVED ONES

A much more casual approach is used for corresponding with those near and dear to you. Only the date is needed in the upper right-hand corner and no inside address is necessary. Simply begin with the salutation, followed by a comma.

SAMPLE LETTER LAYOUT 1

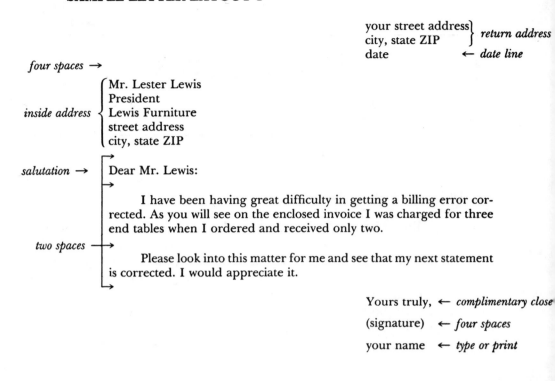

your street address ⎫
city, state ZIP   ⎬ *return address*
date   ⎭ ← *date line*

four spaces →

inside address {
Mr. Lester Lewis
President
Lewis Furniture
street address
city, state ZIP

salutation →   Dear Mr. Lewis:

    I have been having great difficulty in getting a billing error corrected. As you will see on the enclosed invoice I was charged for three end tables when I ordered and received only two.

two spaces →

    Please look into this matter for me and see that my next statement is corrected. I would appreciate it.

Yours truly, ← *complimentary close*

(signature) ← *four spaces*

your name ← *type or print*

Enclosure mark → Enclosure(s)

SAMPLE ENVELOPE LAYOUT 1

your name
your street address
city, state ZIP

    Mr. Lester Lewis
    President
    Lewis Furniture
    street address
    city, state ZIP

SAMPLE LETTER LAYOUT 2

your street address⎤ *return address*
city, state ZIP   ⎦
date   ← *date line*

Order #000 00   ← *reference line*

← *four spaces*

inside address ⎰ Lewis Furniture
                    ⎱ street address
                       city, state ZIP

                       Attention: Mr. Lester Lewis
                               President

salutation → Dear Mr. Lewis:

two spaces — It has become evident that your firm is not willing to correct the billing error on the above order which I called to your attention a month ago. As a result, I am turning the matter over to the Better Business Bureau. They will be receiving copies of all correspondence, along with the original receipt and the incorrect invoice.

Yours truly, ← *complimentary close*

(signature) ← *four spaces*

your name ← *type or print*

Enclosure mark → Enclosures
copy to → cc: Better Business Bureau

SAMPLE ENVELOPE LAYOUT 2

your name
street address
city, state ZIP

                    Lewis Furniture
                    street address
                    city, state ZIP

Attention: Mr. Lester Lewis
        President

COMPLIMENTARY CLOSE EXAMPLES

For Business Letters	For Letters to Friends and Loved Ones
Yours truly,	Love,
Yours very truly,	All my love,
Very truly yours,	Love and kisses,
Sincerely,	With love,
Sincerely yours,	Lots of love,
Yours sincerely,	Loving you,
Cordially,	Fondly,
Cordially yours,	Affectionately,
Yours cordially,	Warmly,
Best regards,	Warm regards,
Expectantly,	With all my heart,
Impatiently,	Forever yours,
With anticipation,	Thank you,
Formerly yours,	Many thanks,
	Thanks again,
	With appreciation,
	Missing you,
	Your friend,
	As ever,
	Best regards,

HOW TO FIND A ZIP CODE

The ZIP codes for addresses in your area can be found in your local telephone directory. When you need a ZIP for a far-away location, you can call your local post office and ask for it, or you can go to the post office and look it up. Copies of the *National ZIP Code Directory* are kept handy for customers' use.

ABBREVIATIONS OF THE STATES

Use the two-letter abbreviation of states on the envelope to speed delivery. There's no need for periods between the letters, nor should you use punctuation between the state abbreviation and the ZIP Code.

Alabama	AL	Missouri	MO
Alaska	AK	Montana	MT
Arizona	AZ	Nebraska	NE
Arkansas	AR	Nevada	NV
California	CA	New Hampshire	NH
Colorado	CO	New Jersey	NJ
Connecticut	CT	New Mexico	NM
		New York	NY
Delaware	DE	North Carolina	NC
District of		North Dakota	ND
Columbia	DC	Ohio	OH
Florida	FL	Oklahoma	OK
Georgia	GA	Oregon	OR
Hawaii	HI	Pennsylvania	PA
Idaho	ID	Rhode Island	RI
Illinois	IL	South Carolina	SC
Indiana	IN	South Dakota	SD
Iowa	IA	Tennessee	TN
Kansas	KS	Texas	TX
Kentucky	KY	Utah	UT
Louisiana	LA	Vermont	VT
Maine	ME	Virginia	VA
Maryland	MD	Washington	WA
Massachusetts	MA	West Virginia	WV
Michigan	MI	Wisconsin	WI
Minnesota	MN	Wyoming	WY
Mississippi	MS		

Index